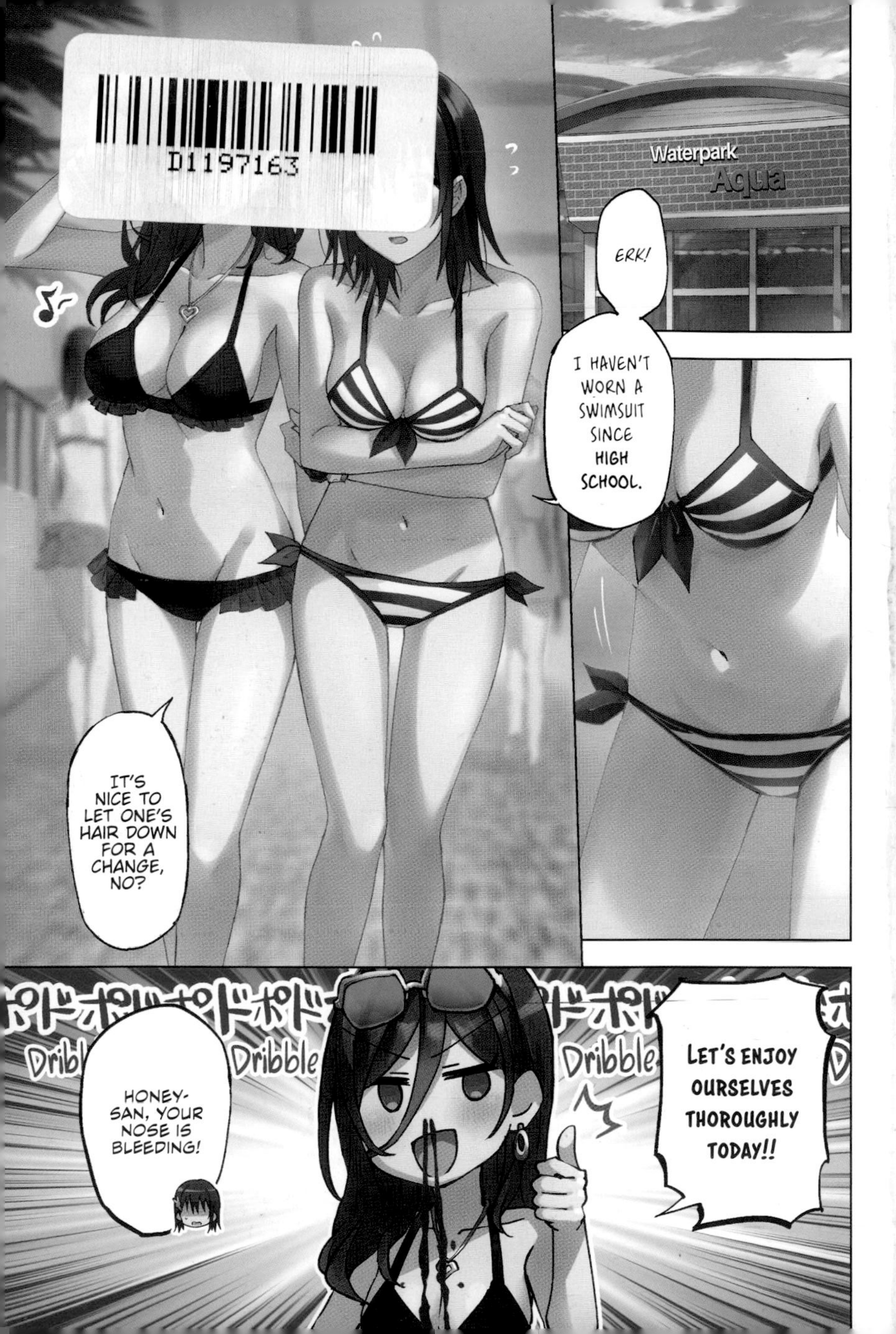
Waterpark Aqua
ERK!
I HAVEN'T WORN A SWIMSUIT SINCE HIGH SCHOOL.
IT'S NICE TO LET ONE'S HAIR DOWN FOR A CHANGE, NO?
LET'S ENJOY OURSELVES THOROUGHLY TODAY!!
Dribble Dribble Dribble
HONEY-SAN, YOUR NOSE IS BLEEDING!

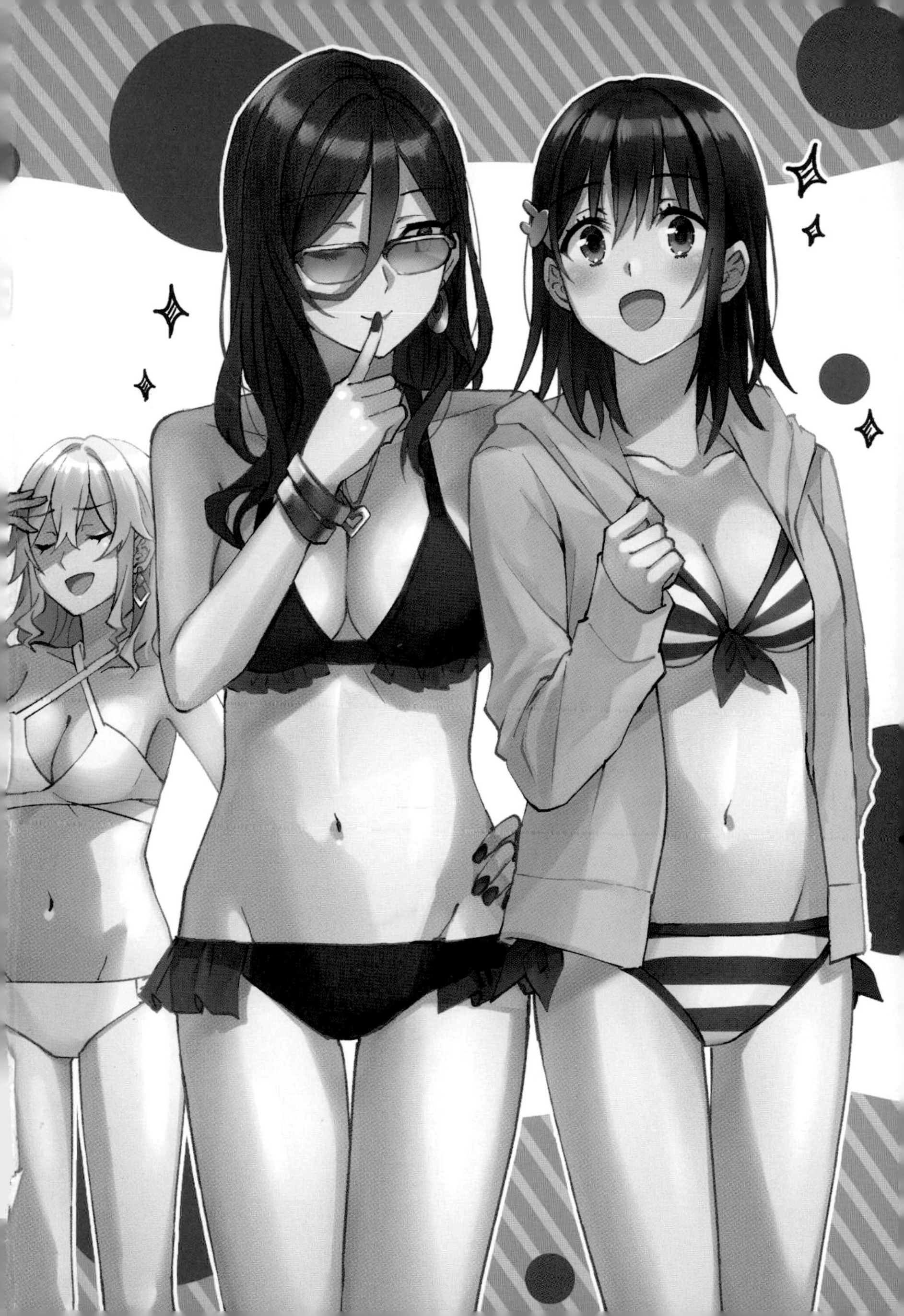

CHAPTER 11 SUMMER! AND SWIMSUITS!!

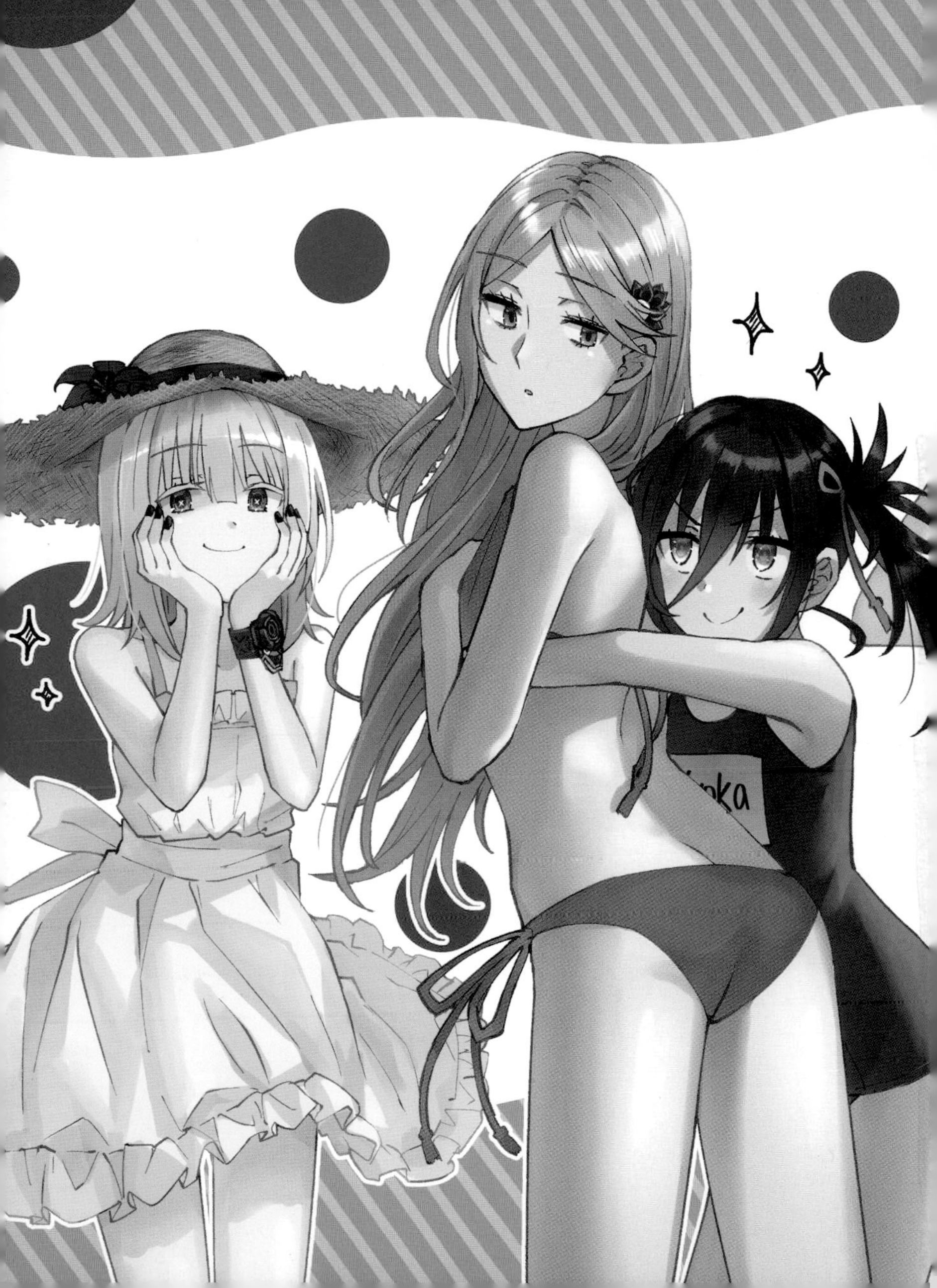

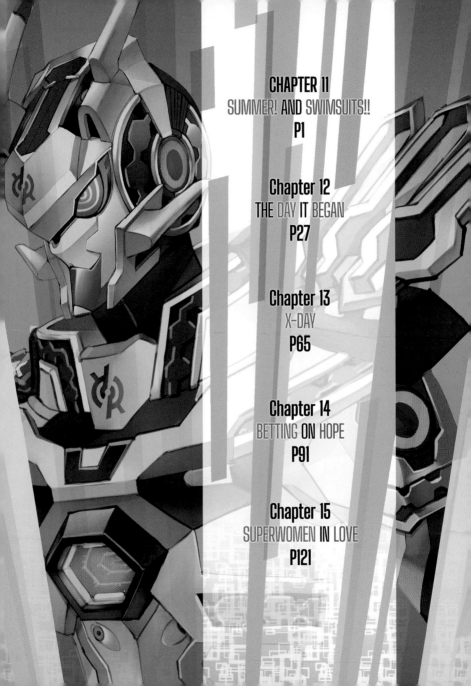

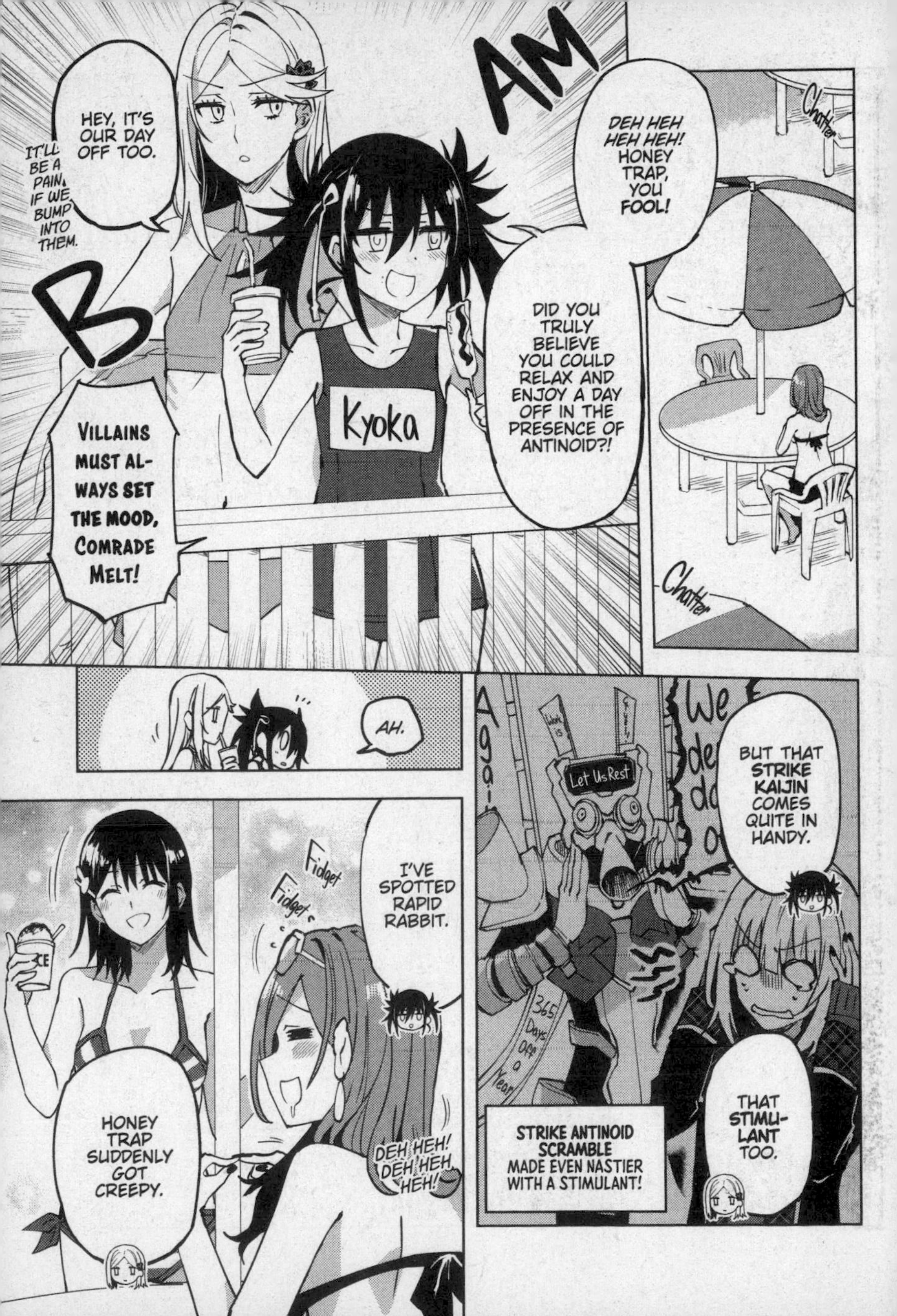
Chatter
Chatter
AM
B
DEH HEH HEH HEH! HONEY TRAP, YOU FOOL!
DID YOU TRULY BELIEVE YOU COULD RELAX AND ENJOY A DAY OFF IN THE PRESENCE OF ANTINOID?!
Kyoka
HEY, IT'S OUR DAY OFF TOO.
IT'LL BE A PAIN IF WE BUMP INTO THEM.
VILLAINS MUST AL-WAYS SET THE MOOD, COMRADE MELT!
Let Us Rest
365 Days Off a Year
BUT THAT STRIKE KAIJIN COMES QUITE IN HANDY.
THAT STIMU-LANT TOO.
STRIKE ANTINOID SCRAMBLE MADE EVEN NASTIER WITH A STIMULANT!
AH.
I'VE SPOTTED RAPID RABBIT.
Fidget Fidget
DEH HEH! DEH HEH HEH!
HONEY TRAP SUDDENLY GOT CREEPY.

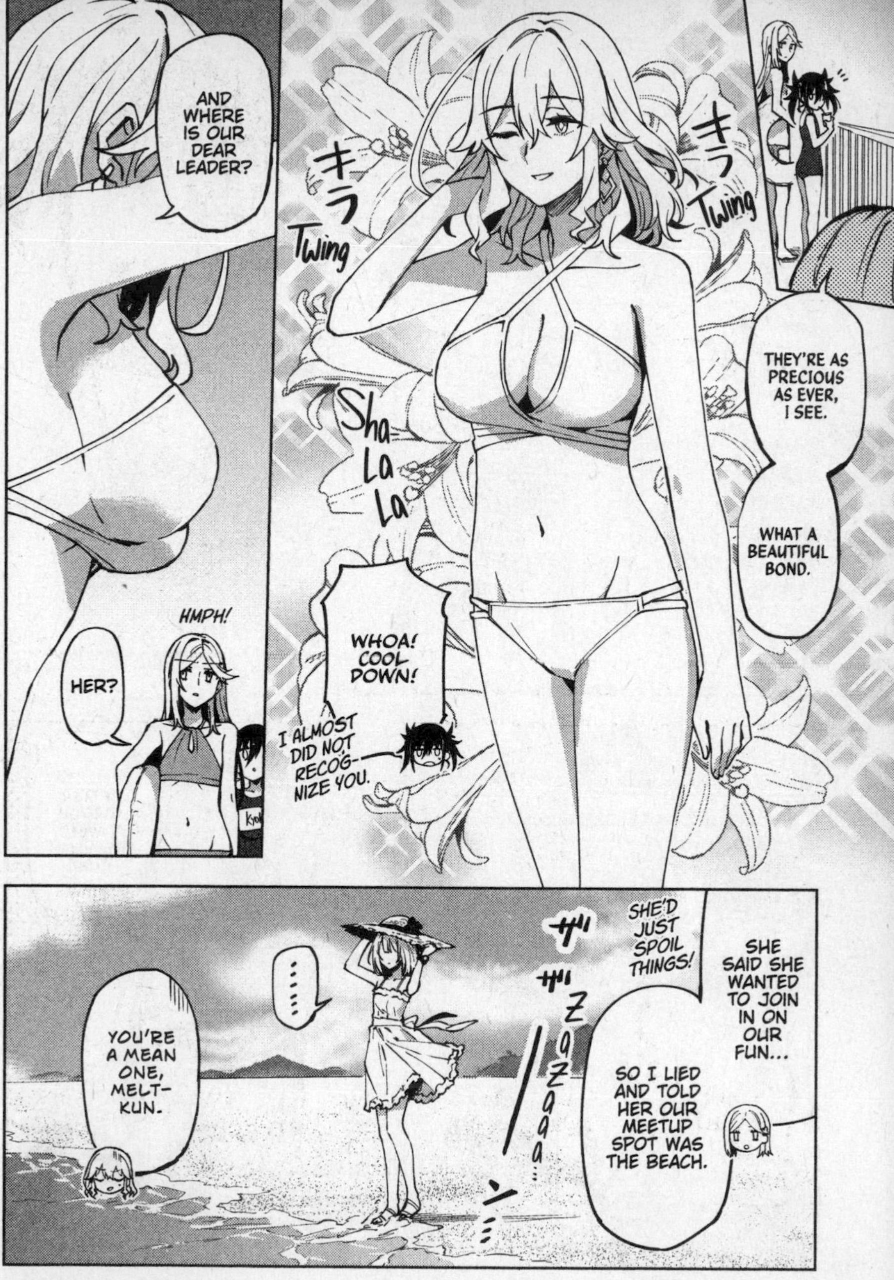
THEY'RE AS PRECIOUS AS EVER, I SEE.
WHAT A BEAUTIFUL BOND.
キラ Twing
キラ Twing
Sha La La
WHOA! COOL DOWN!
I ALMOST DID NOT RECOG-NIZE YOU.
AND WHERE IS OUR DEAR LEADER?
HMPH!
HER?
SHE SAID SHE WANTED TO JOIN IN ON OUR FUN...
SO I LIED AND TOLD HER OUR MEETUP SPOT WAS THE BEACH.
SHE'D JUST SPOIL THINGS!
ザ ザ
Zaza Zaaa...
......
YOU'RE A MEAN ONE, MELT-KUN.

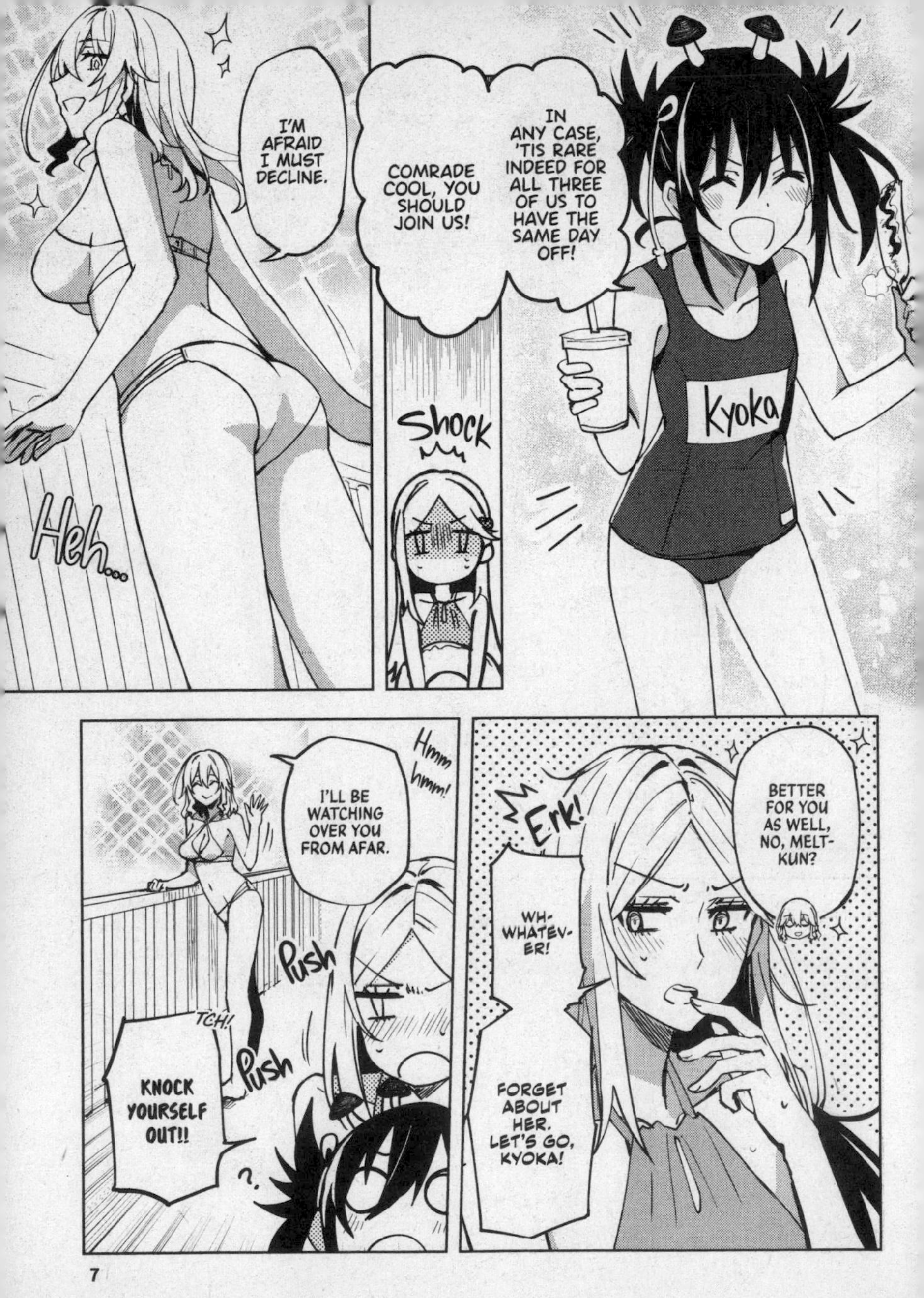
IN ANY CASE, 'TIS RARE INDEED FOR ALL THREE OF US TO HAVE THE SAME DAY OFF!
COMRADE COOL, YOU SHOULD JOIN US!
Shock
I'M AFRAID I MUST DECLINE.
Heh...
BETTER FOR YOU AS WELL, NO, MELT-KUN?
Erk!
WH-WHATEVER!
FORGET ABOUT HER. LET'S GO, KYOKA!
Hmm hmm!
I'LL BE WATCHING OVER YOU FROM AFAR.
Push
TCH!
Push
KNOCK YOURSELF OUT!!
?

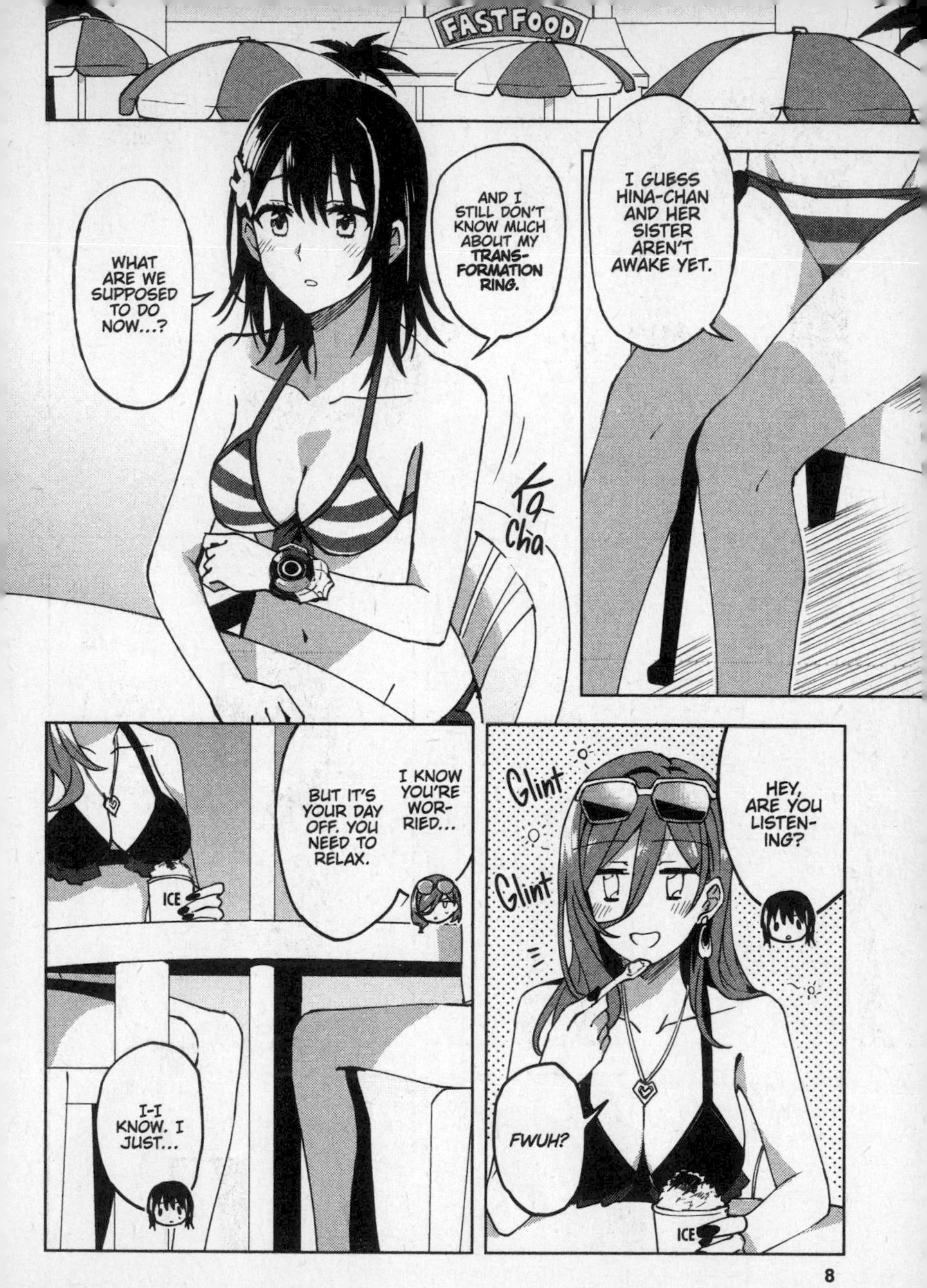
I GUESS HINA-CHAN AND HER SISTER AREN'T AWAKE YET.
FAST FOOD
AND I STILL DON'T KNOW MUCH ABOUT MY TRANS-FORMATION RING.
WHAT ARE WE SUPPOSED TO DO NOW...?
Ka-Cha
HEY, ARE YOU LISTEN-ING?
Glint
Glint
FWUH?
I KNOW YOU'RE WOR-RIED...
BUT IT'S YOUR DAY OFF. YOU NEED TO RELAX.
ICE
I-I KNOW. I JUST...
ICE

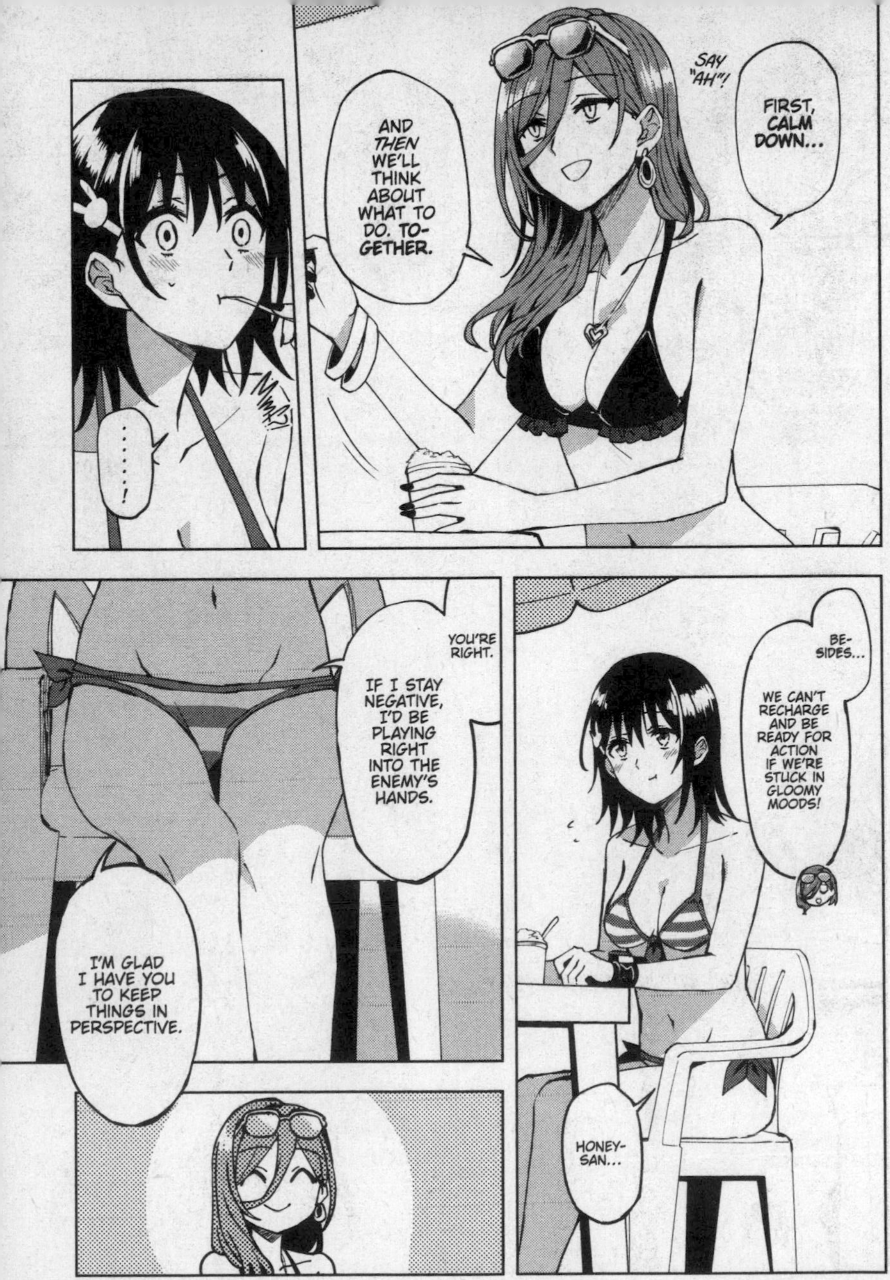
SAY "AH"!
FIRST, CALM DOWN...
AND *THEN* WE'LL THINK ABOUT WHAT TO DO. TO-GETHER.
......!
BE-SIDES...
WE CAN'T RECHARGE AND BE READY FOR ACTION IF WE'RE STUCK IN GLOOMY MOODS!
HONEY-SAN...
YOU'RE RIGHT.
IF I STAY NEGATIVE, I'D BE PLAYING RIGHT INTO THE ENEMY'S HANDS.
I'M GLAD I HAVE YOU TO KEEP THINGS IN PERSPECTIVE.

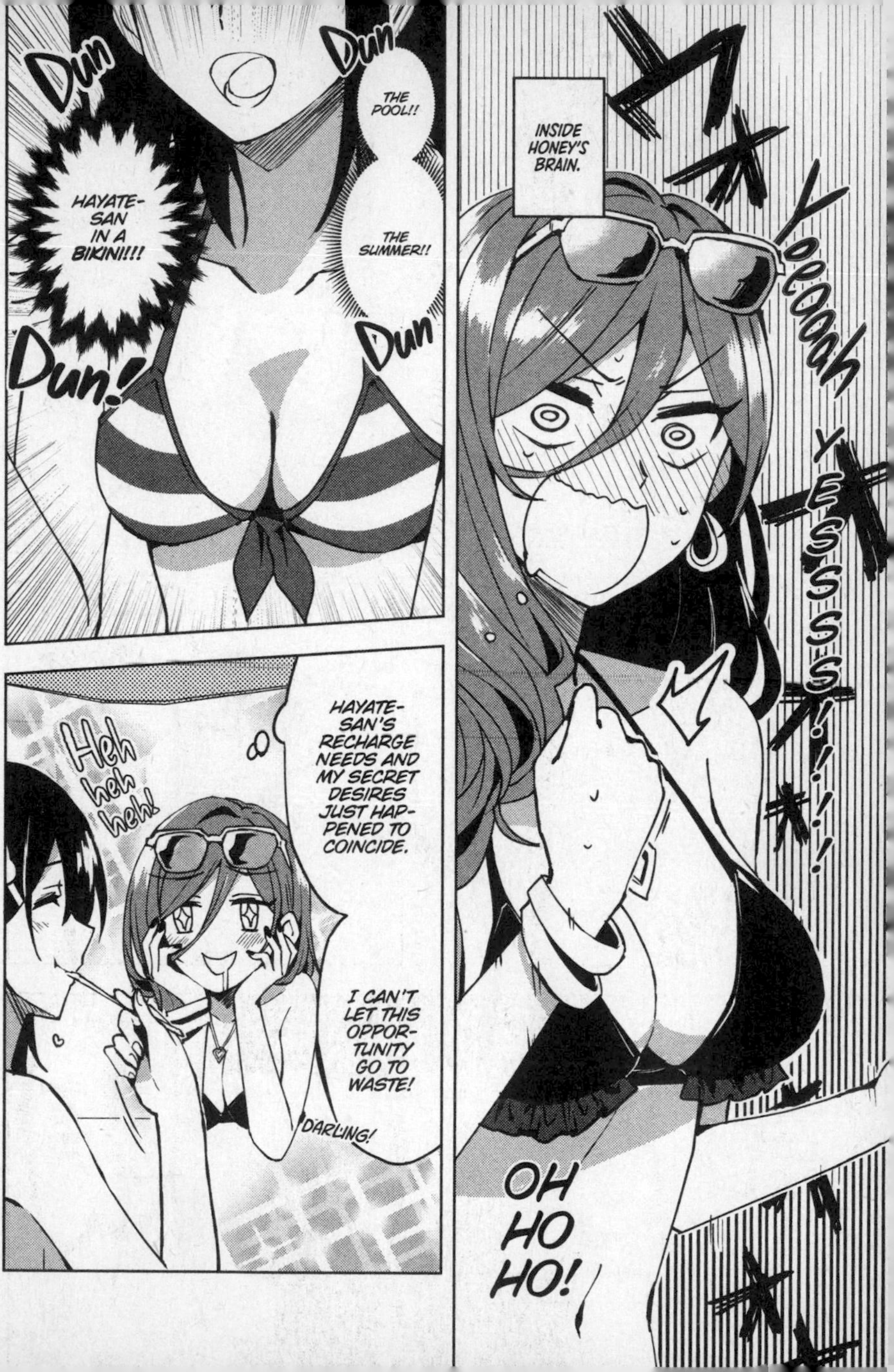
INSIDE HONEY'S BRAIN.
Yeeaaah YESSSSS!!!
OH HO HO!
Dun
Dun
THE POOL!!
THE SUMMER!!
HAYATE-SAN IN A BIKINI!!!
Dun
Dun!
HAYATE-SAN'S RECHARGE NEEDS AND MY SECRET DESIRES JUST HAPPENED TO COINCIDE.
I CAN'T LET THIS OPPORTUNITY GO TO WASTE!
Heh heh heh!
DARLING!

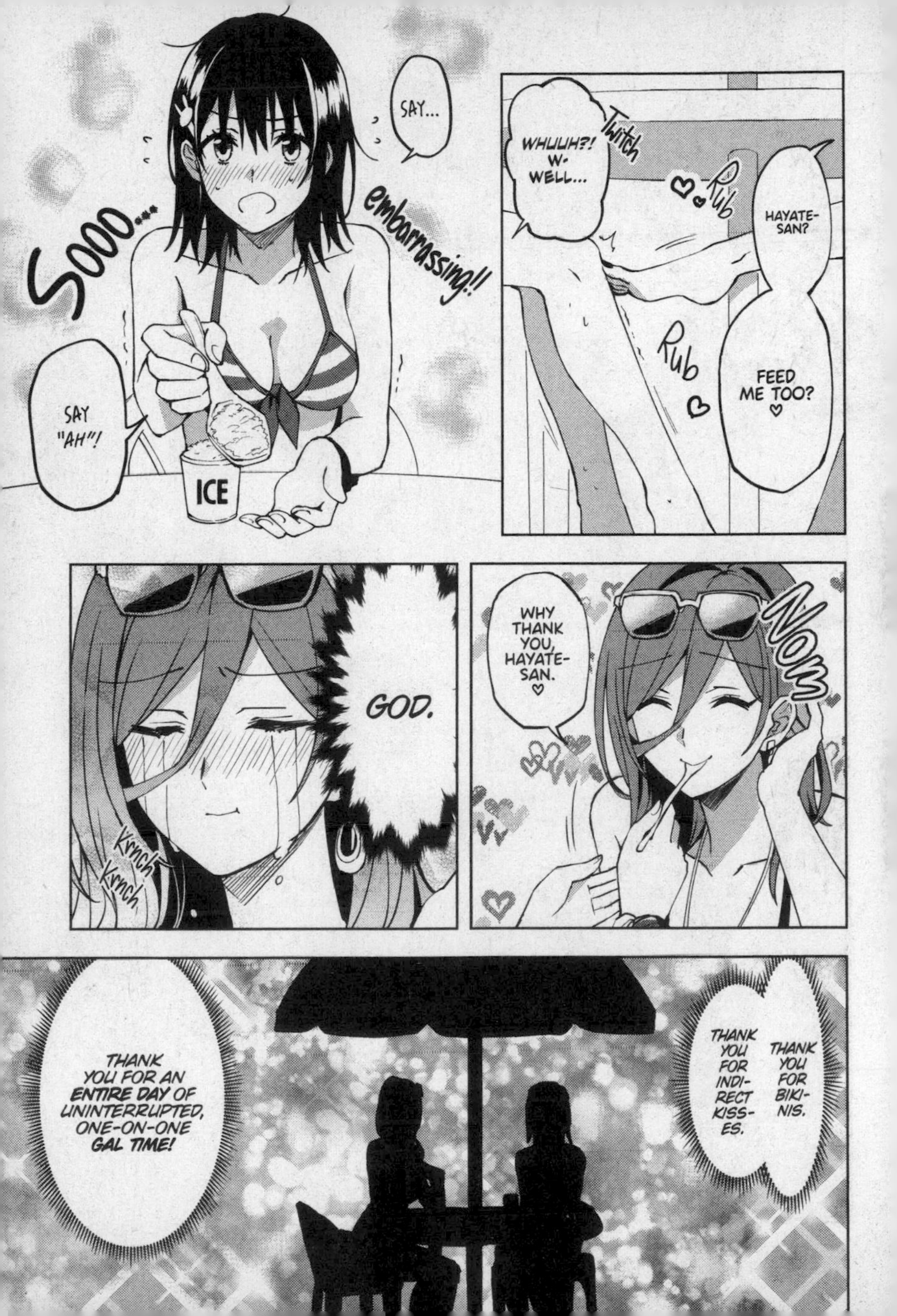
HAYATE-SAN? FEED ME TOO? ♡
Rub ♡
Rub ♡
Twitch
WHUUH?! W-WELL...
SAY...
SOOO... embarrassing!!
SAY "AH"!
ICE
Nom
WHY THANK YOU, HAYATE-SAN. ♡
GOD.
Krnch Krnch
THANK YOU FOR BIKI-NIS.
THANK YOU FOR INDI-RECT KISS-ES.
THANK YOU FOR AN ENTIRE DAY OF UNINTERRUPTED, ONE-ON-ONE GAL TIME!

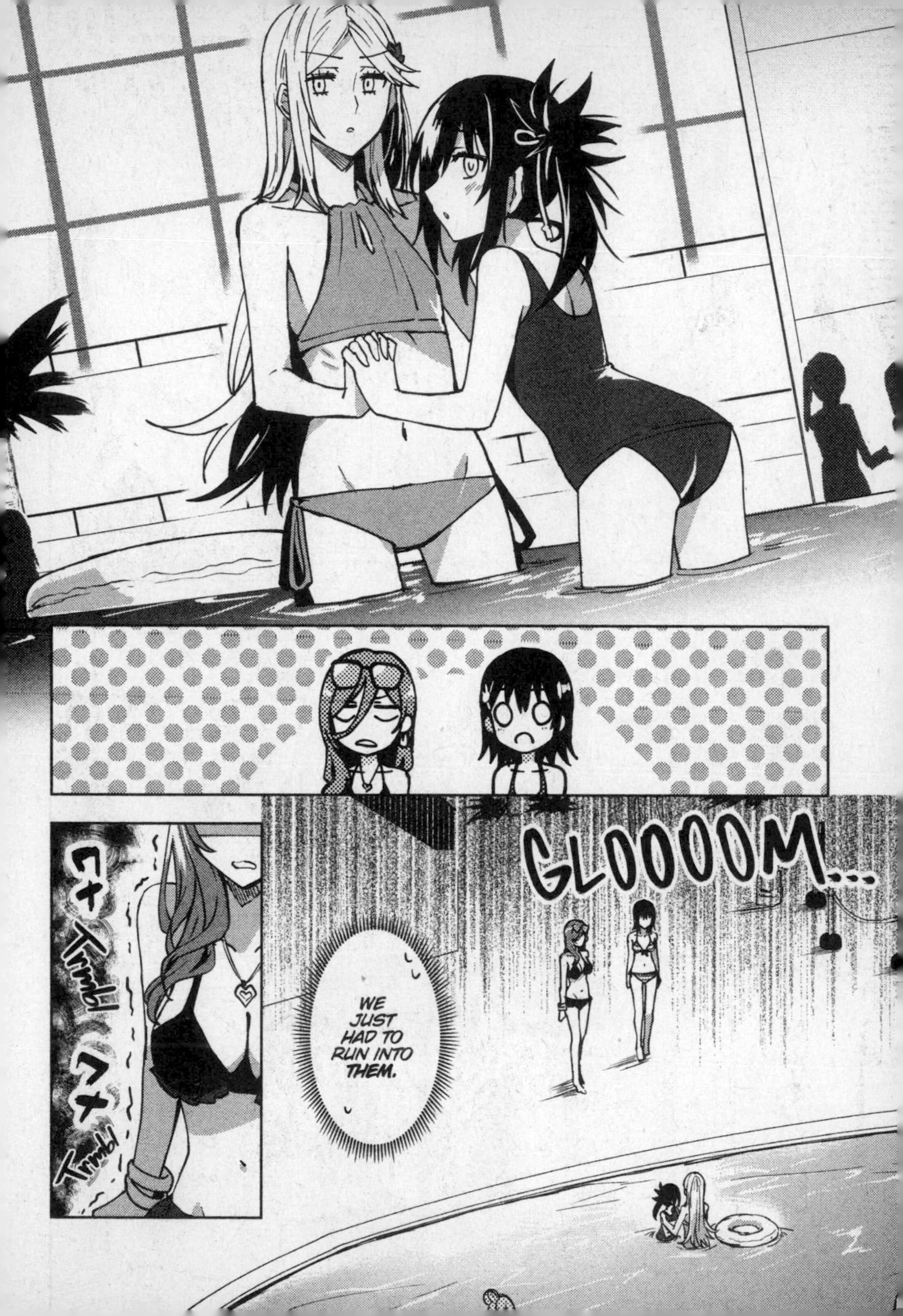
GLOOOOM...
WE JUST HAD TO RUN INTO THEM.
Trmbl
Trmbl

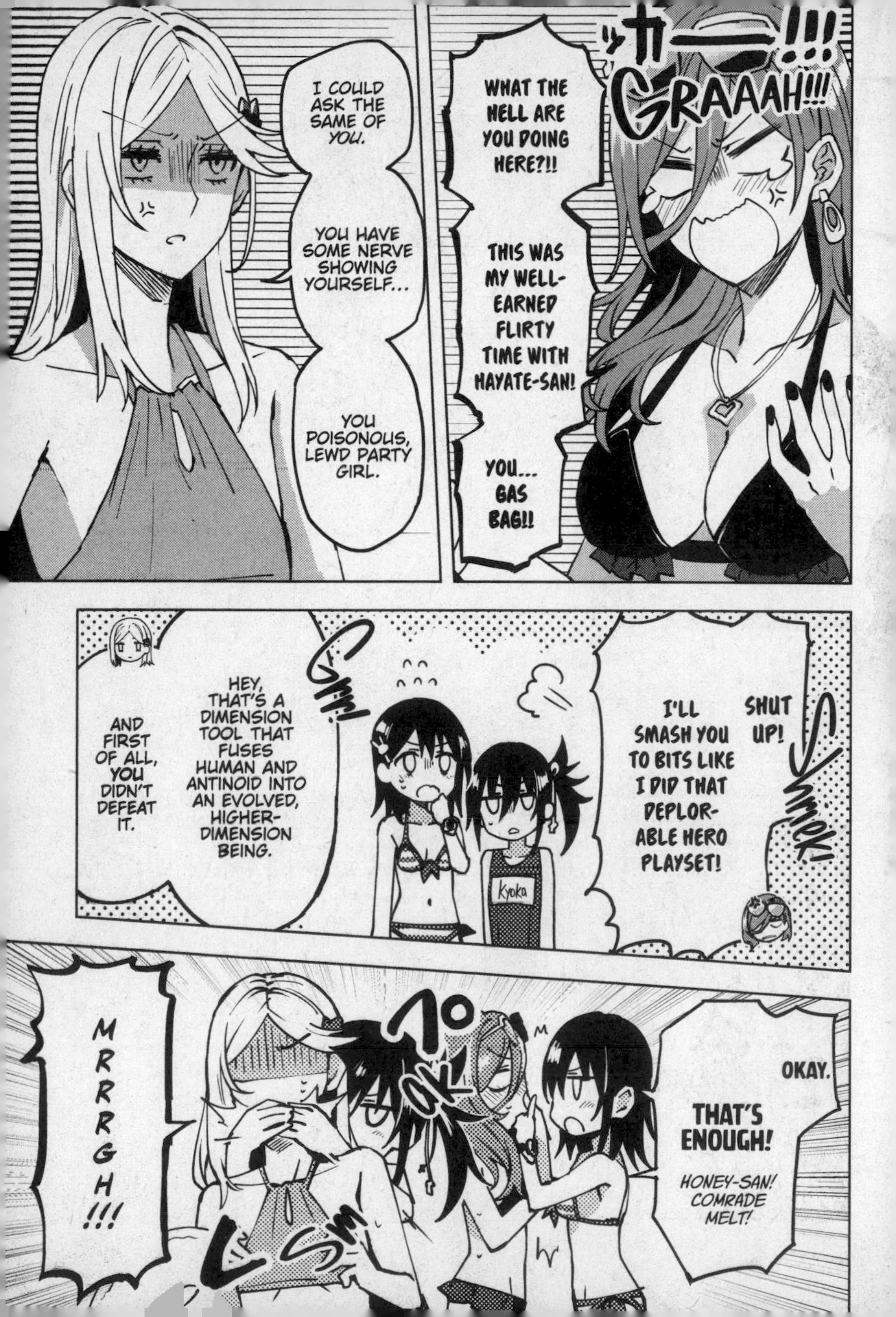
GRAAAH!!!
WHAT THE HELL ARE YOU DOING HERE?!!
THIS WAS MY WELL-EARNED FLIRTY TIME WITH HAYATE-SAN!
YOU... GAS BAG!!
I COULD ASK THE SAME OF YOU.
YOU HAVE SOME NERVE SHOWING YOURSELF...
YOU POISONOUS, LEWD PARTY GIRL.
SHUT UP!
Shmek!
I'LL SMASH YOU TO BITS LIKE I DID THAT DEPLORABLE HERO PLAYSET!
Kyoka
Grrr!
HEY, THAT'S A DIMENSION TOOL THAT FUSES HUMAN AND ANTINOID INTO AN EVOLVED, HIGHER-DIMENSION BEING.
AND FIRST OF ALL, YOU DIDN'T DEFEAT IT.
OKAY.
THAT'S ENOUGH!
HONEY-SAN! COMRADE MELT!
MRRRGH!!!

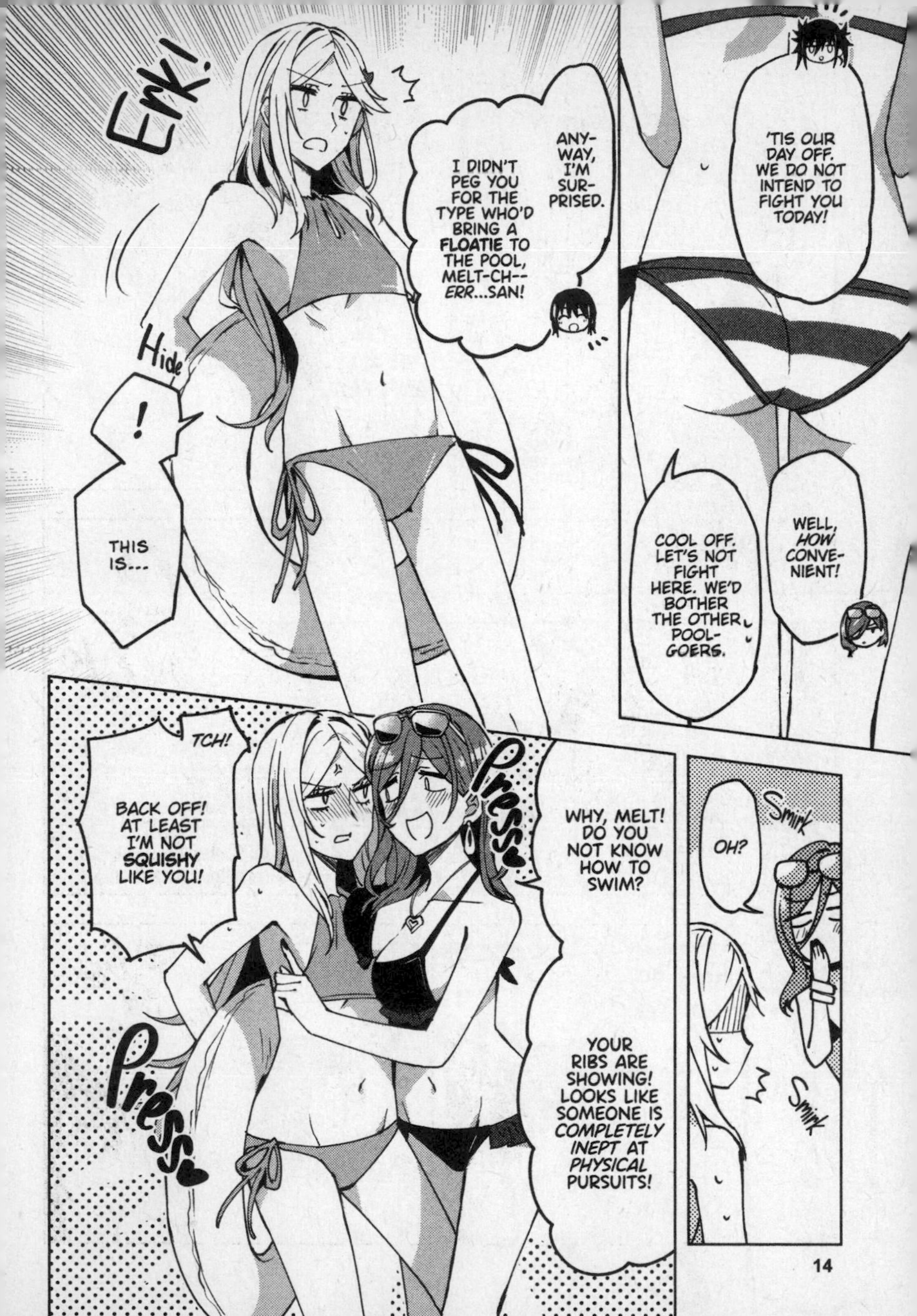
'TIS OUR DAY OFF. WE DO NOT INTEND TO FIGHT YOU TODAY!
WELL, HOW CONVENIENT!
COOL OFF. LET'S NOT FIGHT HERE. WE'D BOTHER THE OTHER POOL-GOERS.
ANY-WAY, I'M SUR-PRISED.
I DIDN'T PEG YOU FOR THE TYPE WHO'D BRING A FLOATIE TO THE POOL, MELT-CH-- ERR...SAN!
Erk!
Hide
!
THIS IS...
Smirk
OH?
Smirk
WHY, MELT! DO YOU NOT KNOW HOW TO SWIM?
Press
TCH!
BACK OFF! AT LEAST I'M NOT SQUISHY LIKE YOU!
YOUR RIBS ARE SHOWING! LOOKS LIKE SOMEONE IS COMPLETELY INEPT AT PHYSICAL PURSUITS!
Press

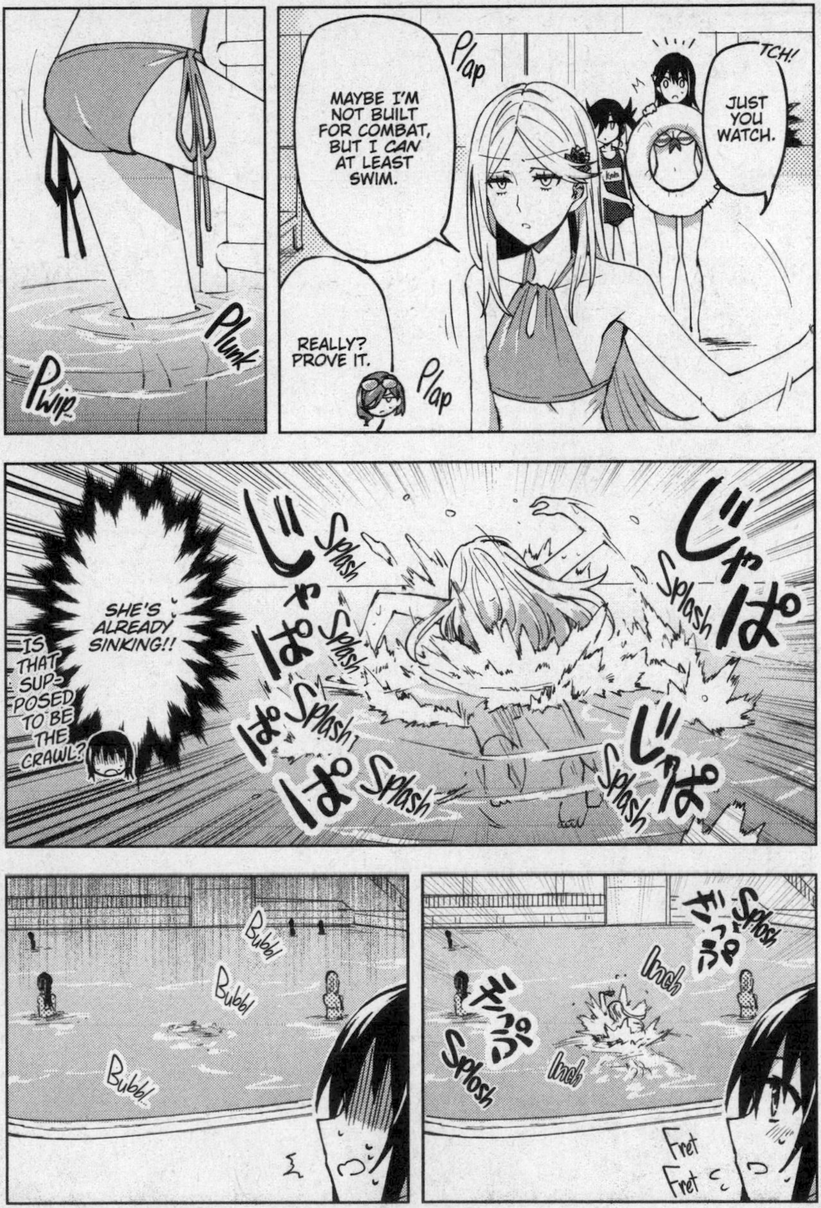
TCH!
JUST YOU WATCH.
MAYBE I'M NOT BUILT FOR COMBAT, BUT I CAN AT LEAST SWIM.
Plap
REALLY? PROVE IT.
Plap
Plunk
Pwip
じゃぱ
Splash
じゃぱ
Splash
じゃぱ
Splash
ぱ
Splash
ぱ
Splash
SHE'S ALREADY SINKING!!
IS THAT SUP-POSED TO BE THE CRAWL?
Bubbl
Bubbl
Bubbl...
ざっぷ
Splosh
Inch
ざっぷ
Splosh
Inch
Fret
Fret

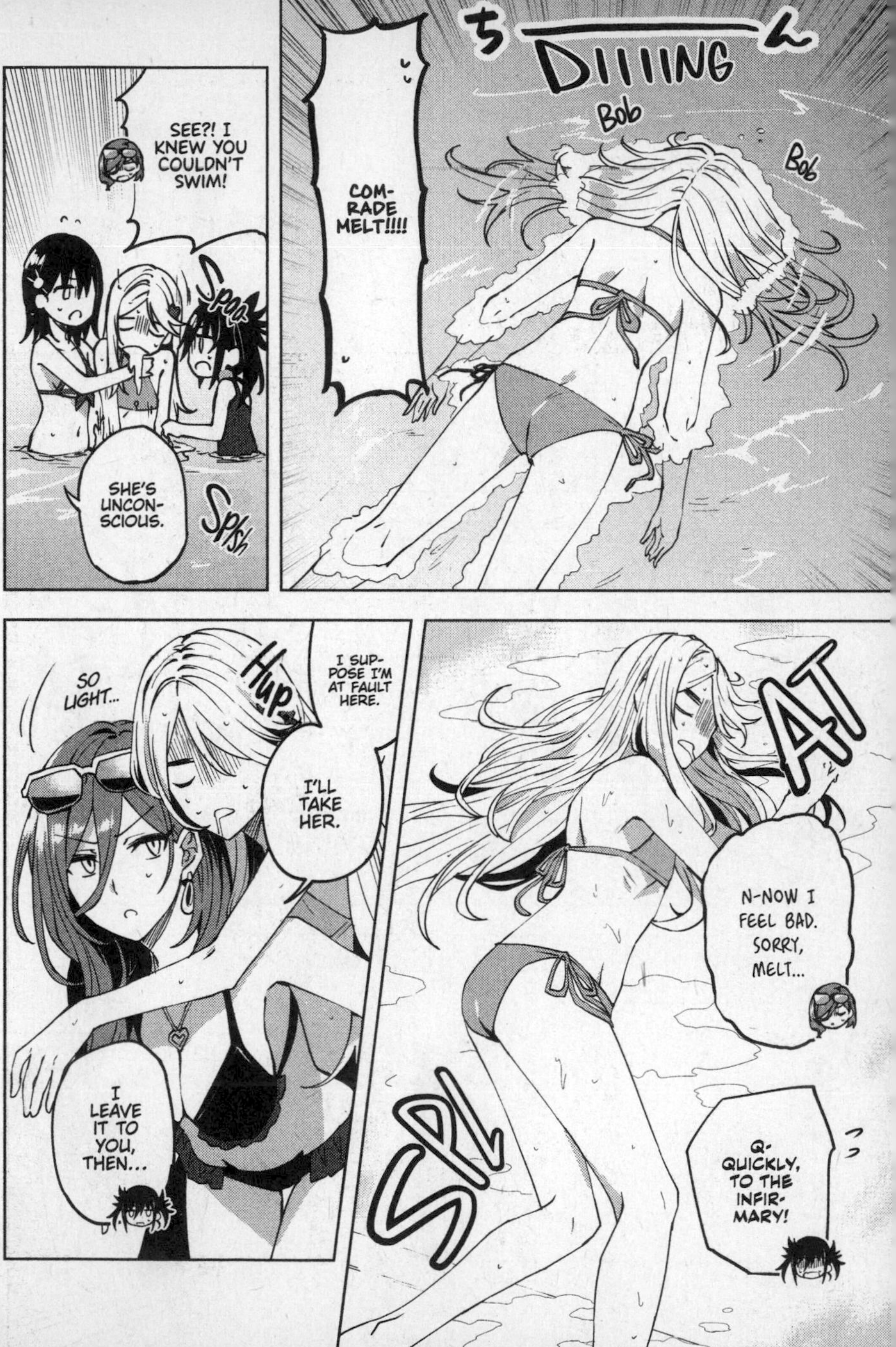
ち——ん
DIIIING
Bob
Bob
COM-RADE MELT!!!!
SEE?! I KNEW YOU COULDN'T SWIM!
Spoo
SHE'S UNCON-SCIOUS.
Splsh
AT
SPL
N-NOW I FEEL BAD. SORRY, MELT...
Q-QUICKLY, TO THE INFIR-MARY!
I SUP-POSE I'M AT FAULT HERE.
Hup
I'LL TAKE HER.
SO LIGHT...
I LEAVE IT TO YOU, THEN...

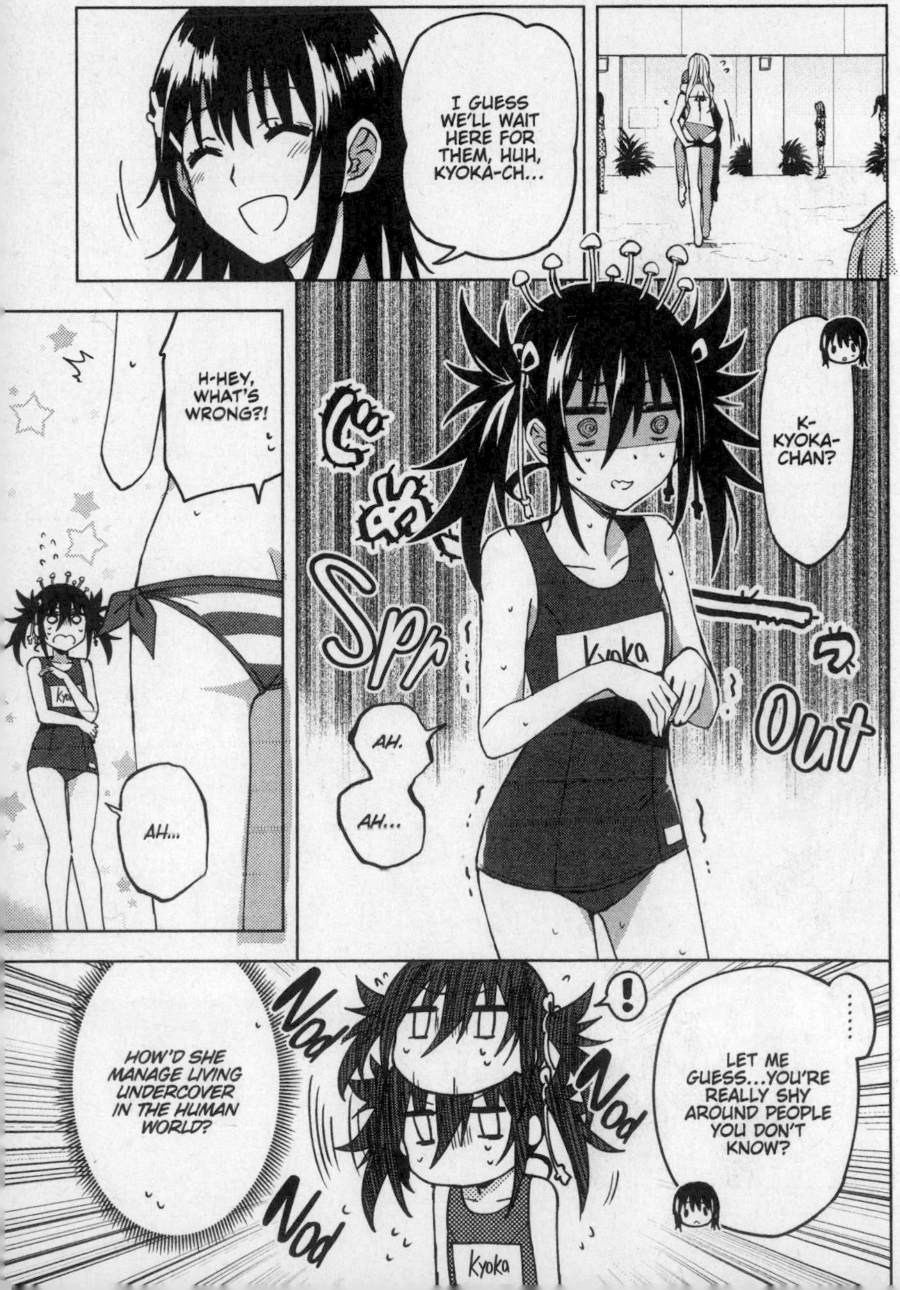
I GUESS WE'LL WAIT HERE FOR THEM, HUH, KYOKA-CH...
K-KYOKA-CHAN?
Spr
Kyoka
Out
AH.
AH...
H-HEY, WHAT'S WRONG?!
Kyoka
AH...
......
LET ME GUESS...YOU'RE REALLY SHY AROUND PEOPLE YOU DON'T KNOW?
!
Nod
Nod
Nod
Nod
Kyoka
HOW'D SHE MANAGE LIVING UNDERCOVER IN THE HUMAN WORLD?

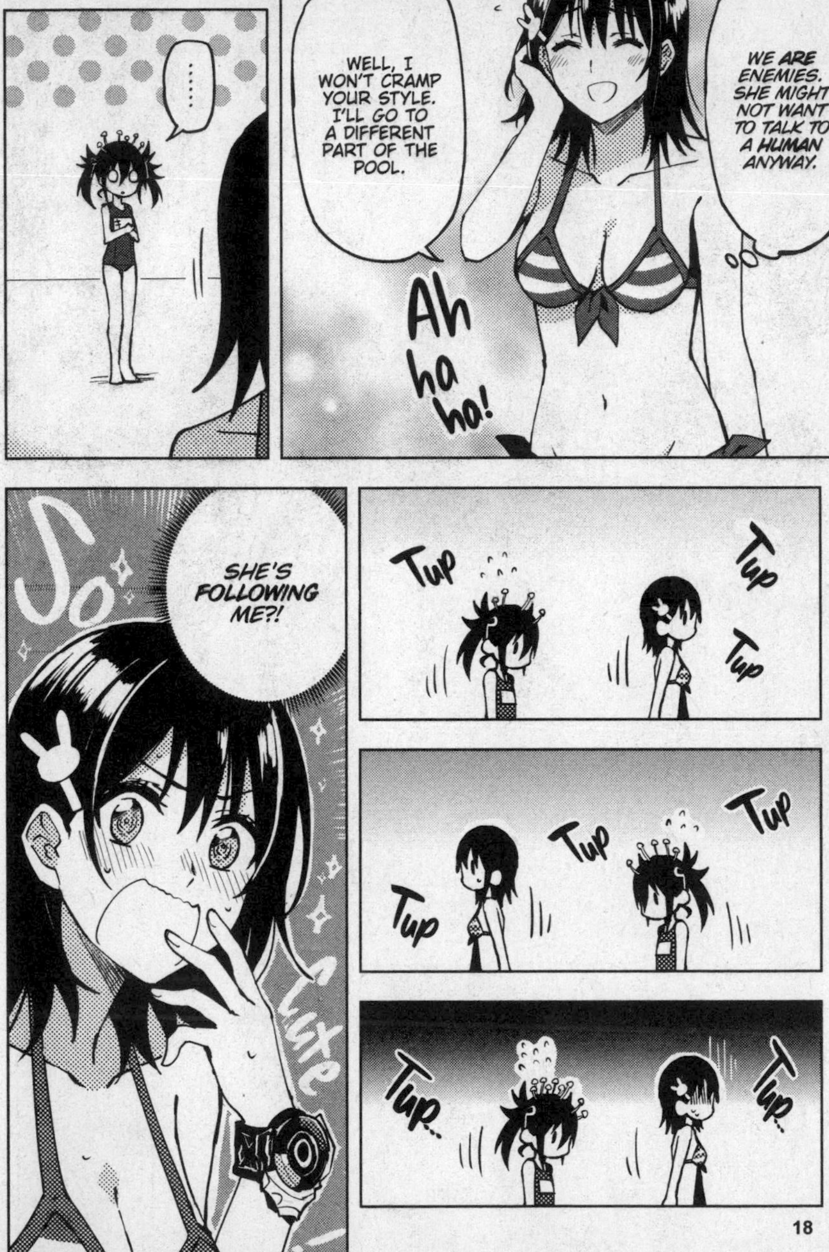
WE ARE ENEMIES. SHE MIGHT NOT WANT TO TALK TO A HUMAN ANYWAY.
WELL, I WON'T CRAMP YOUR STYLE. I'LL GO TO A DIFFERENT PART OF THE POOL.
Ah ha ha!
......
Tup
Tup
Tup
Tup
Tup
Tup
Tup...
Tup...
SHE'S FOLLOWING ME?!
So
cute

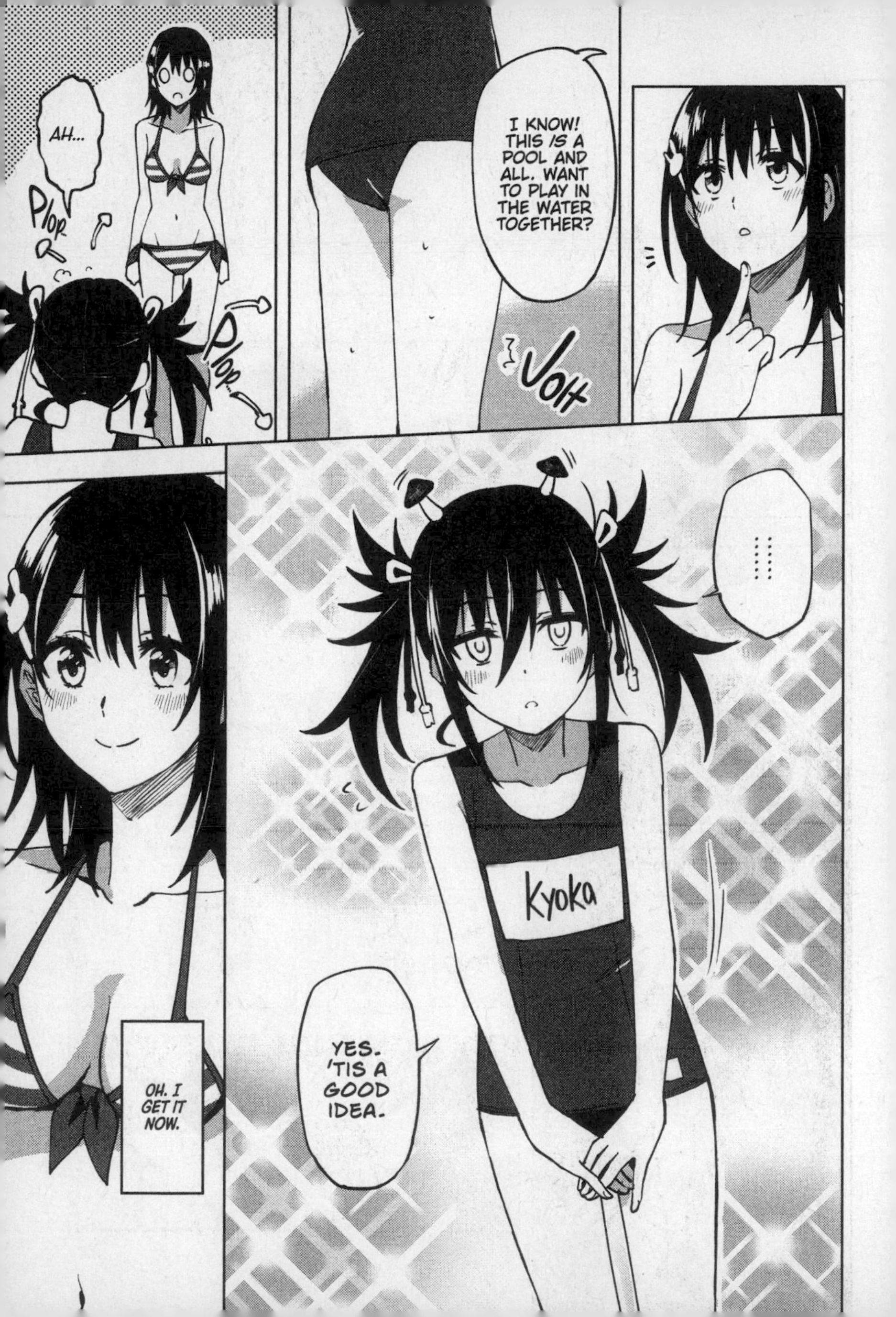
I KNOW! THIS IS A POOL AND ALL. WANT TO PLAY IN THE WATER TOGETHER?
Volt
AH...
Plop
Plop...
......
YES. 'TIS A GOOD IDEA.
Kyoka
OH. I GET IT NOW.

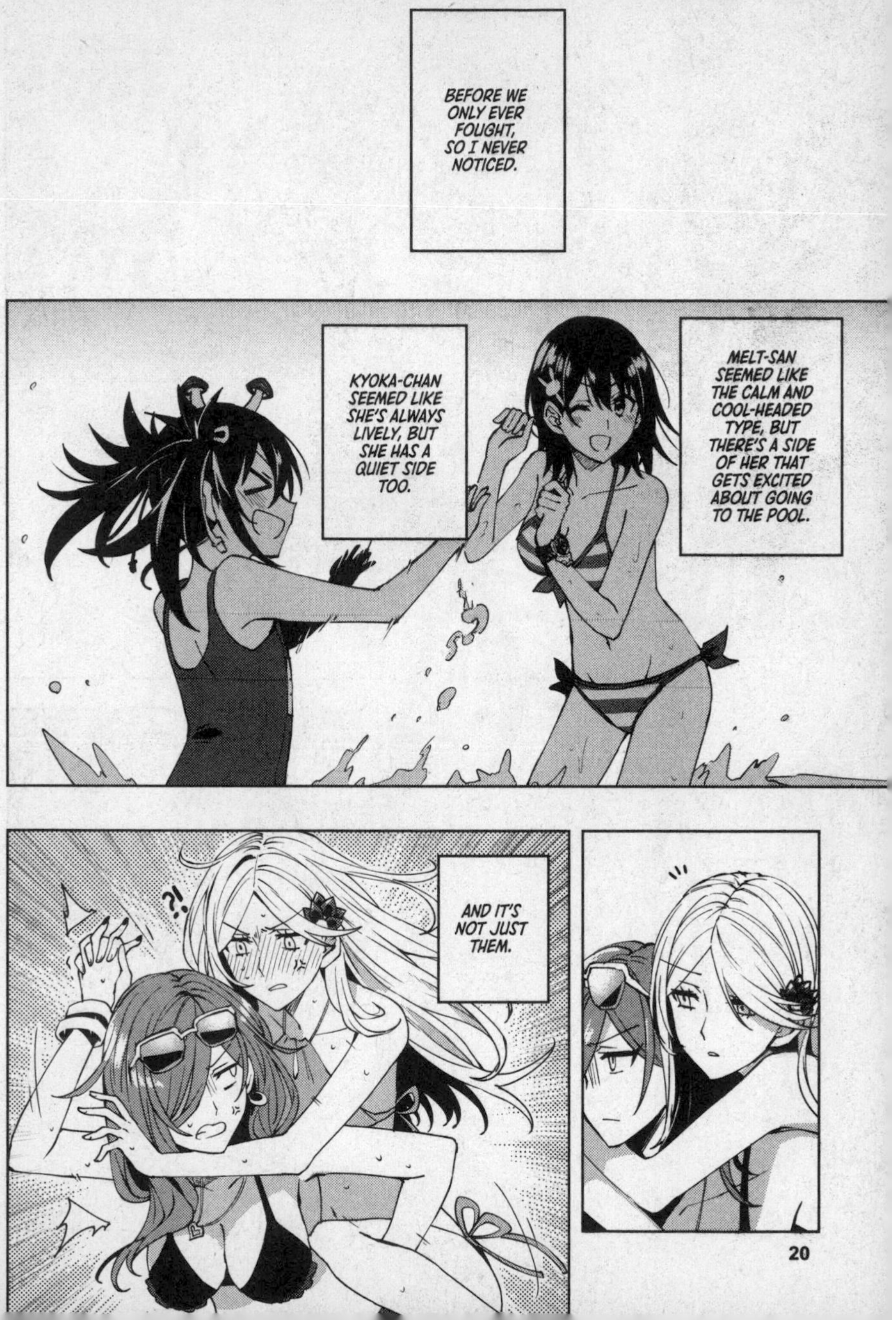
BEFORE WE ONLY EVER FOUGHT, SO I NEVER NOTICED.
MELT-SAN SEEMED LIKE THE CALM AND COOL-HEADED TYPE, BUT THERE'S A SIDE OF HER THAT GETS EXCITED ABOUT GOING TO THE POOL.
KYOKA-CHAN SEEMED LIKE SHE'S ALWAYS LIVELY, BUT SHE HAS A QUIET SIDE TOO.
AND IT'S NOT JUST THEM.
?!

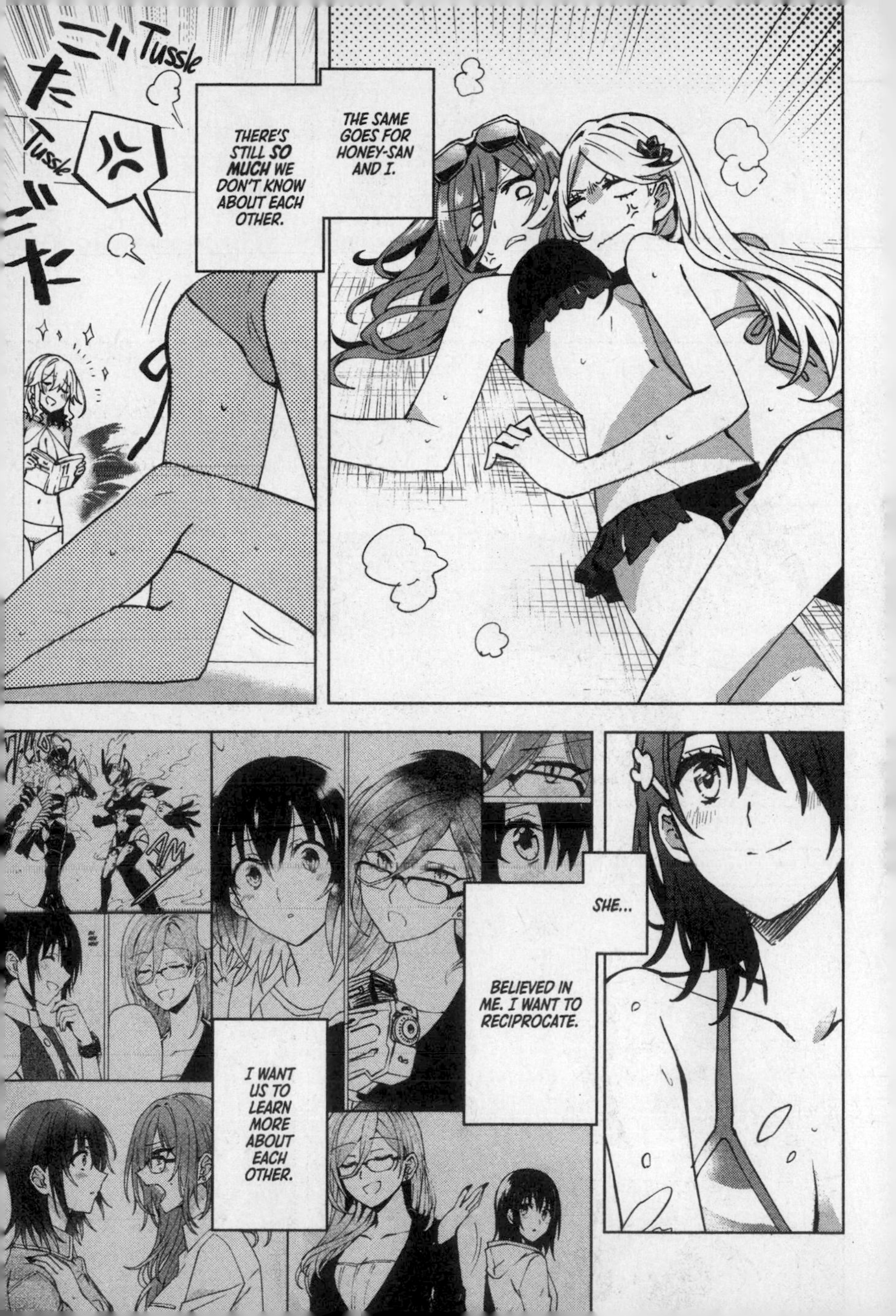
THE SAME GOES FOR HONEY-SAN AND I.
THERE'S STILL **SO MUCH** WE DON'T KNOW ABOUT EACH OTHER.
Tussle
Tussle
SHE...
BELIEVED IN ME. I WANT TO RECIPROCATE.
I WANT US TO LEARN MORE ABOUT EACH OTHER.

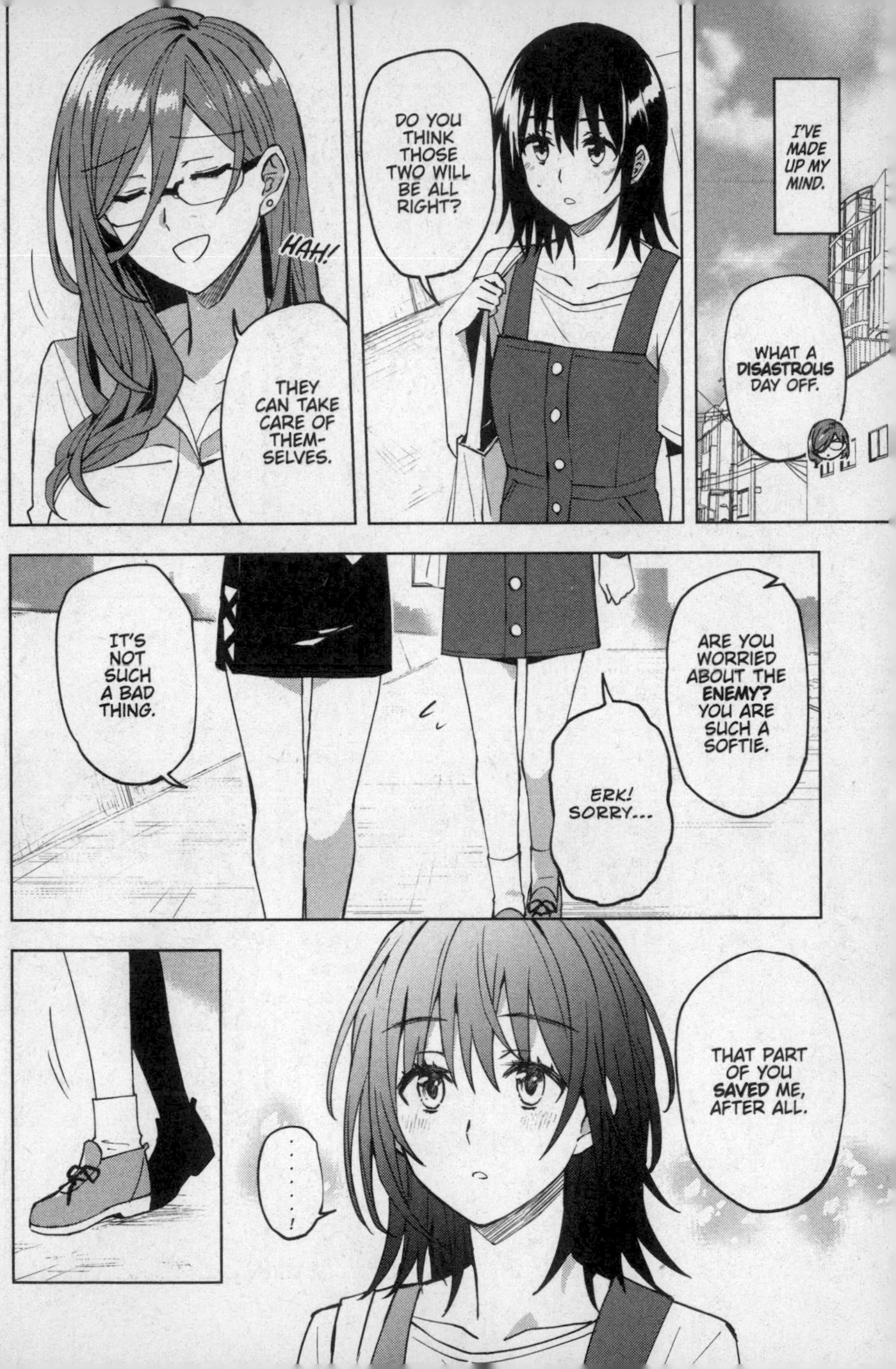
I'VE MADE UP MY MIND.
WHAT A **DISASTROUS** DAY OFF.
DO YOU THINK THOSE TWO WILL BE ALL RIGHT?
HAH!
THEY CAN TAKE CARE OF THEMSELVES.
ARE YOU WORRIED ABOUT THE **ENEMY?** YOU ARE SUCH A SOFTIE.
ERK! SORRY...
IT'S NOT SUCH A BAD THING.
THAT PART OF YOU **SAVED** ME, AFTER ALL.
......!

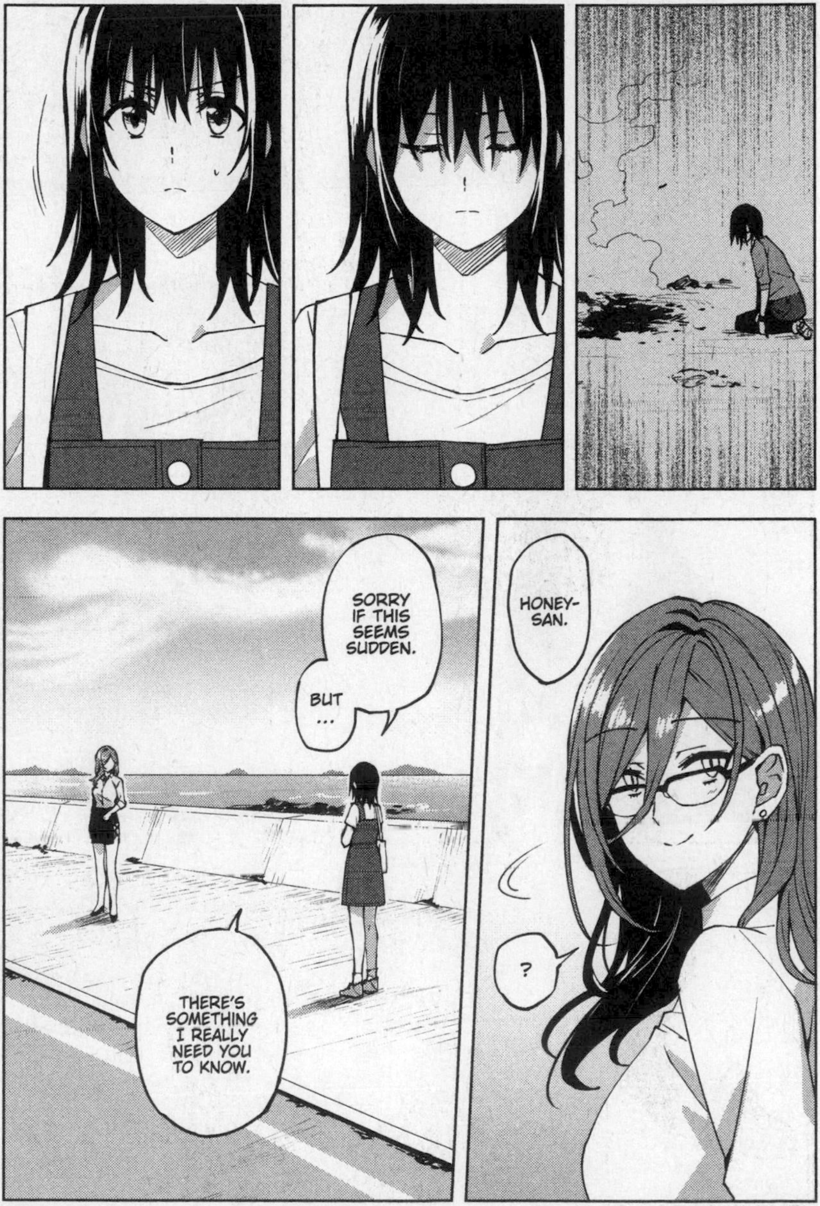
HONEY-SAN.
?
SORRY IF THIS SEEMS SUDDEN.
BUT ...
THERE'S SOMETHING I REALLY NEED YOU TO KNOW.

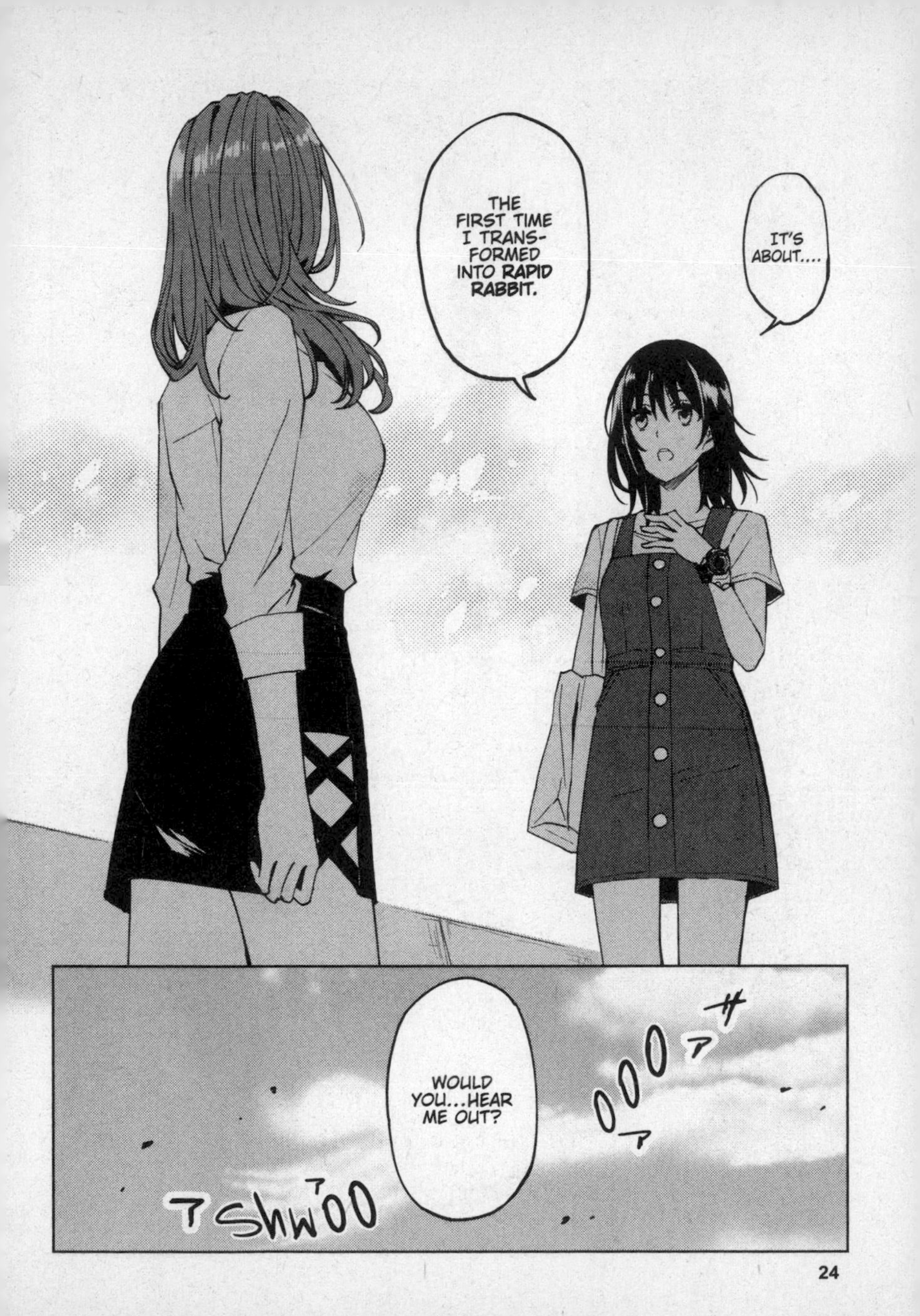
IT'S ABOUT....
THE FIRST TIME I TRANS-FORMED INTO RAPID RABBIT.
WOULD YOU...HEAR ME OUT?
SHWOO

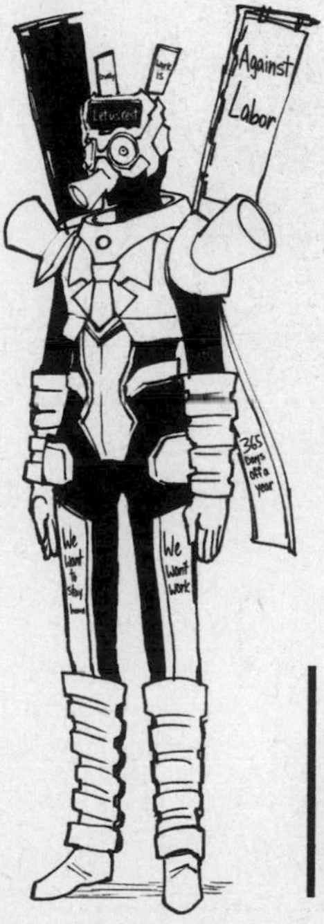
Let us rest
Against Labor
365 Days off a year
We want to stay home
We want work

Strike Antinoid Scramble (Enhanced Kaijin)
Superwomen in Love!
Honey Trap & Rapid Rabbit
Character Data

SUPERWOMEN IN LOVE!

HONEY TRAP & RAPID RABBIT

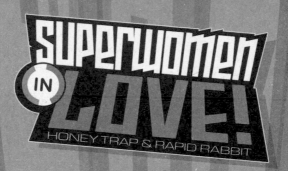

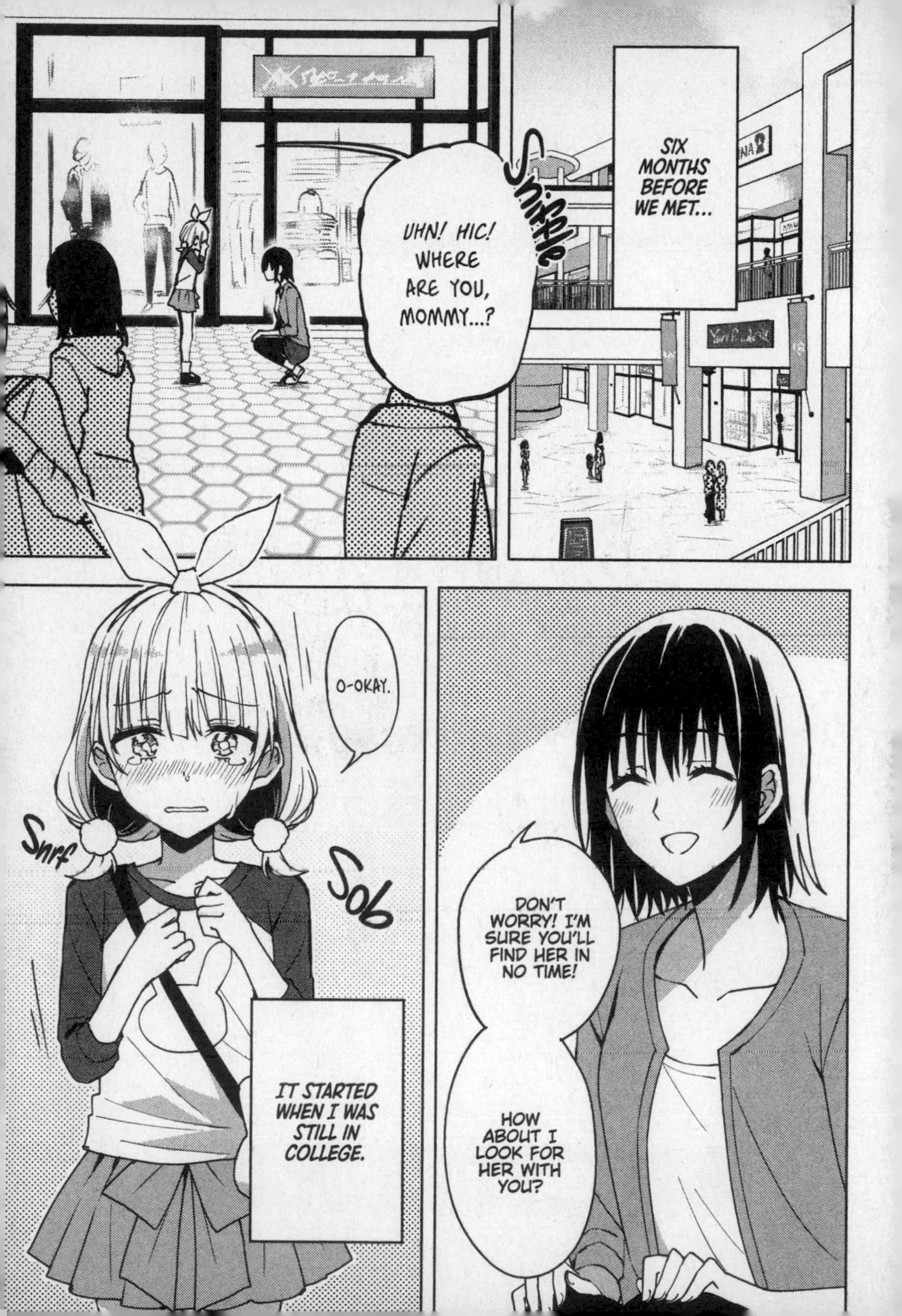
SIX MONTHS BEFORE WE MET...
Sniffle
UHN! HIC! WHERE ARE YOU, MOMMY...?
DON'T WORRY! I'M SURE YOU'LL FIND HER IN NO TIME!
HOW ABOUT I LOOK FOR HER WITH YOU?
O-OKAY.
Sob
Snrf
IT STARTED WHEN I WAS STILL IN COLLEGE.

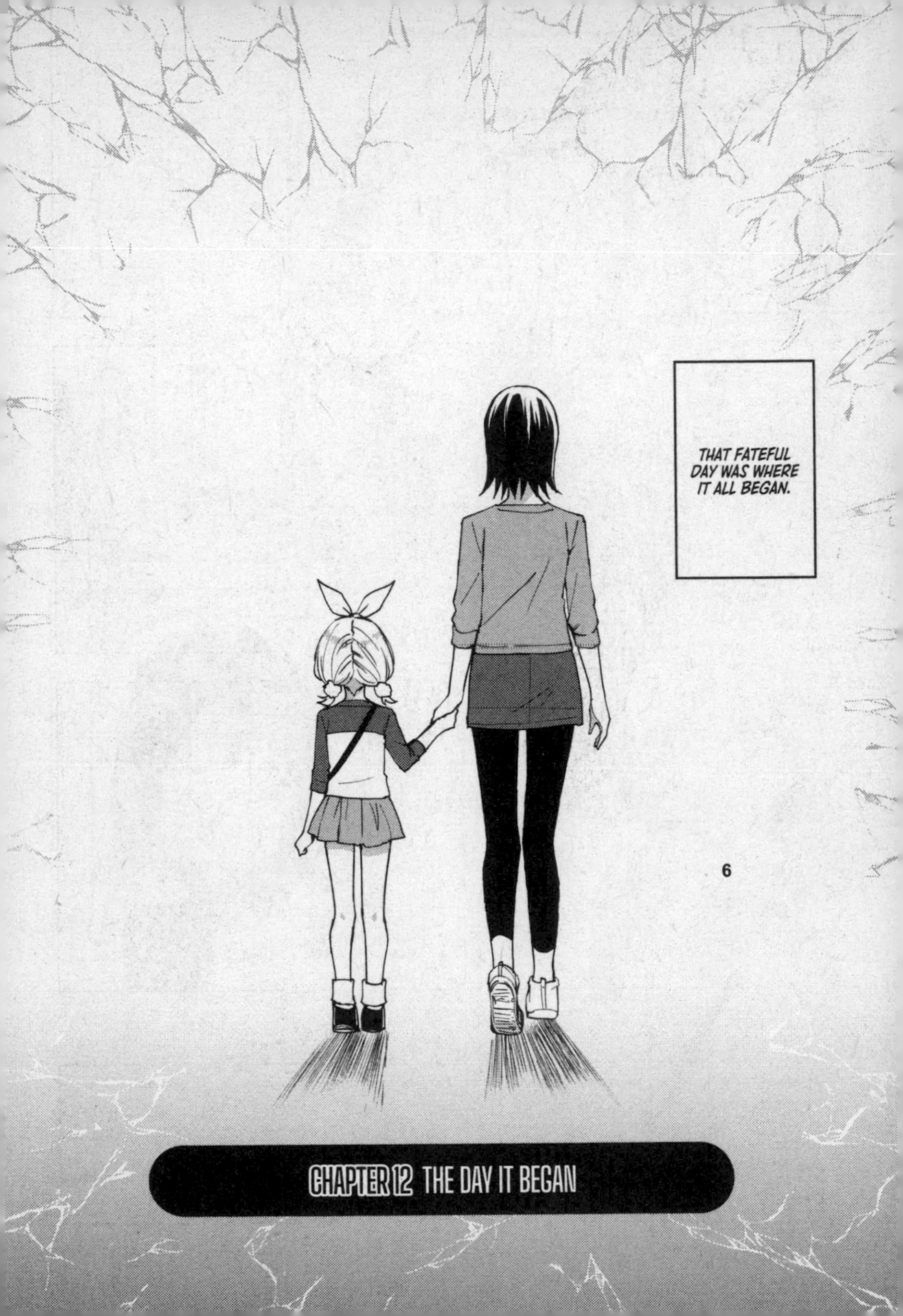
THAT FATEFUL DAY WAS WHERE IT ALL BEGAN.
6
CHAPTER 12 THE DAY IT BEGAN

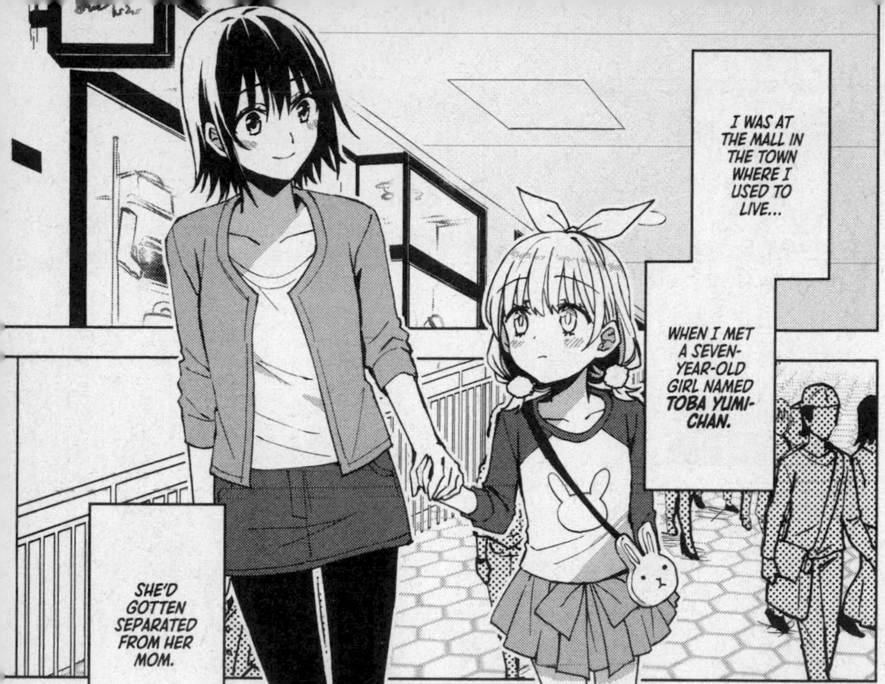
I WAS AT THE MALL IN THE TOWN WHERE I USED TO LIVE...
WHEN I MET A SEVEN-YEAR-OLD GIRL NAMED **TOBA YUMI-CHAN.**
SHE'D GOTTEN SEPARATED FROM HER MOM.
I DECIDED TO STICK WITH HER UNTIL THEY FOUND EACH OTHER.

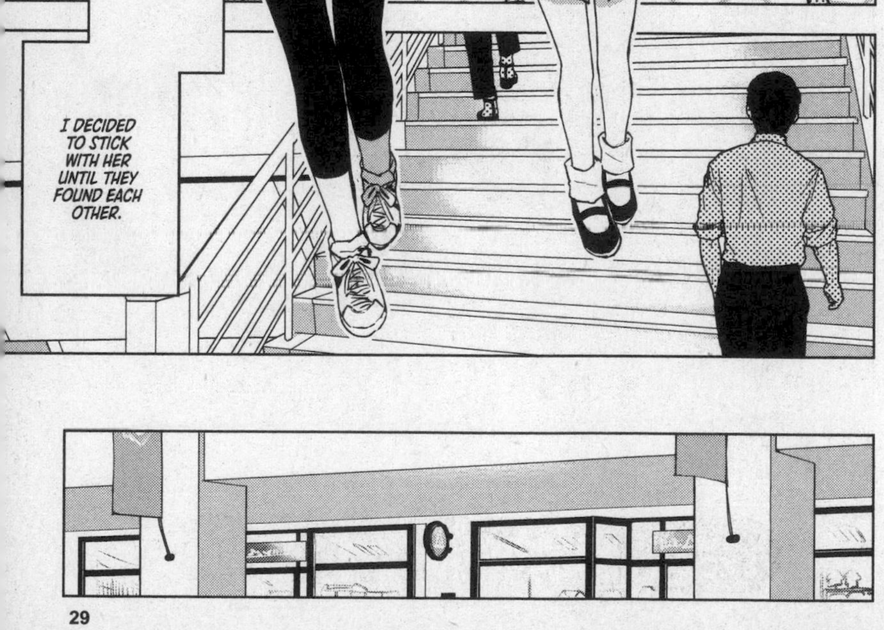

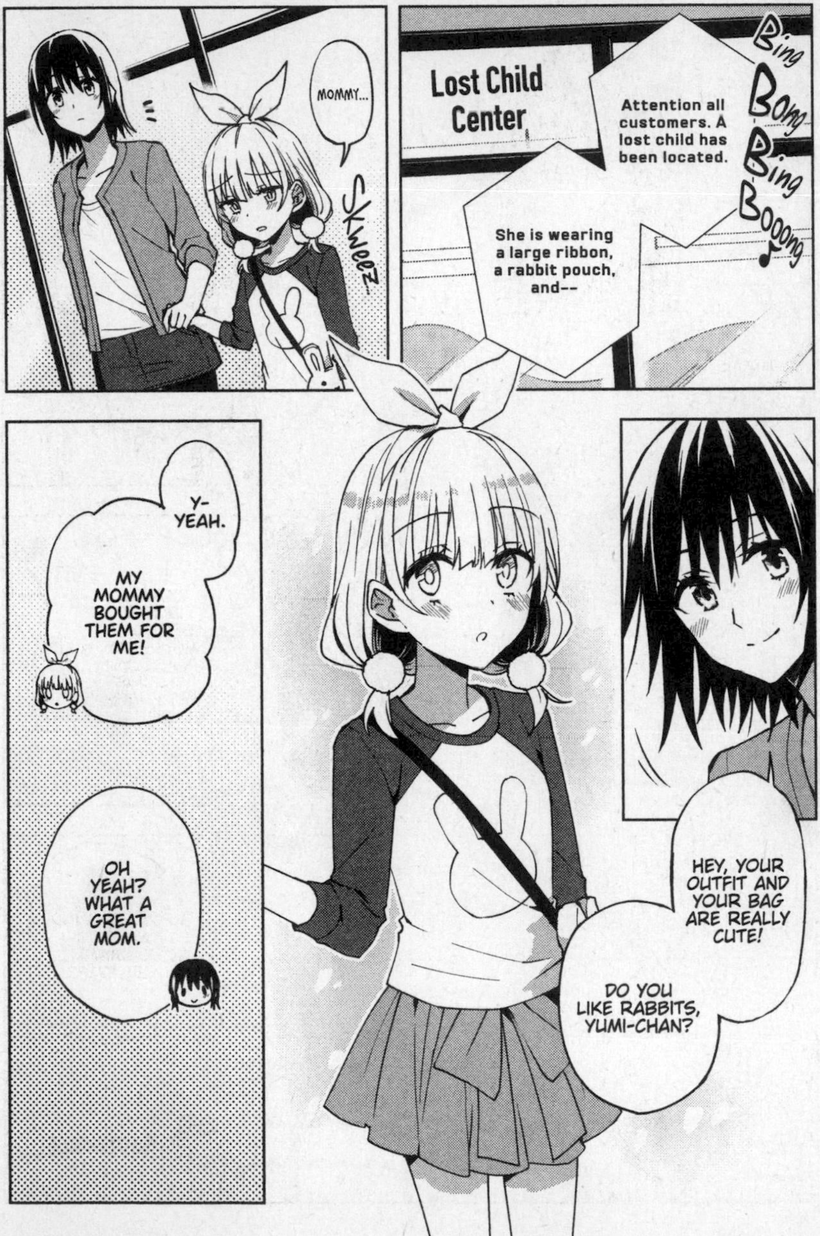
Lost Child Center
Attention all customers. A lost child has been located.
She is wearing a large ribbon, a rabbit pouch, and--
Bing Bong Bing Booong
MOMMY...
SKWEEZ
HEY, YOUR OUTFIT AND YOUR BAG ARE REALLY CUTE!
DO YOU LIKE RABBITS, YUMI-CHAN?
Y-YEAH.
MY MOMMY BOUGHT THEM FOR ME!
OH YEAH? WHAT A GREAT MOM.

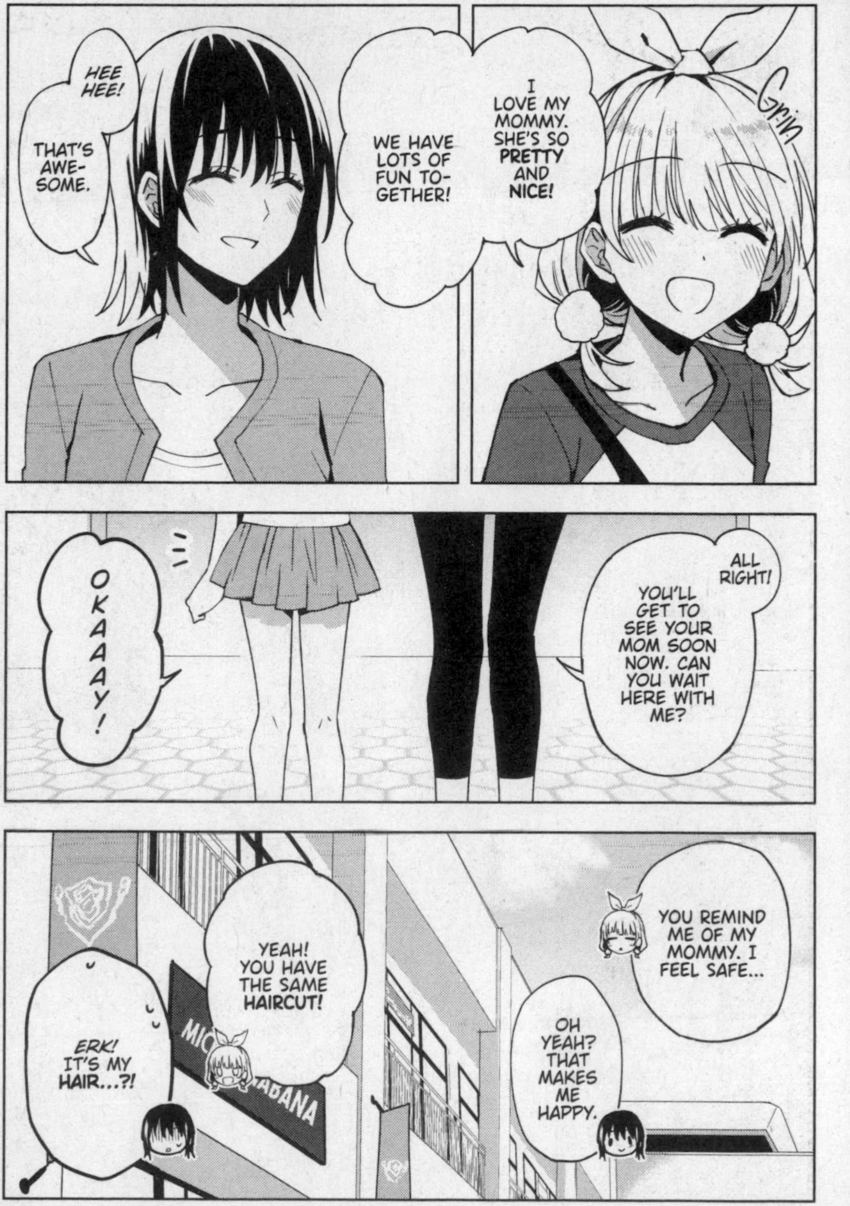
Grin
I LOVE MY MOMMY. SHE'S SO PRETTY AND NICE!
WE HAVE LOTS OF FUN TO-GETHER!
HEE HEE!
THAT'S AWE-SOME.
ALL RIGHT!
YOU'LL GET TO SEE YOUR MOM SOON NOW. CAN YOU WAIT HERE WITH ME?
OKAAAAY!
YOU REMIND ME OF MY MOMMY. I FEEL SAFE...
OH YEAH? THAT MAKES ME HAPPY.
YEAH! YOU HAVE THE SAME HAIRCUT!
ERK! IT'S MY HAIR...?!

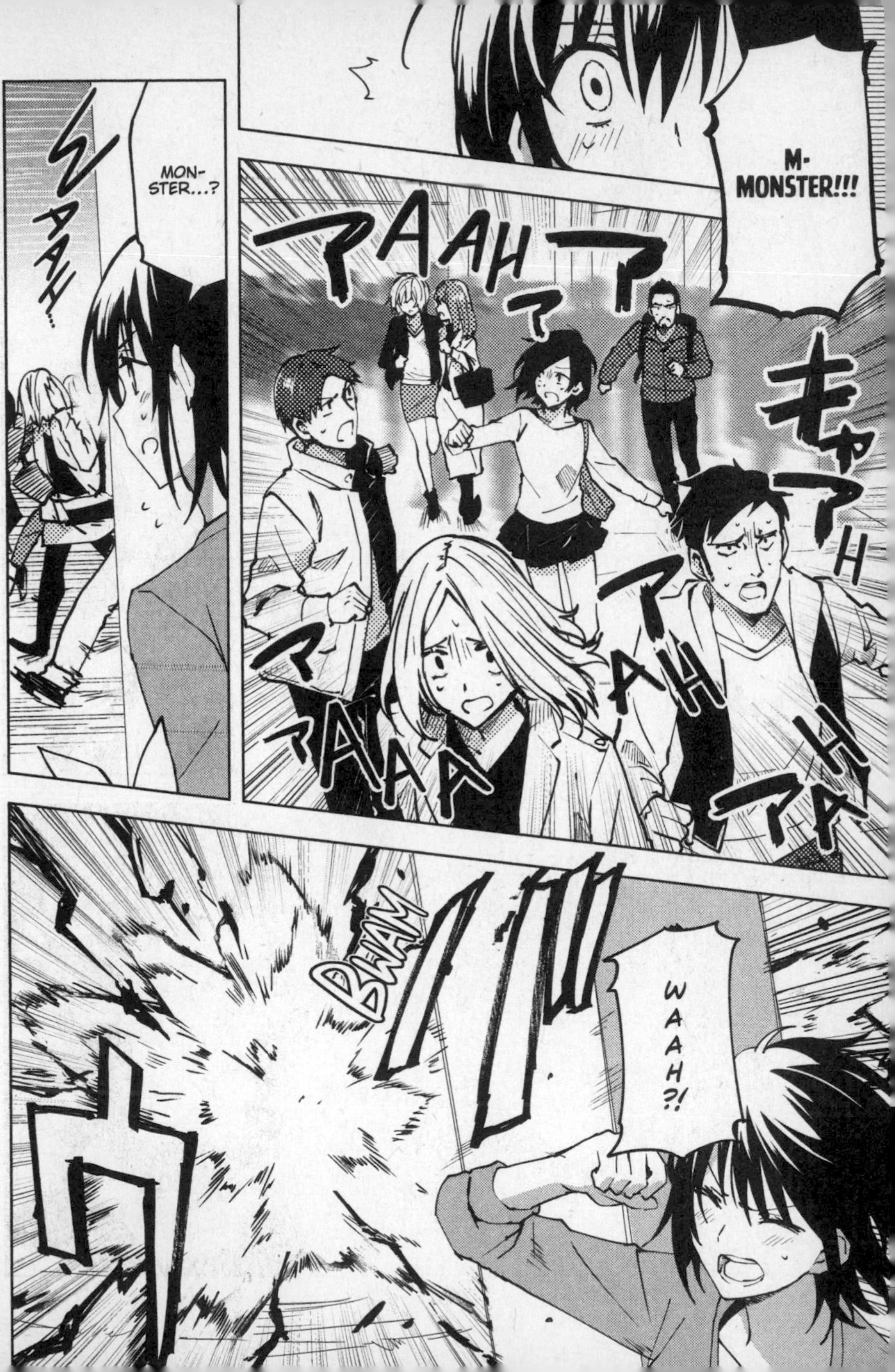
M-MONSTER!!!
AAH
キャア
AAH
AAAA
MON-STER...?
WAAH...
BWAM
WAAH?!

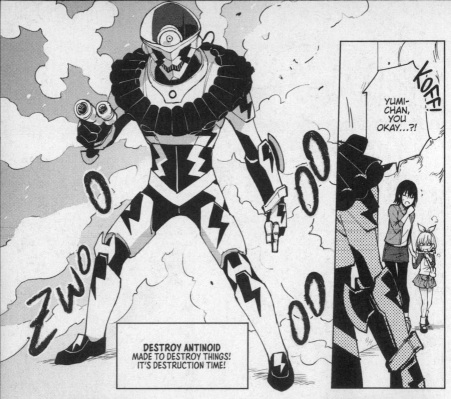

KOFF!

YUMI-CHAN, YOU OKAY...?!

ZWO OO OO OO

DESTROY ANTINOID
MADE TO DESTROY THINGS!
IT'S DESTRUCTION TIME!

IT WAS THE FIRST TIME I'D EVER SEEN AN ANTINOID.

GLORP

Shivr

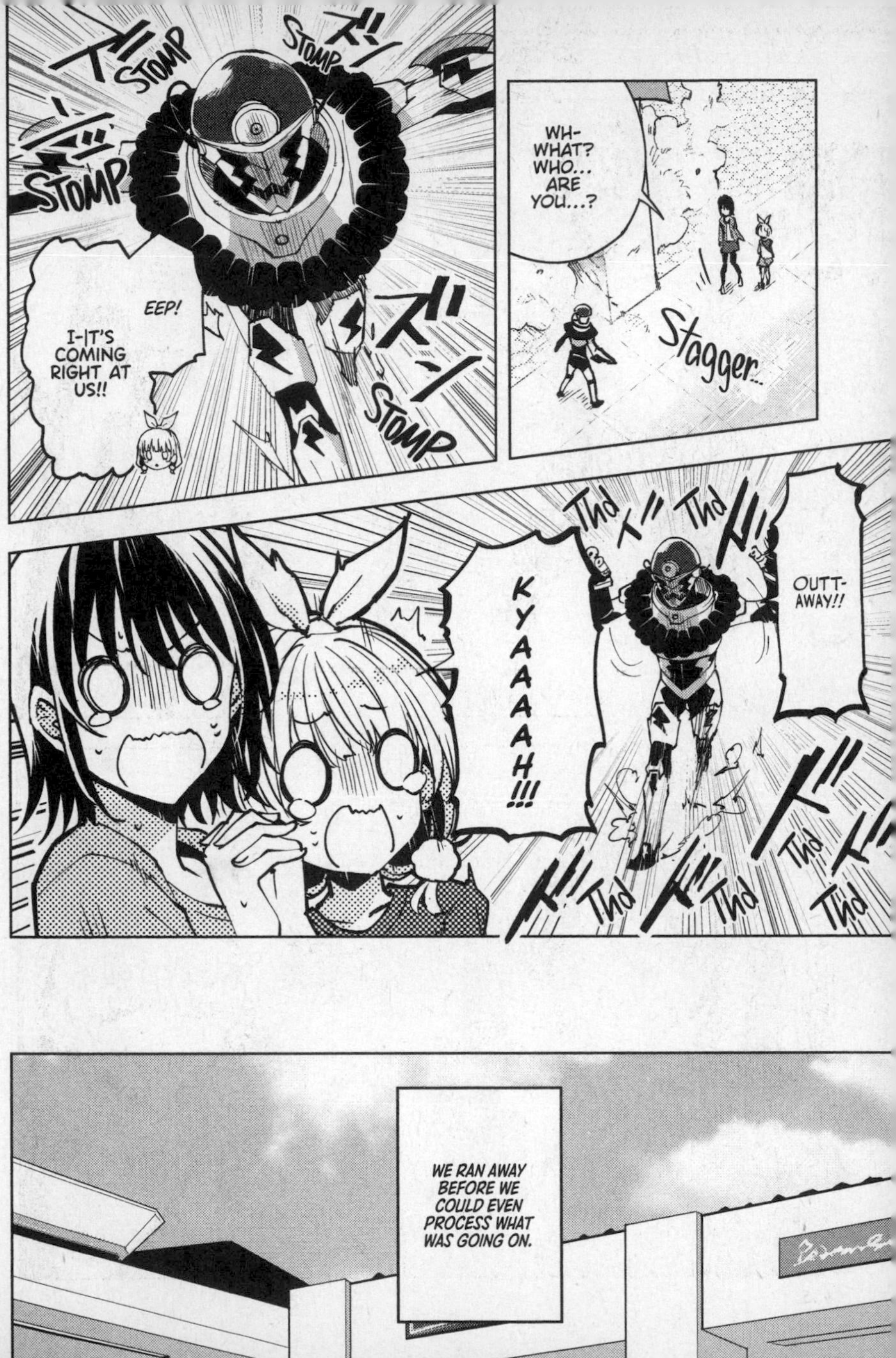
WH-WHAT? WHO... ARE YOU...?
Stagger...
STOMP
STOMP
STOMP
STOMP
EEP!
I-IT'S COMING RIGHT AT US!!
Thd Thd
OUTT-AWAY!!
KYAAAAAH!!!
Thd Thd Thd Thd
WE RAN AWAY BEFORE WE COULD EVEN PROCESS WHAT WAS GOING ON.

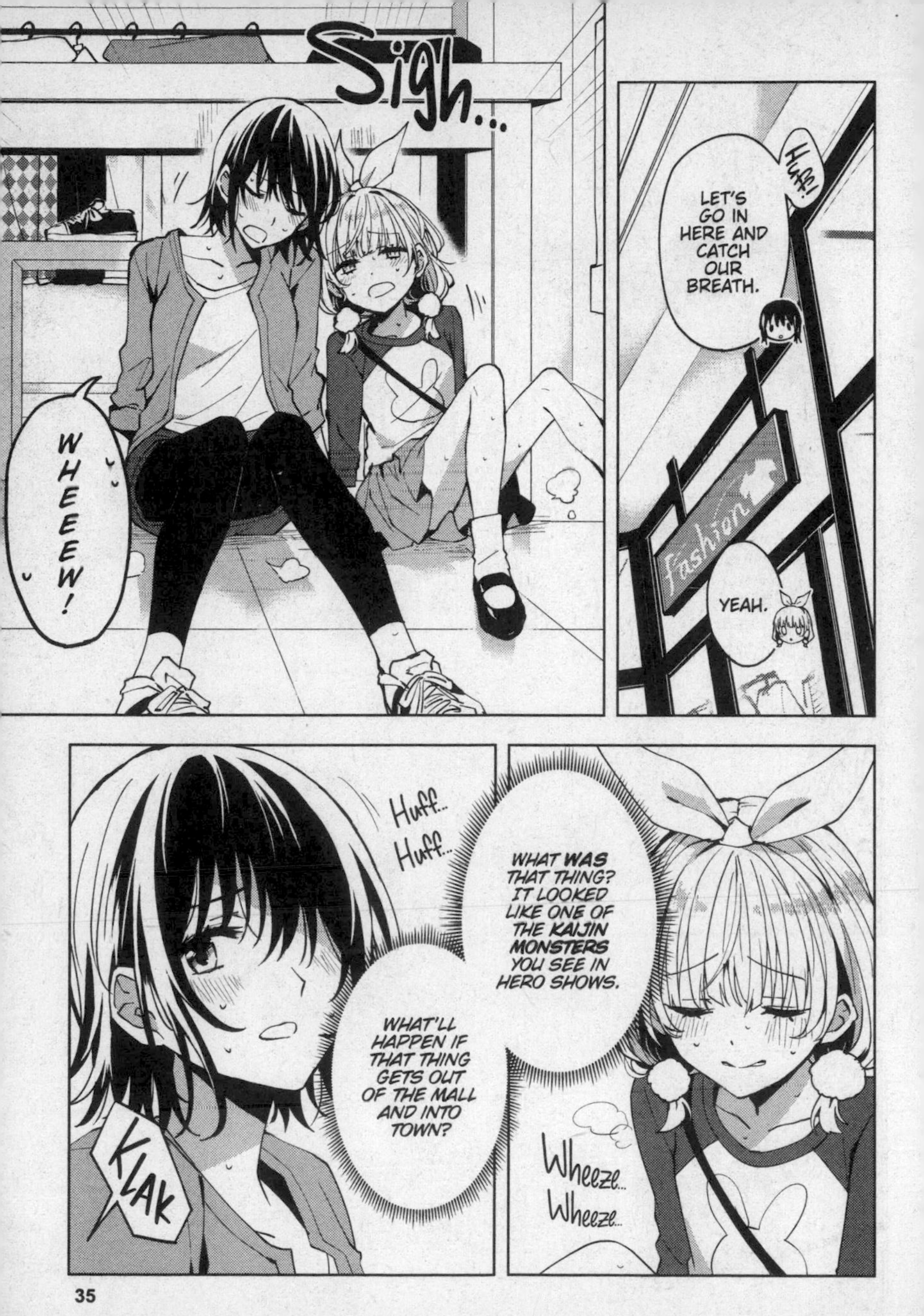
Huff!
LET'S GO IN HERE AND CATCH OUR BREATH.
fashion
YEAH.
Sigh...
WHEEEEW!
WHAT WAS THAT THING? IT LOOKED LIKE ONE OF THE KAIJIN MONSTERS YOU SEE IN HERO SHOWS.
Wheeze... Wheeze...
Huff... Huff...
WHAT'LL HAPPEN IF THAT THING GETS OUT OF THE MALL AND INTO TOWN?
KLAK

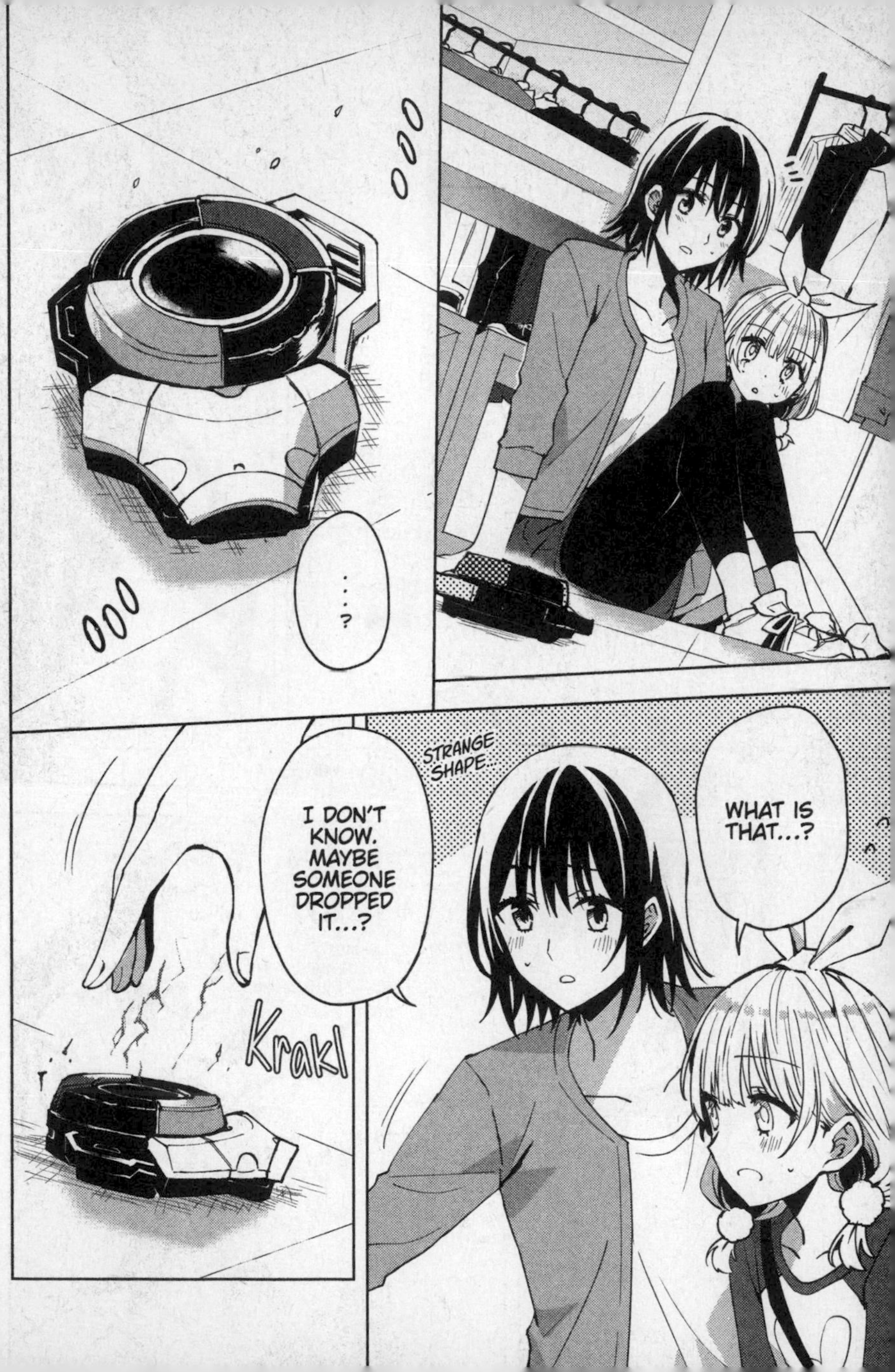
...?
WHAT IS THAT...?
STRANGE SHAPE...
I DON'T KNOW. MAYBE SOMEONE DROPPED IT...?
Krak!

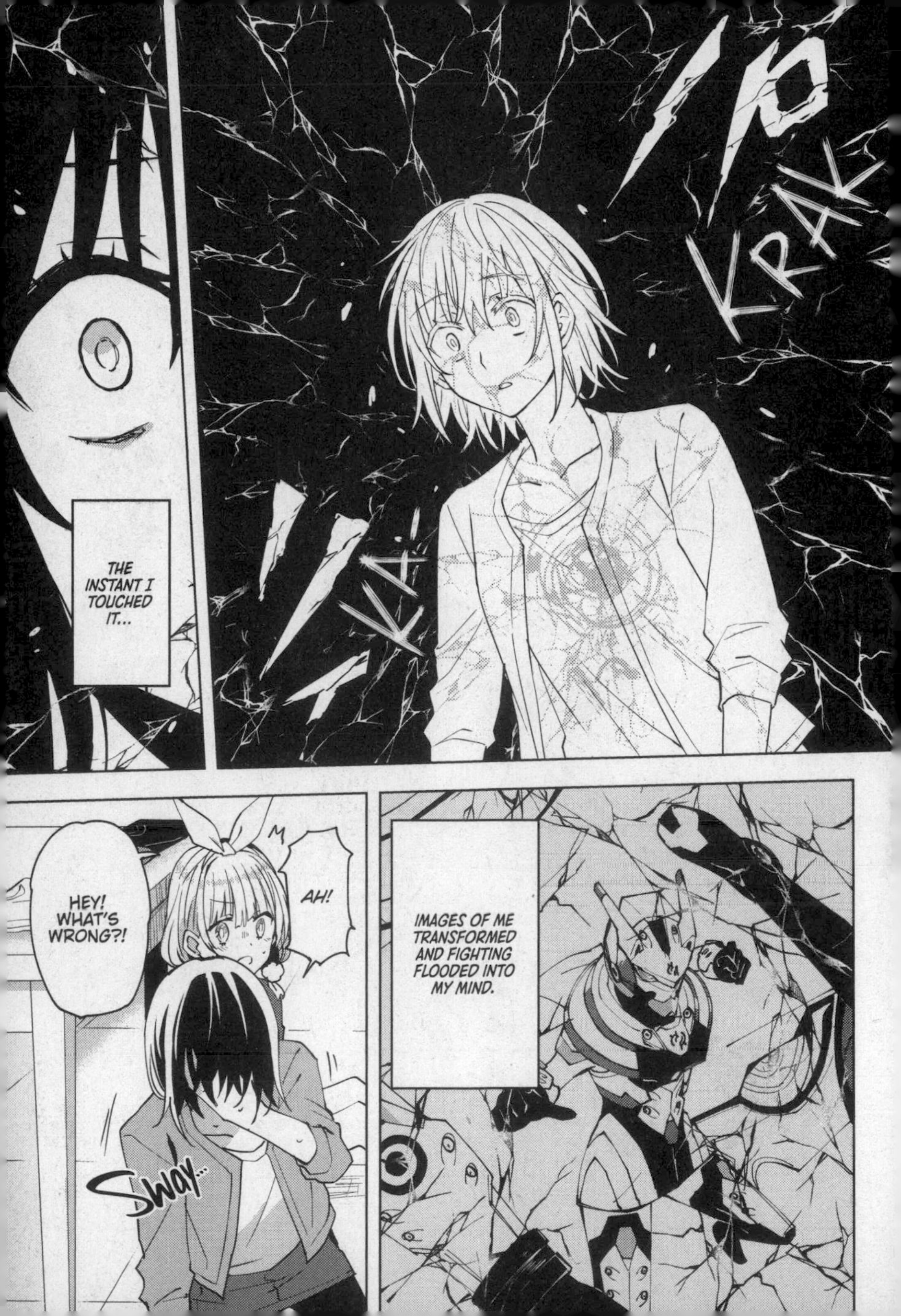
KRAK
THE INSTANT I TOUCHED IT...
IMAGES OF ME TRANSFORMED AND FIGHTING FLOODED INTO MY MIND.
AH!
HEY! WHAT'S WRONG?!
Sway...

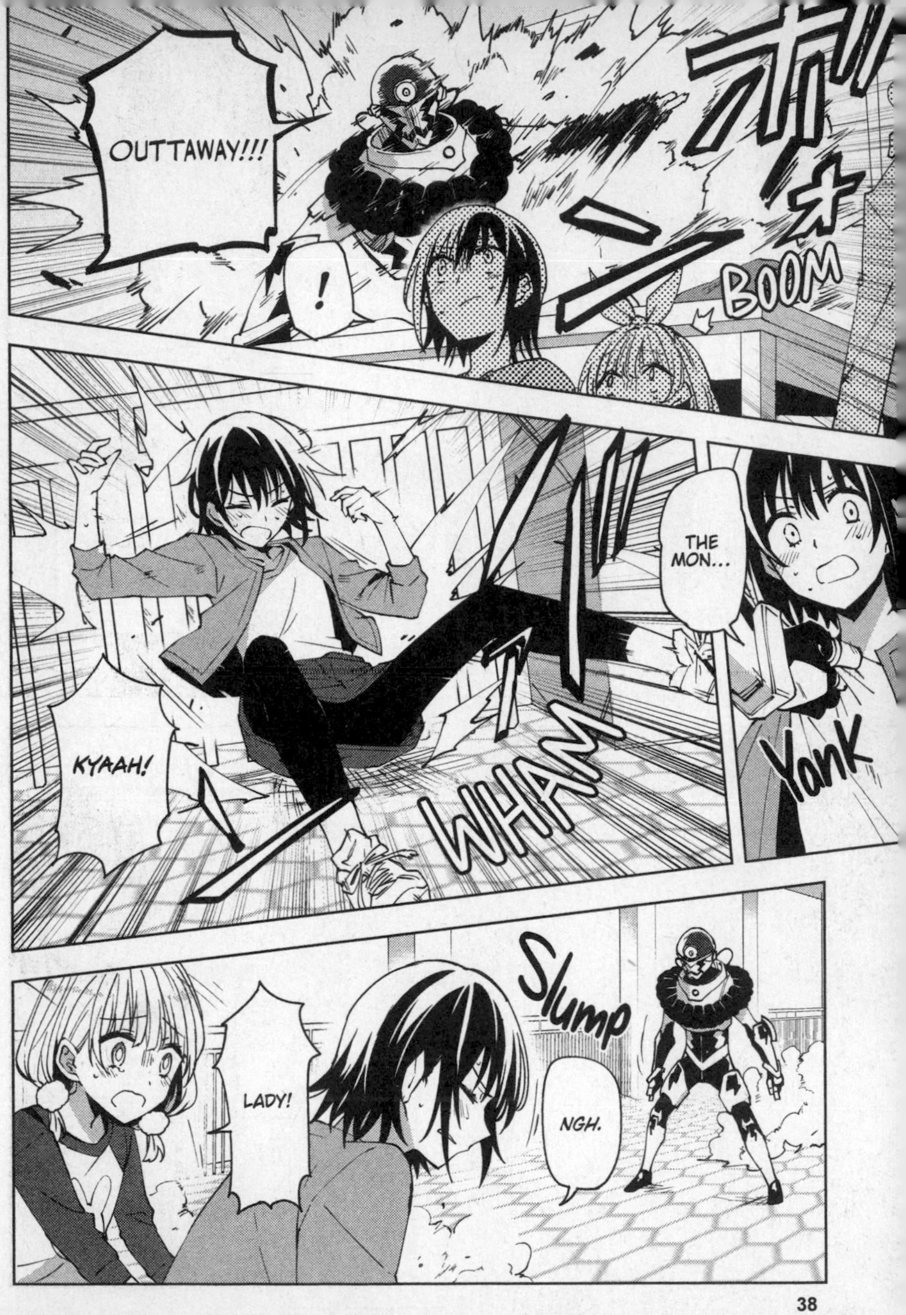
BOOM
OUTTAWAY!!!
!
THE MON...
Yonk
KYAAH!
WHAM
Slump
NGH.
LADY!

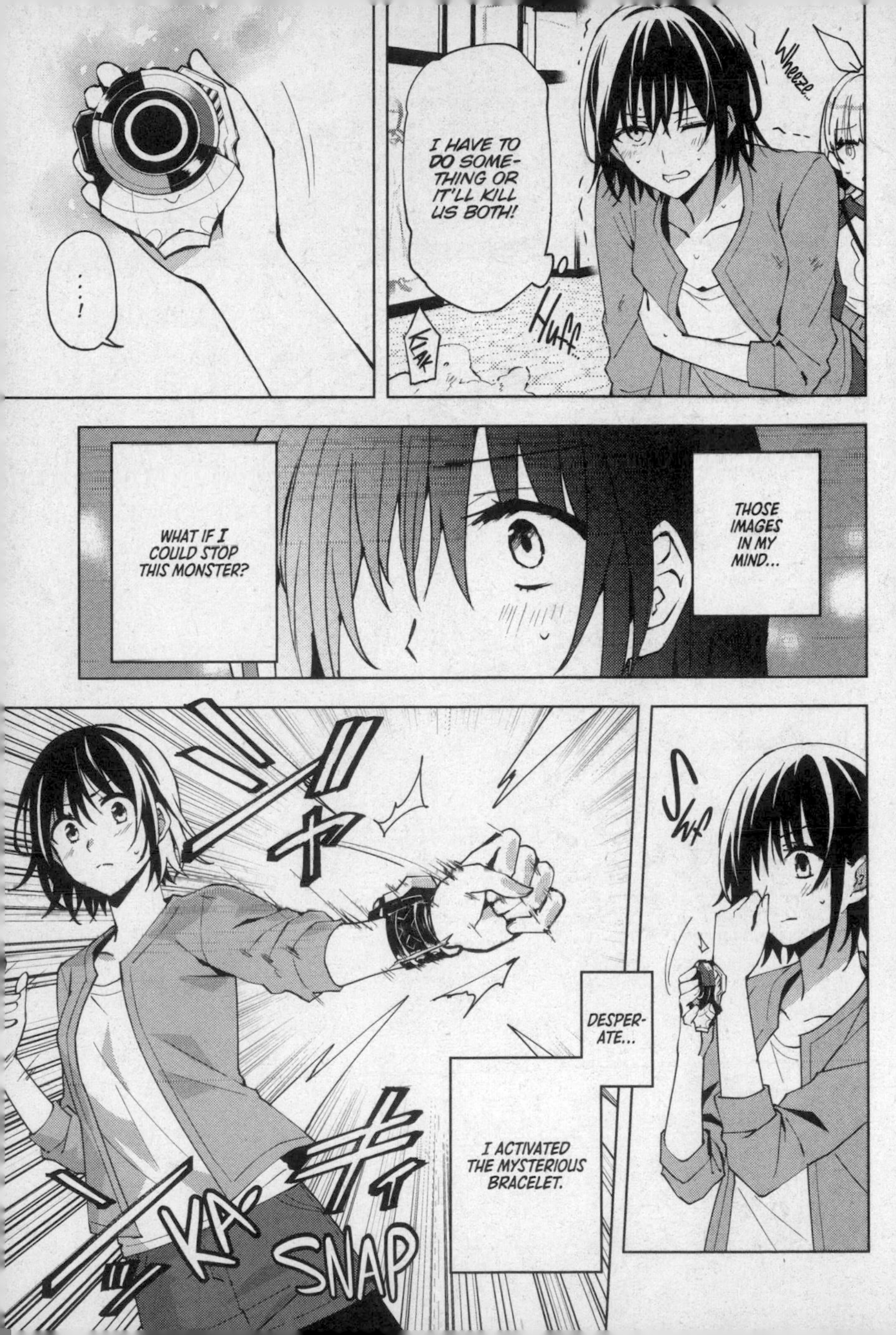
Wheeze...
I HAVE TO DO SOME-THING OR IT'LL KILL US BOTH!
Huff...
Klak
...!
THOSE IMAGES IN MY MIND...
WHAT IF I COULD STOP THIS MONSTER?
Swf
DESPER-ATE...
I ACTIVATED THE MYSTERIOUS BRACELET.
KA-
SNAP

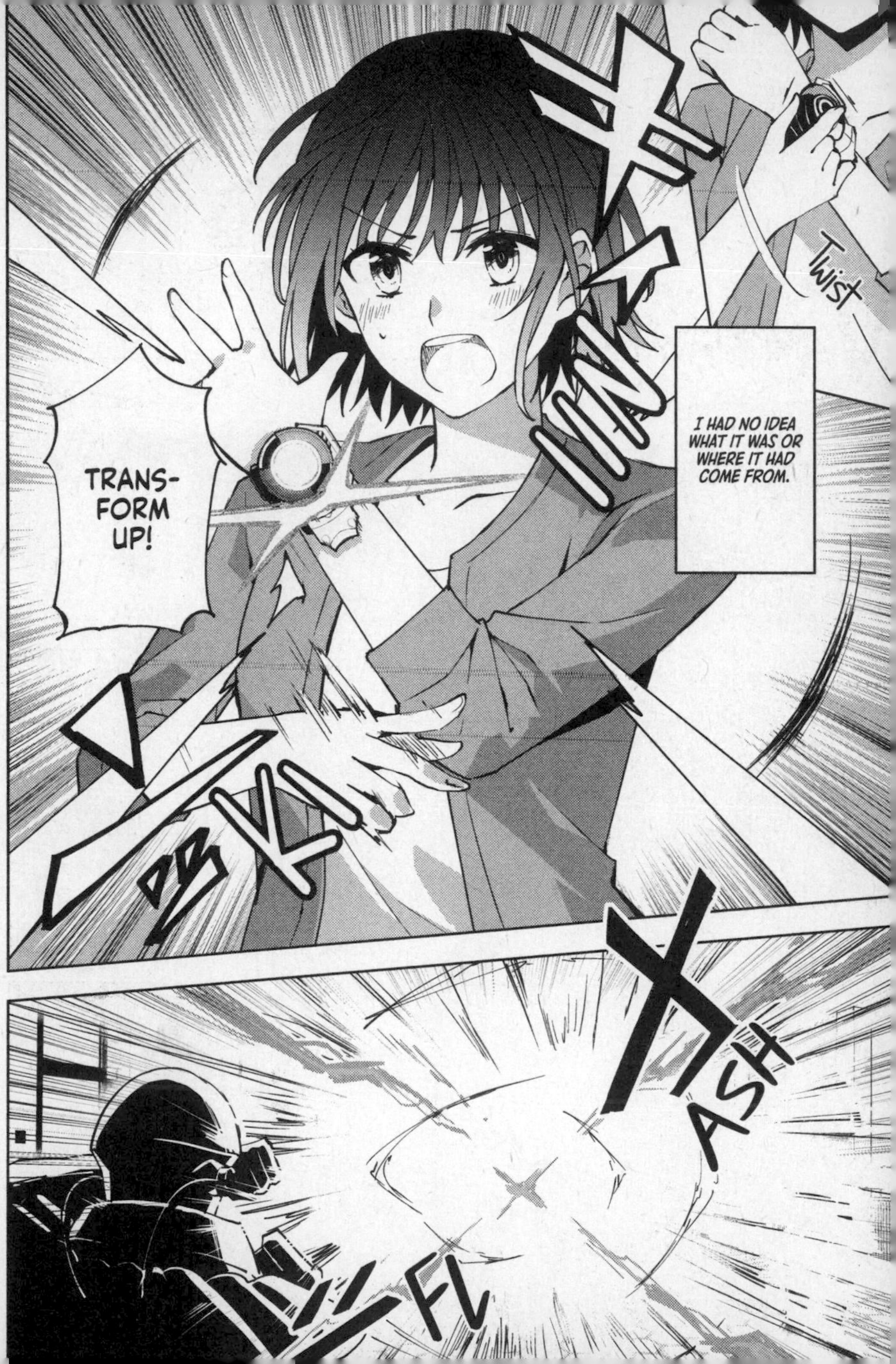
Twist
I HAD NO IDEA WHAT IT WAS OR WHERE IT HAD COME FROM.
TRANS-FORM UP!
FLASH

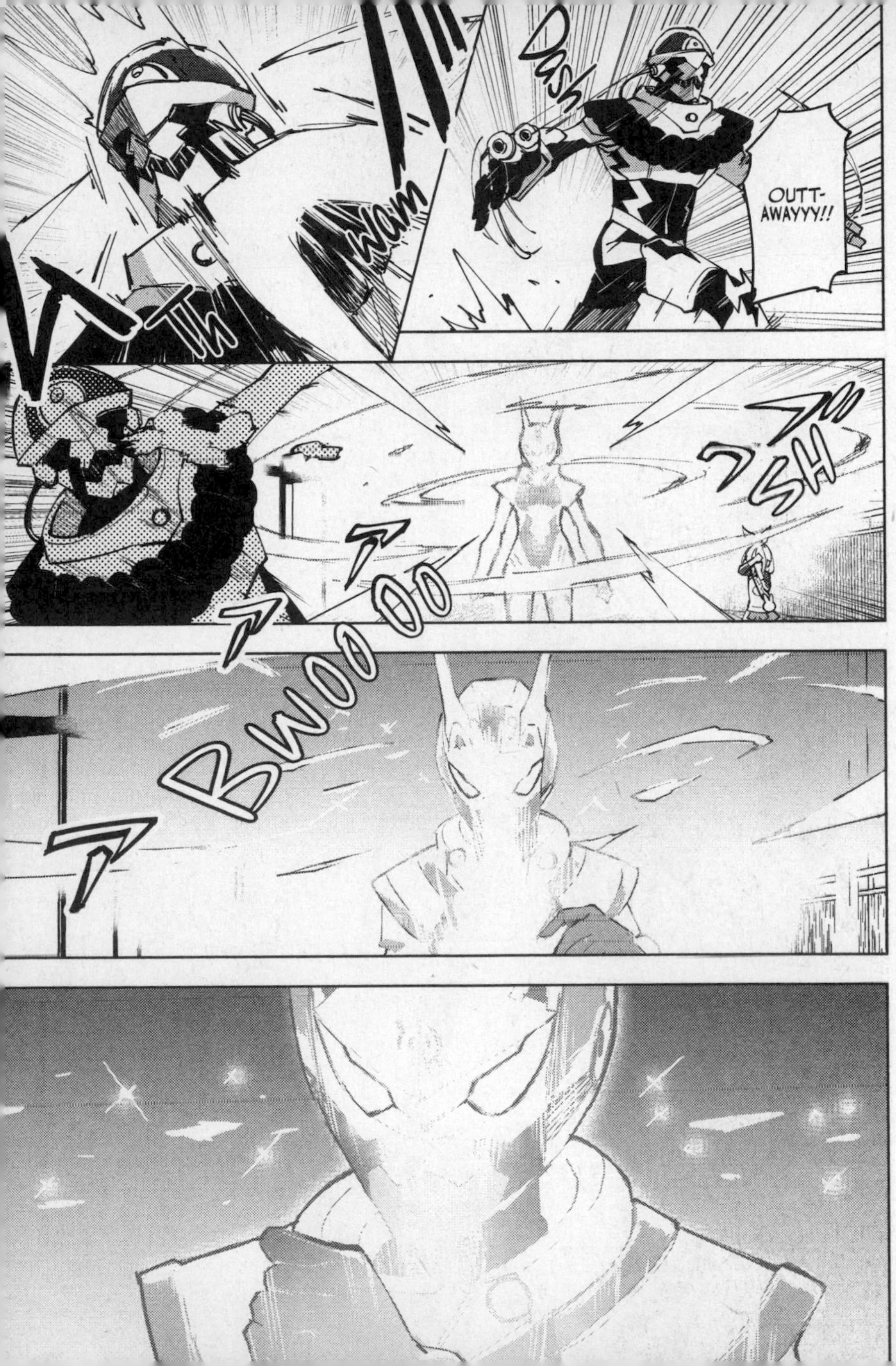
Dash
OUTT-AWAYYY!!
Wam
Th
SH
BWOOOO

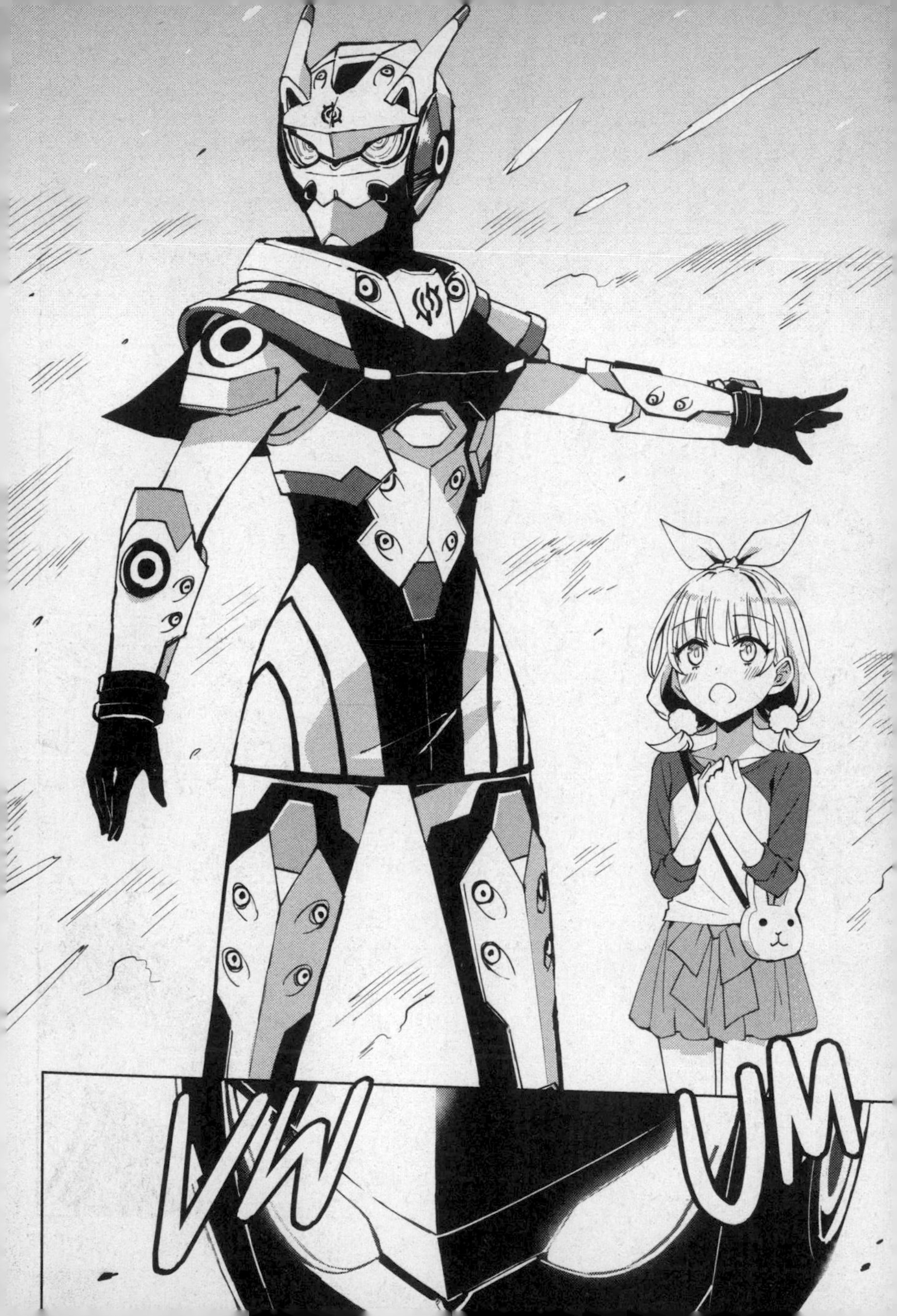
VWUM

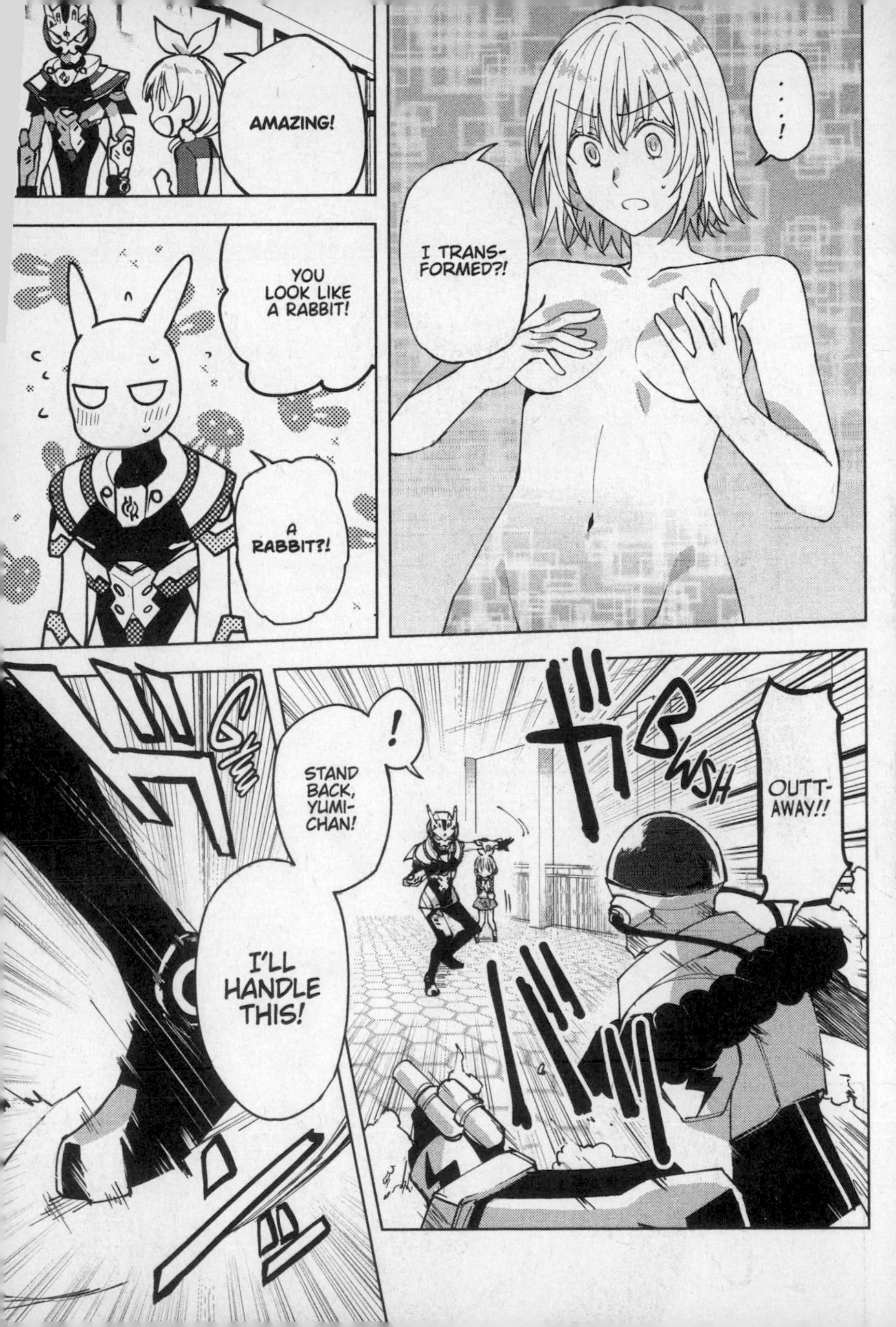
...!
I TRANS-FORMED?!
AMAZING!
YOU LOOK LIKE A RABBIT!
A RABBIT?!
OUTT-AWAY!!
BWSH
!
STAND BACK, YUMI-CHAN!
I'LL HANDLE THIS!
GYUU

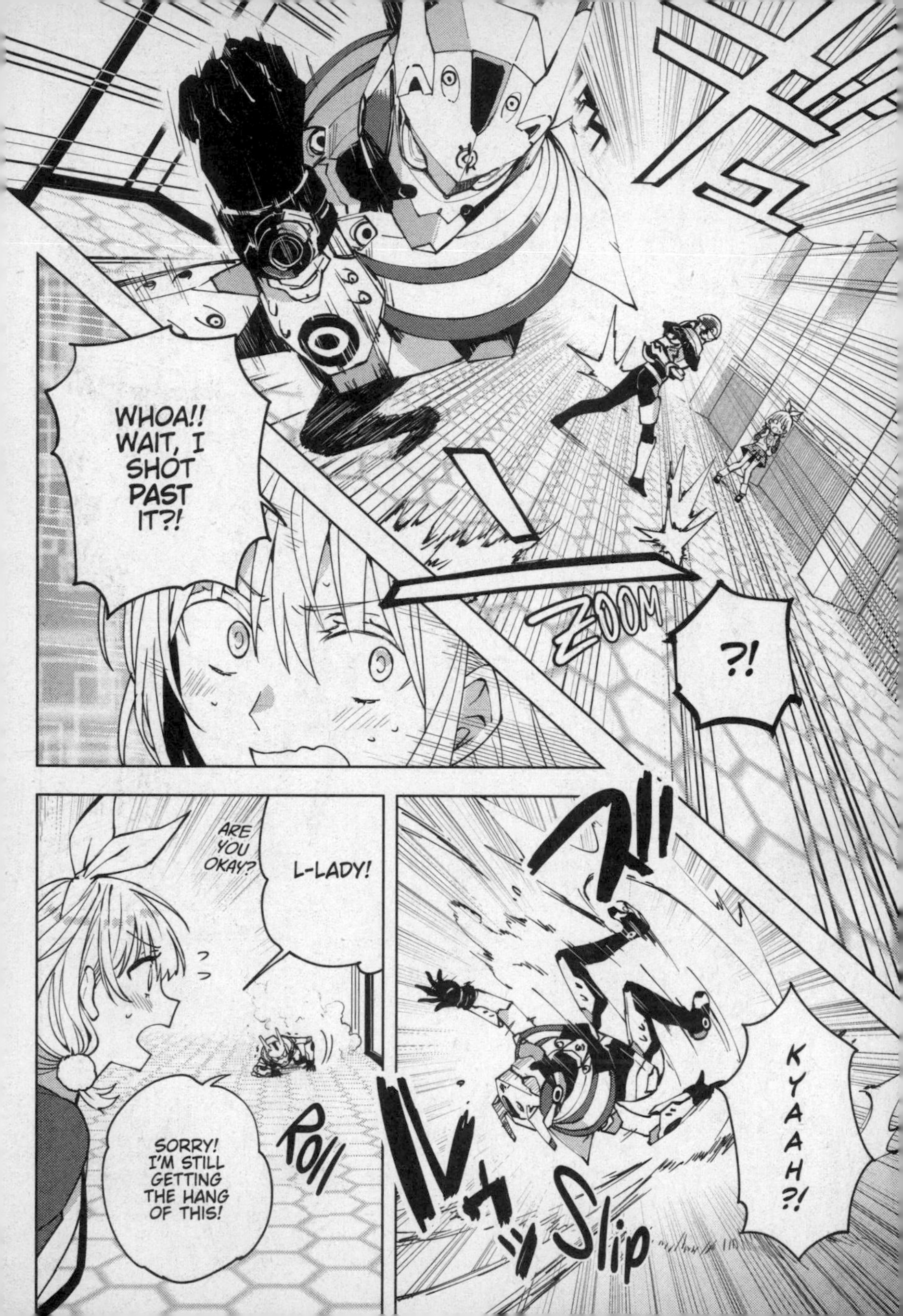
?!
ZOOM
WHOA!! WAIT, I SHOT PAST IT?!
KYAAAH?!
Slip
L-LADY!
ARE YOU OKAY?
Roll
SORRY! I'M STILL GETTING THE HANG OF THIS!

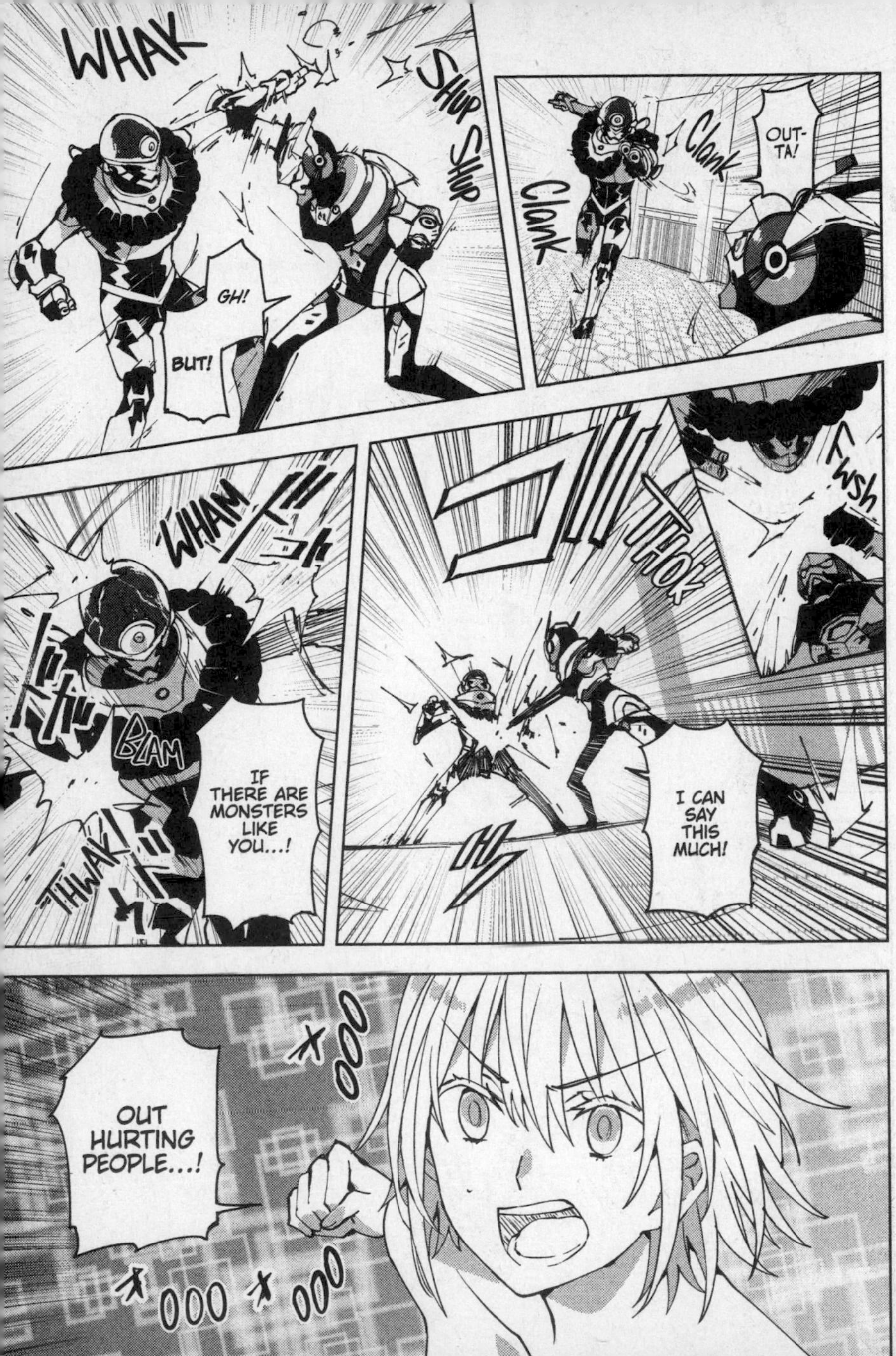
OUT-TA!
Clank
Clank
WHAK
SHUP SHUP
GH!
BUT!
Fwsh
THOK
I CAN SAY THIS MUCH!
WHAM
BLAM
THWAK
IF THERE ARE MONSTERS LIKE YOU...!
OUT HURTING PEOPLE...!

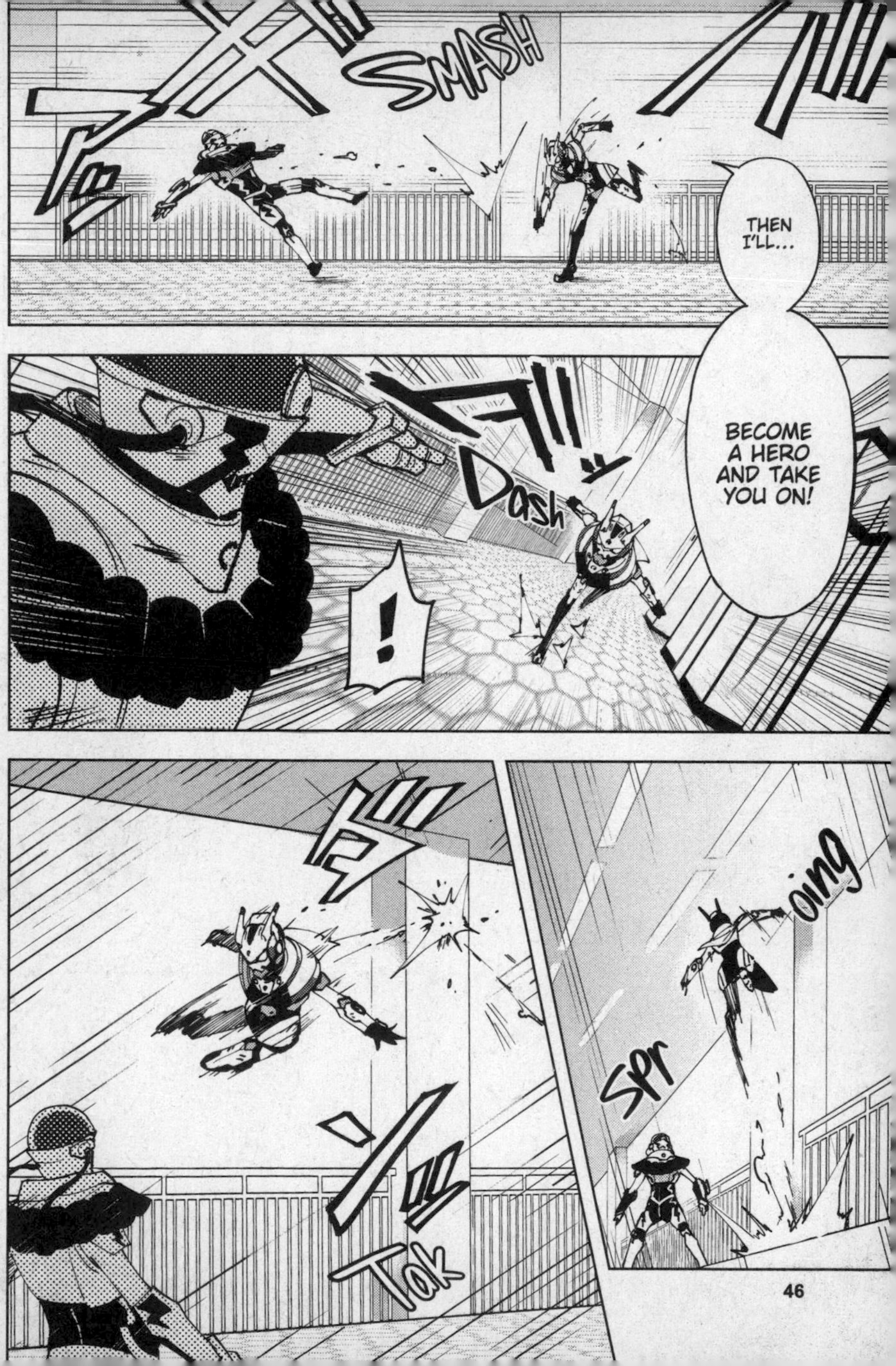
SMASH
THEN I'LL…
BECOME A HERO AND TAKE YOU ON!
Dash
!
Spr
oing
Tak

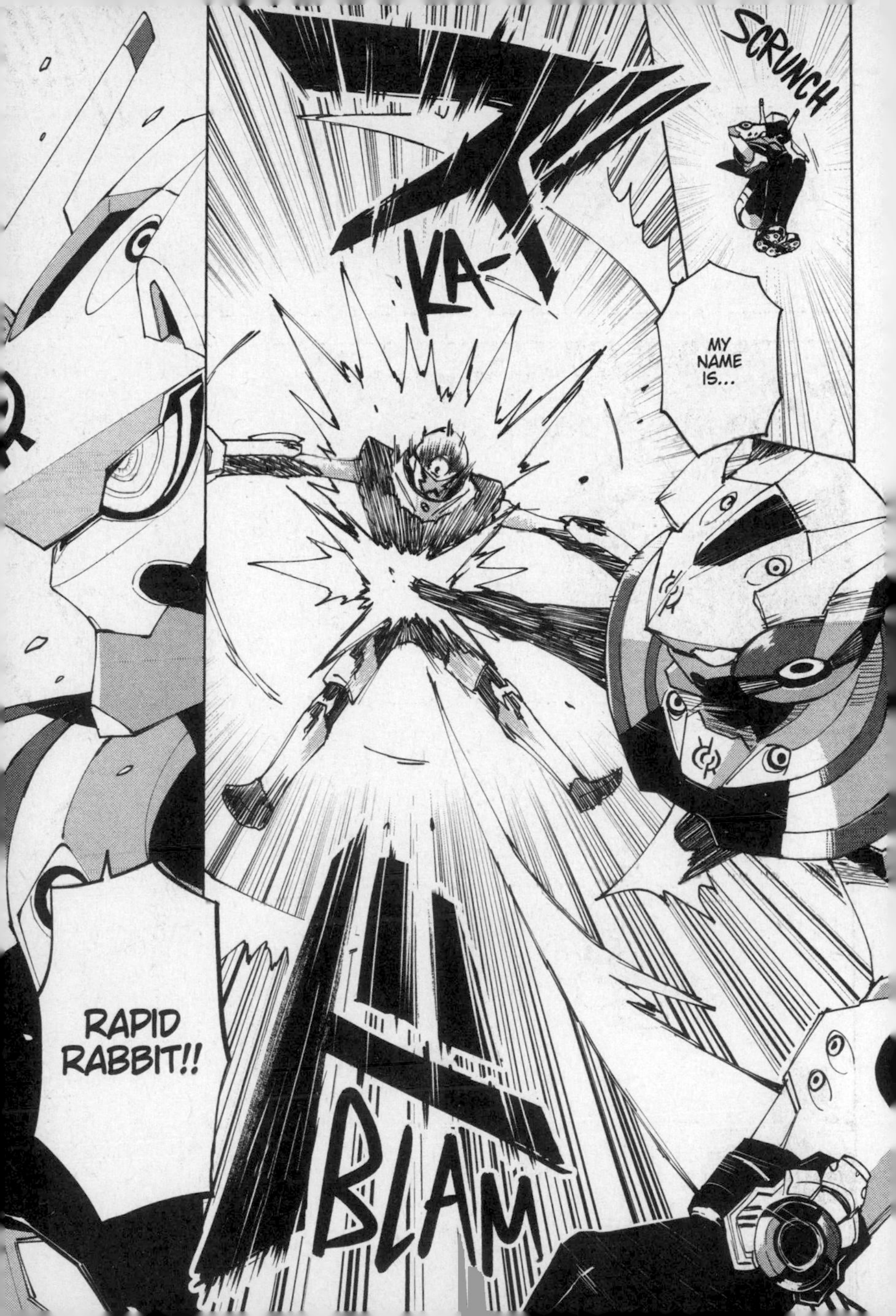
SCRUNCH
MY NAME IS...
KA-
BLAM
RAPID RABBIT!!

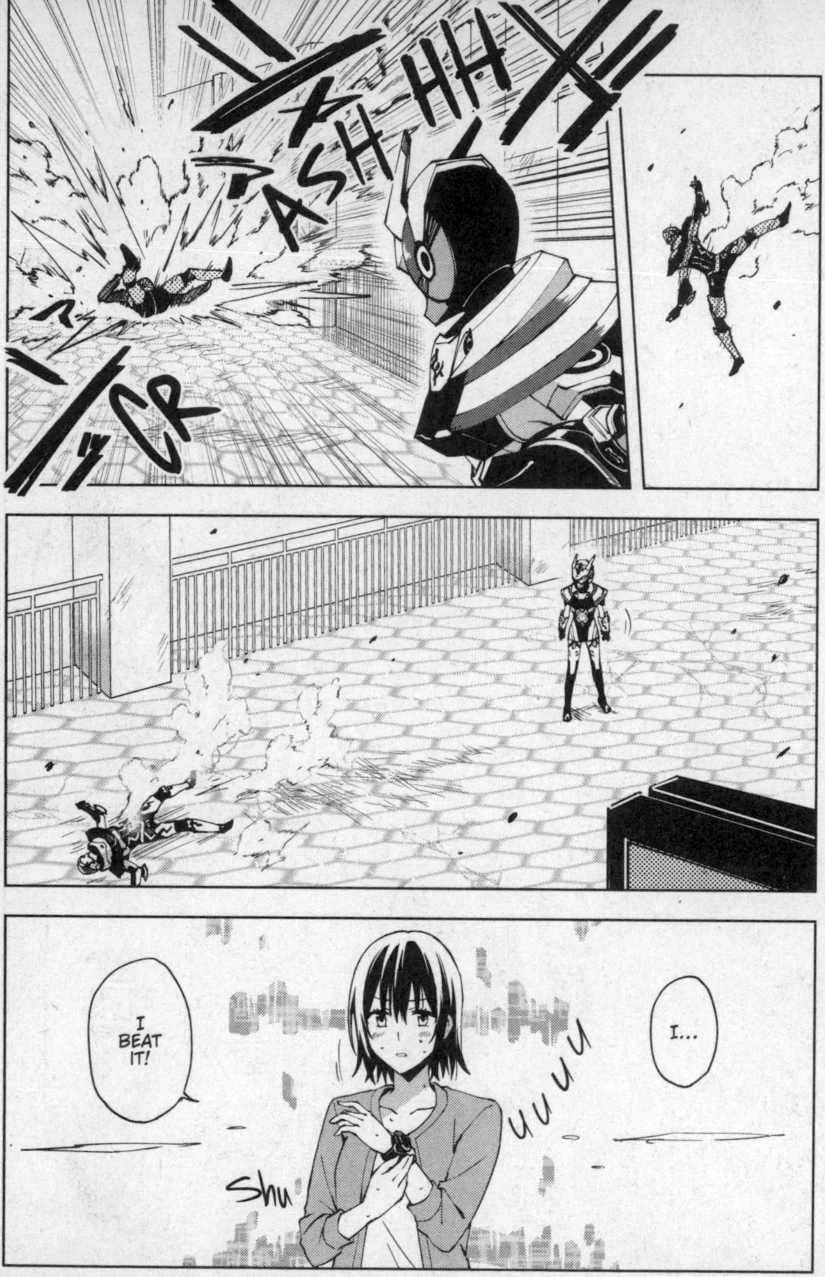
CRASHHH
I...
UUUU
I BEAT IT!
Shu

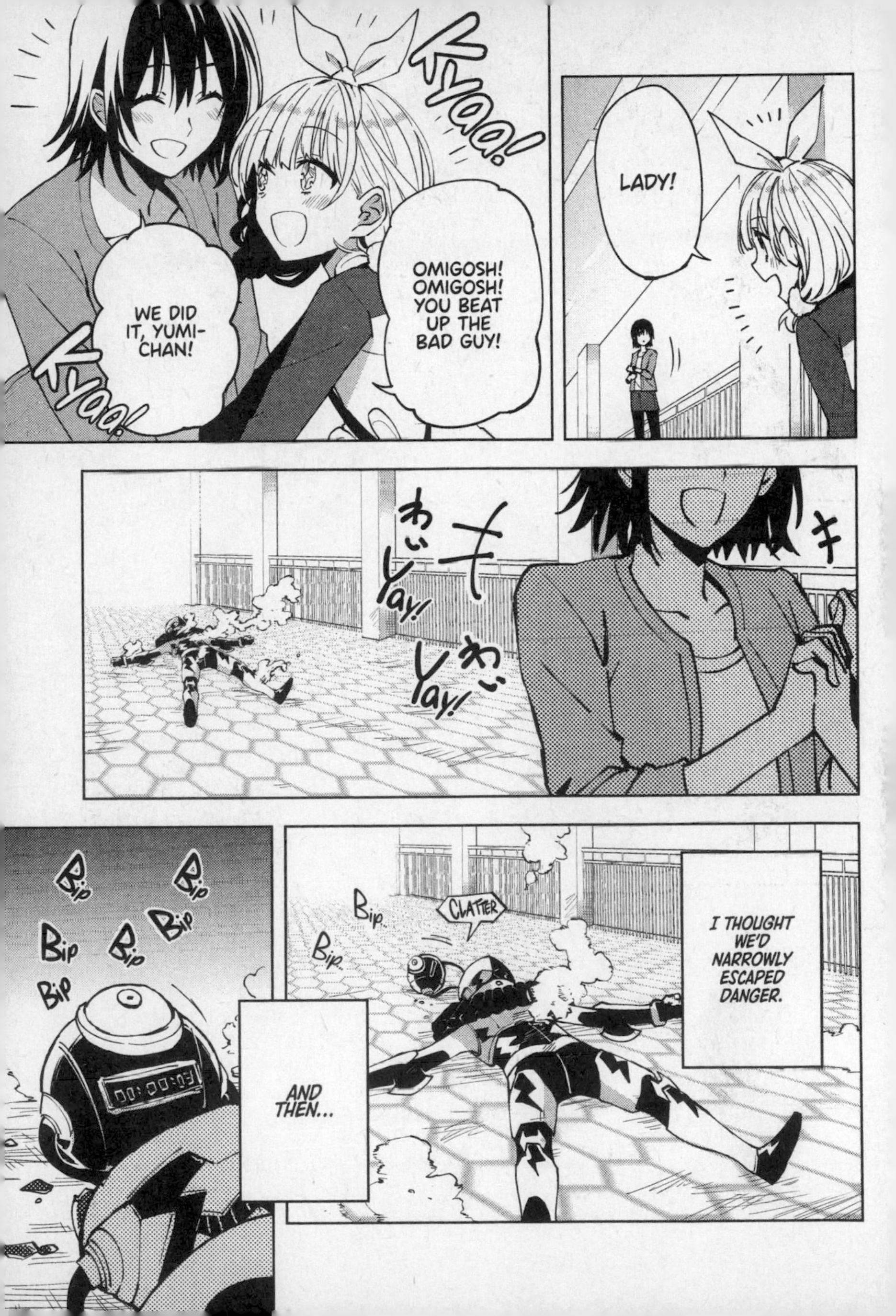
LADY!
Kyaa!
OMIGOSH! OMIGOSH! YOU BEAT UP THE BAD GUY!
WE DID IT, YUMI-CHAN!
Kyaa!
Yay!
Yay!
I THOUGHT WE'D NARROWLY ESCAPED DANGER.
CLATTER
Bip..
Bip..
AND THEN...
Bip
Bip
Bip
Bip
Bip
Bip
00:00:03

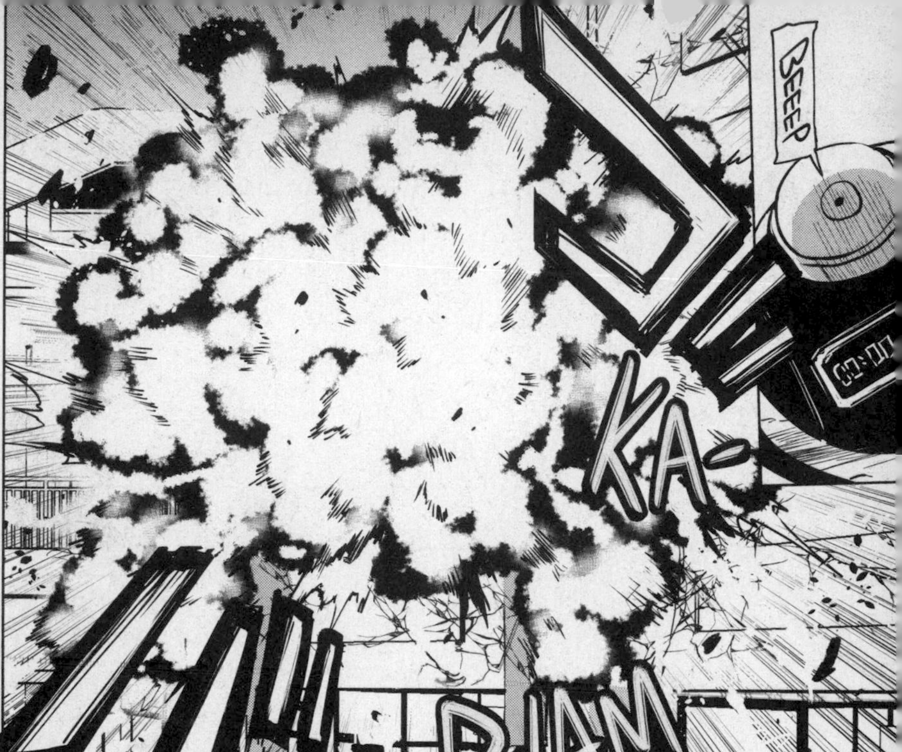
BEEEP
KA-
BLAM

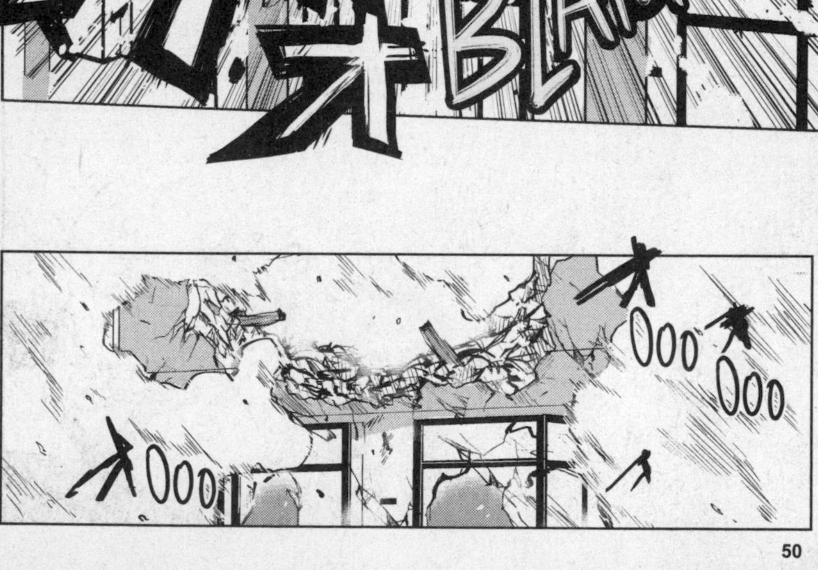

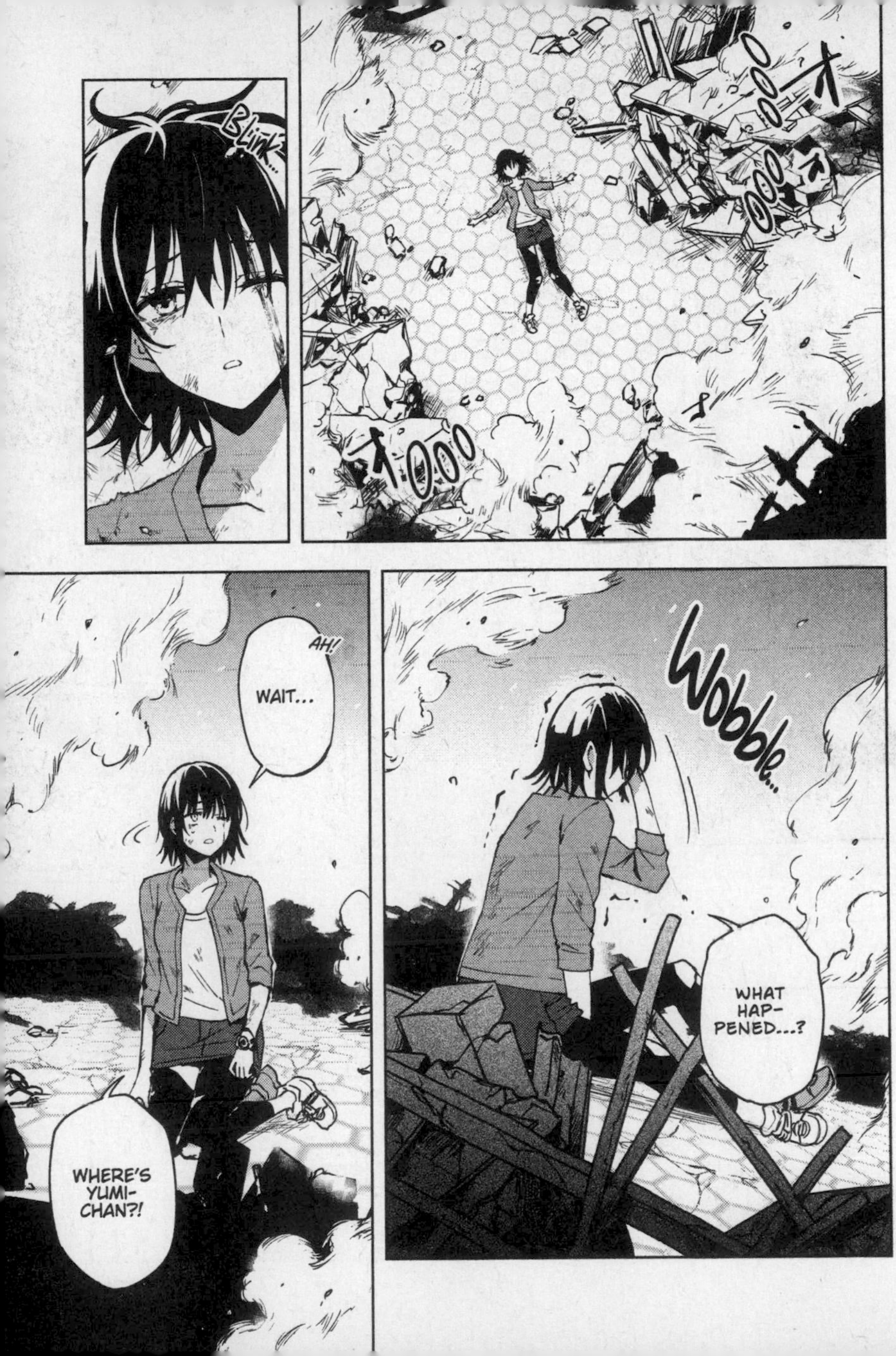
BLINK...
WOBBLE...
WHAT HAPPENED...?
AH!
WAIT...
WHERE'S YUMI-CHAN?!

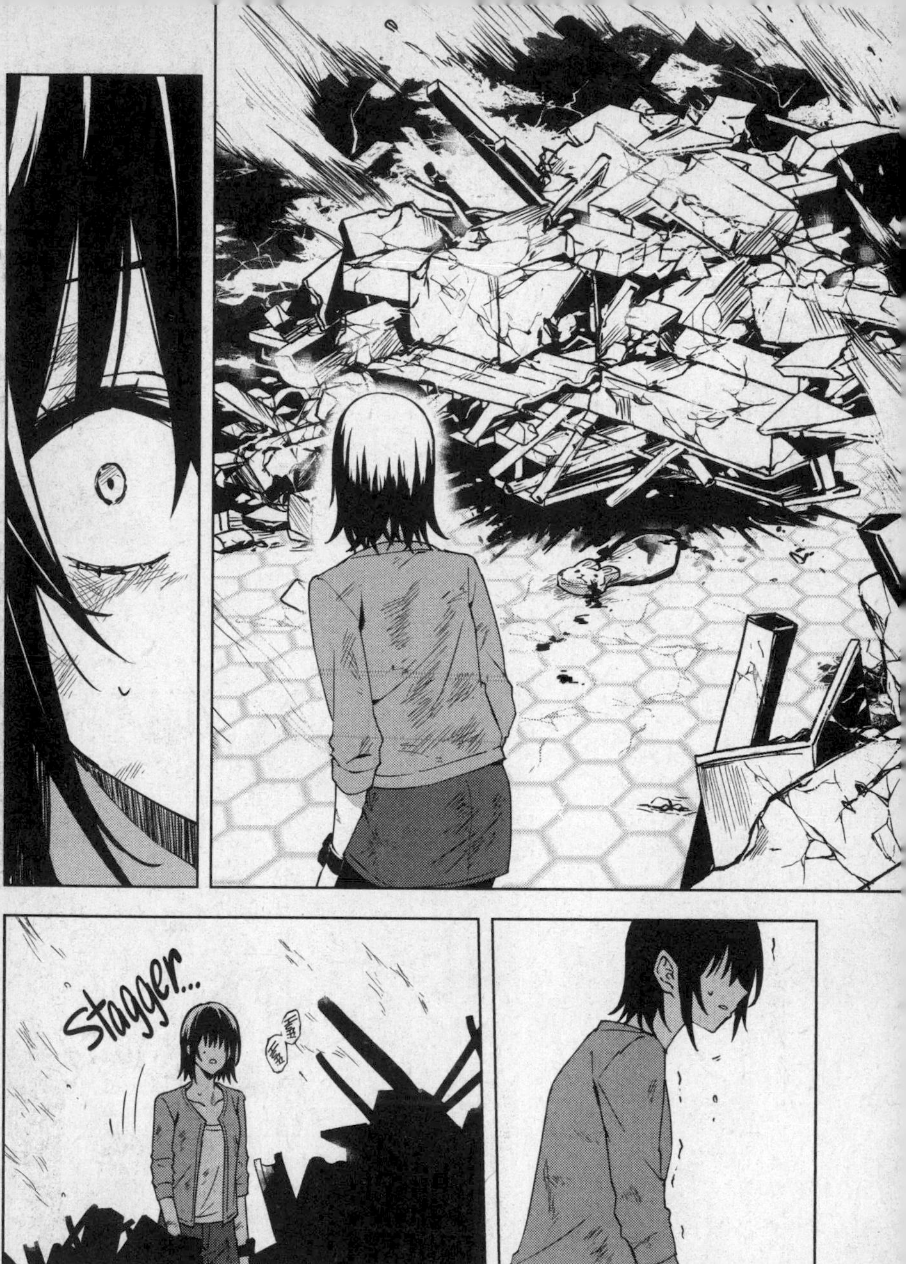
Stagger...
HUFF!
HUFF!

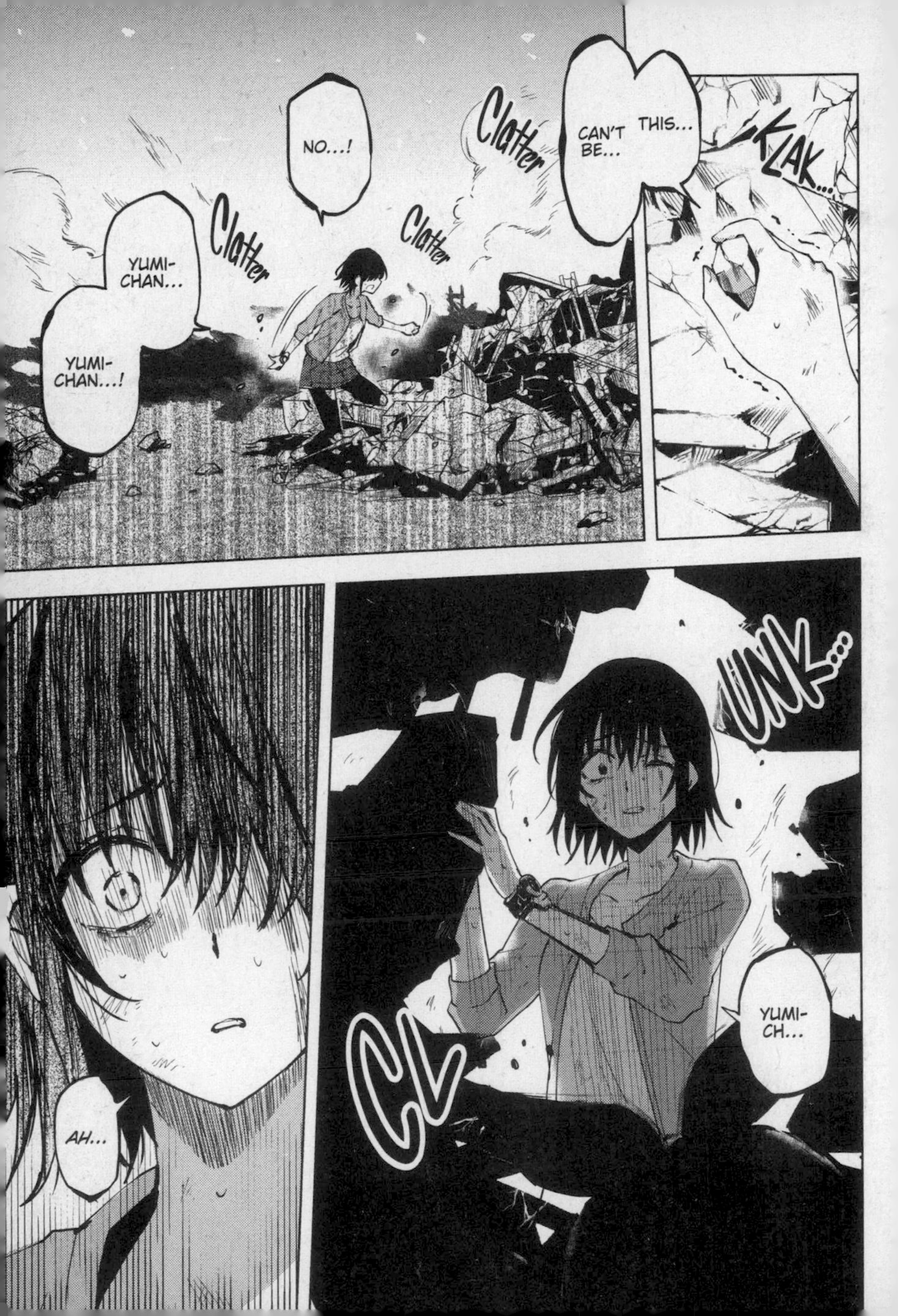
KLAK...
THIS...
CAN'T BE...
Clatter
NO...!
Clatter
Clatter
YUMI-CHAN...
YUMI-CHAN...!
UNK...
CL
YUMI-CH...
AH...

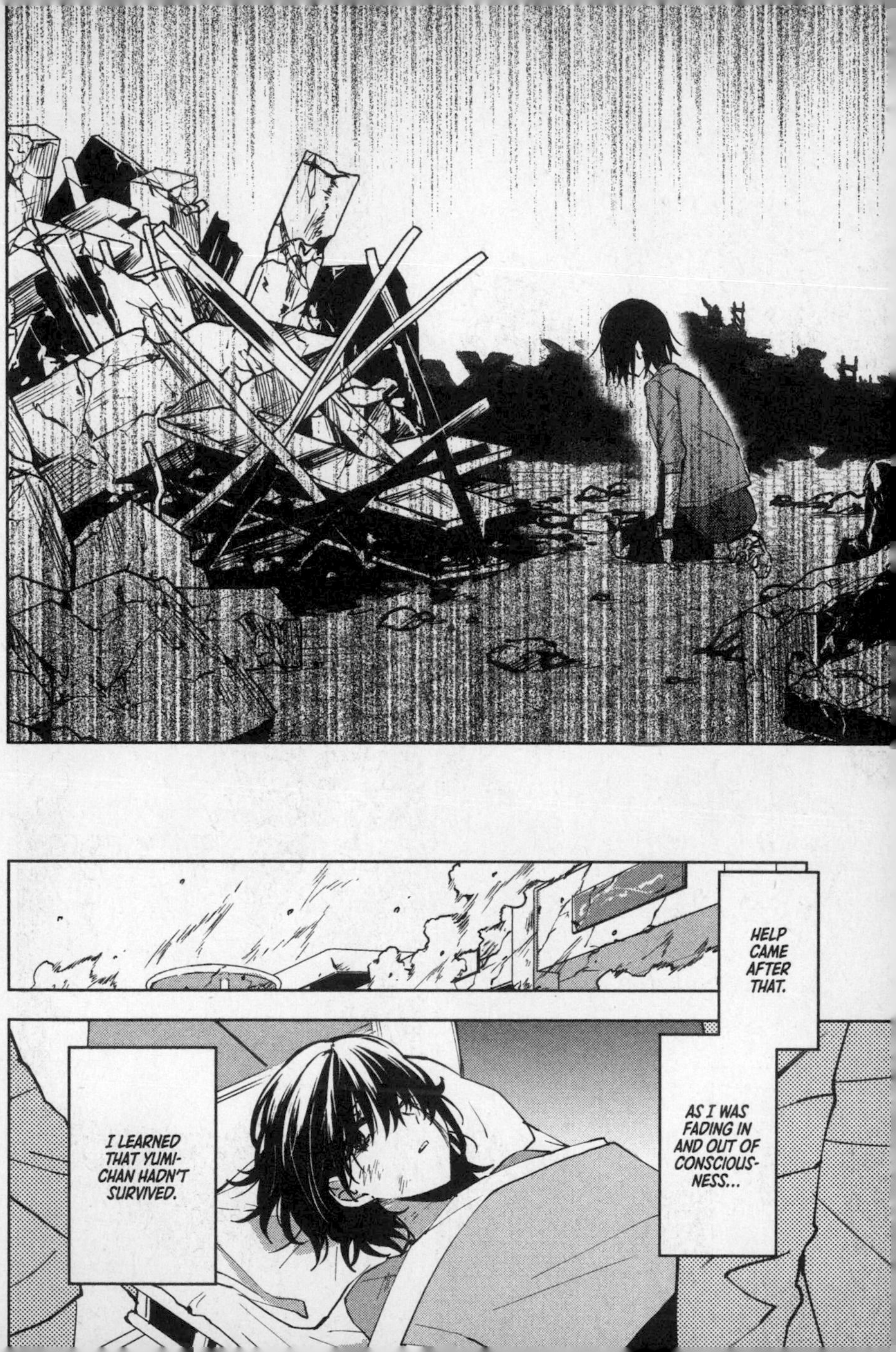
HELP CAME AFTER THAT.
AS I WAS FADING IN AND OUT OF CONSCIOUSNESS...
I LEARNED THAT YUMI-CHAN HADN'T SURVIVED.

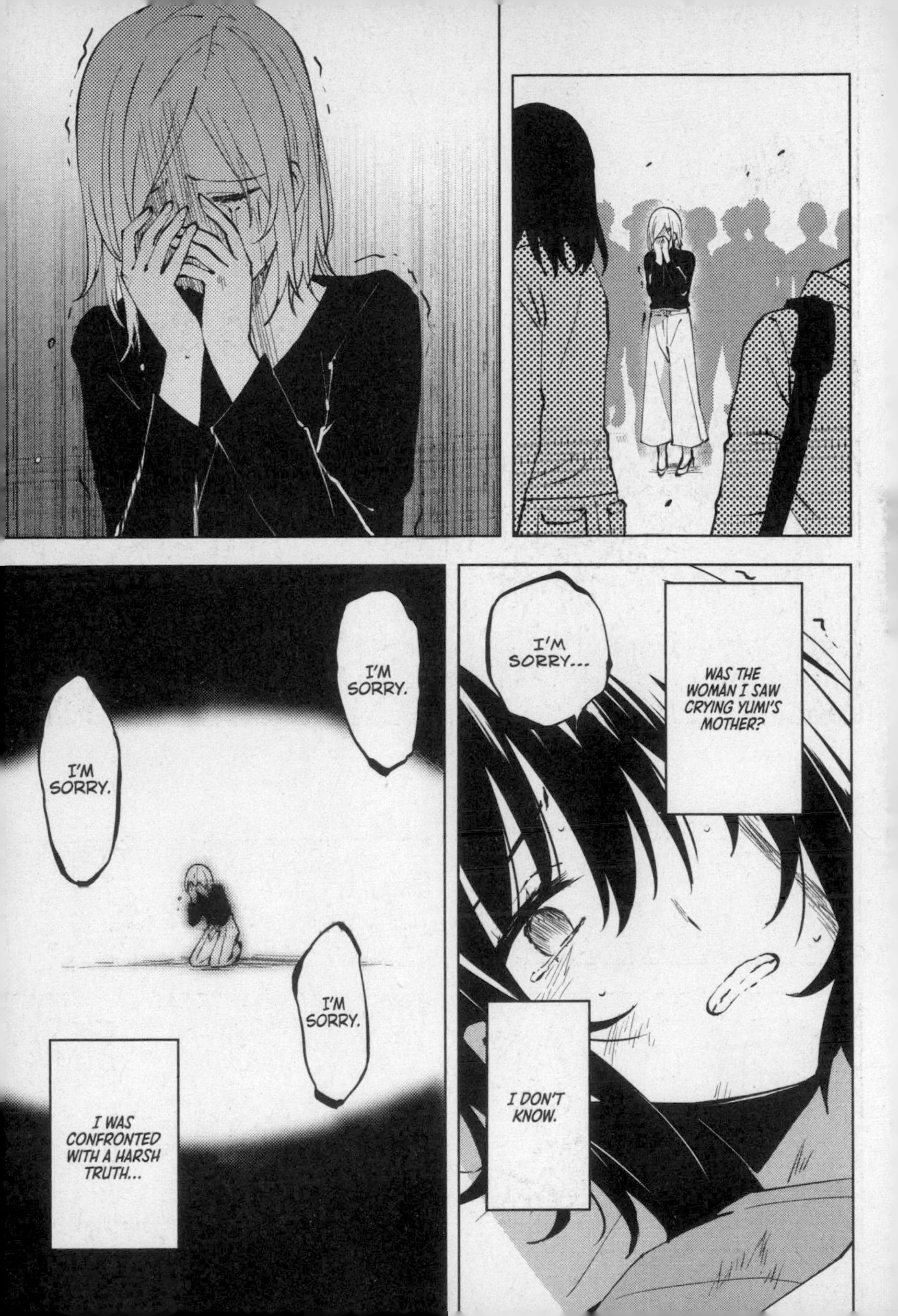
I'M SORRY...
WAS THE WOMAN I SAW CRYING YUMI'S MOTHER?
I DON'T KNOW.
I'M SORRY.
I'M SORRY.
I'M SORRY.
I WAS CONFRONTED WITH A HARSH TRUTH...

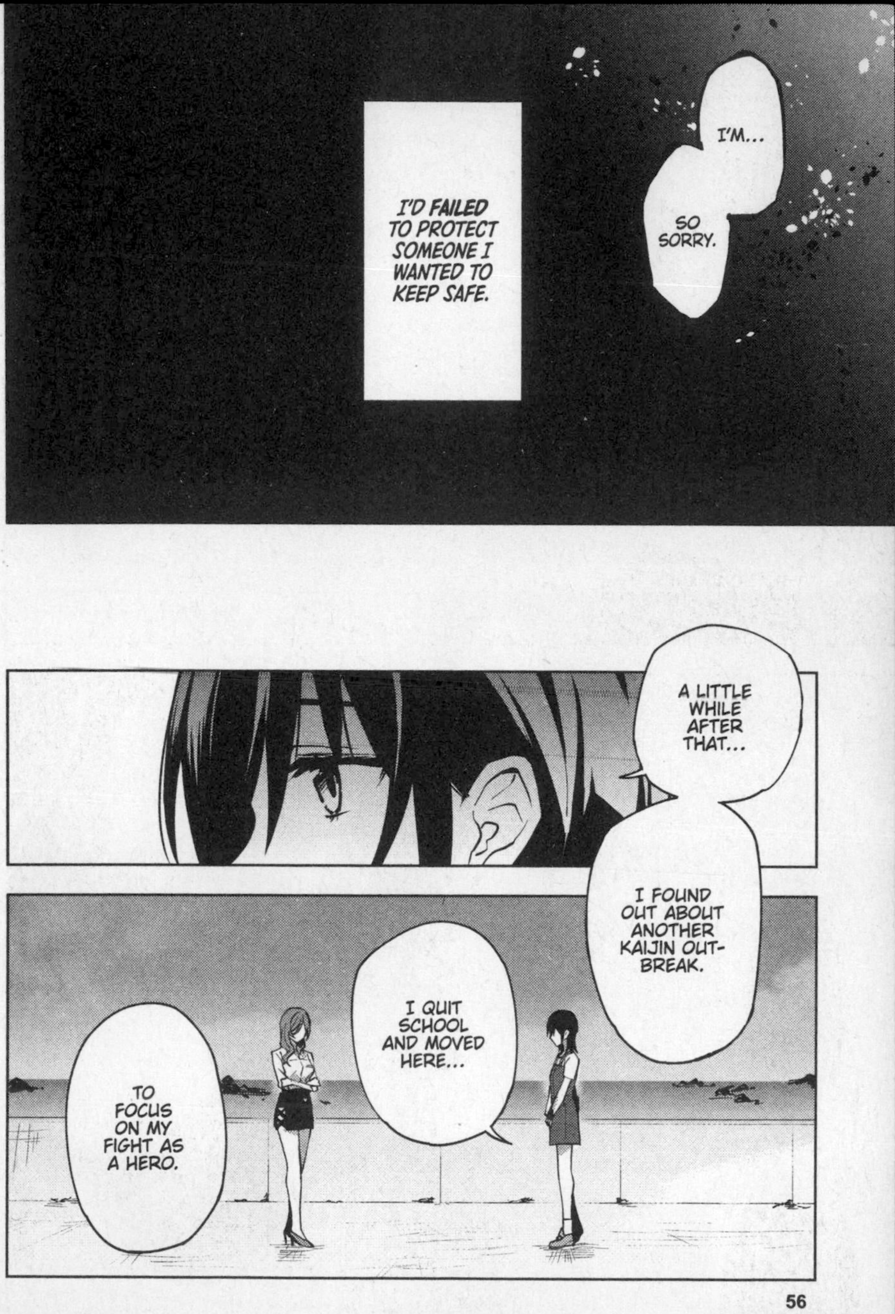
I'M...
SO SORRY.
I'D FAILED TO PROTECT SOMEONE I WANTED TO KEEP SAFE.
A LITTLE WHILE AFTER THAT...
I FOUND OUT ABOUT ANOTHER KAIJIN OUT-BREAK.
I QUIT SCHOOL AND MOVED HERE...
TO FOCUS ON MY FIGHT AS A HERO.

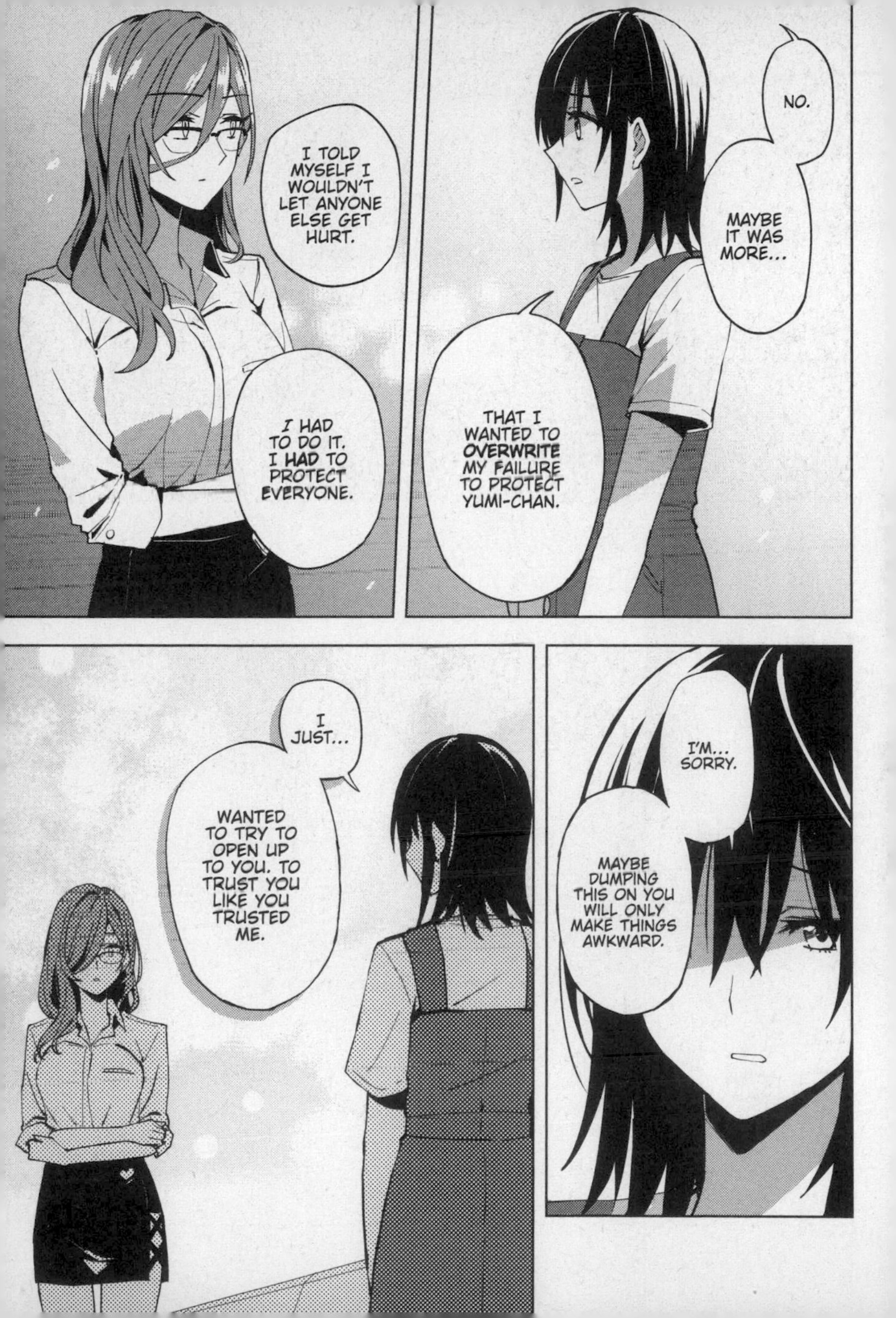
NO.
MAYBE IT WAS MORE...
THAT I WANTED TO **OVERWRITE** MY FAILURE TO PROTECT YUMI-CHAN.
I TOLD MYSELF I WOULDN'T LET ANYONE ELSE GET HURT.
I HAD TO DO IT. I **HAD** *TO PROTECT EVERYONE.*
I'M... SORRY.
MAYBE DUMPING THIS ON YOU WILL ONLY MAKE THINGS AWKWARD.
I JUST...
WANTED TO TRY TO OPEN UP TO YOU. TO TRUST YOU LIKE YOU TRUSTED ME.

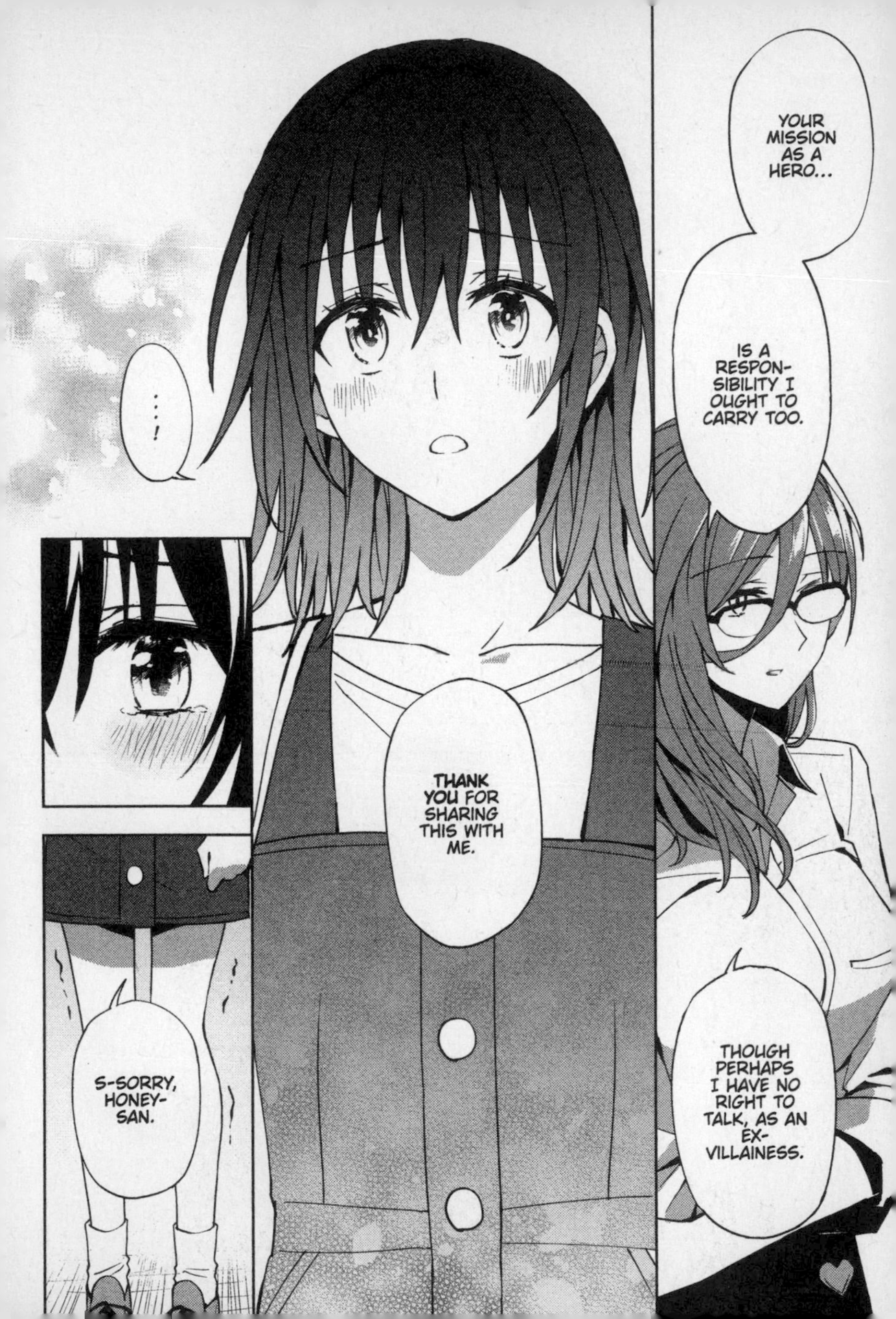
YOUR MISSION AS A HERO...
IS A RESPONSIBILITY I OUGHT TO CARRY TOO.
THOUGH PERHAPS I HAVE NO RIGHT TO TALK, AS AN EX-VILLAINESS.
...!
THANK YOU FOR SHARING THIS WITH ME.
S-SORRY, HONEY-SAN.

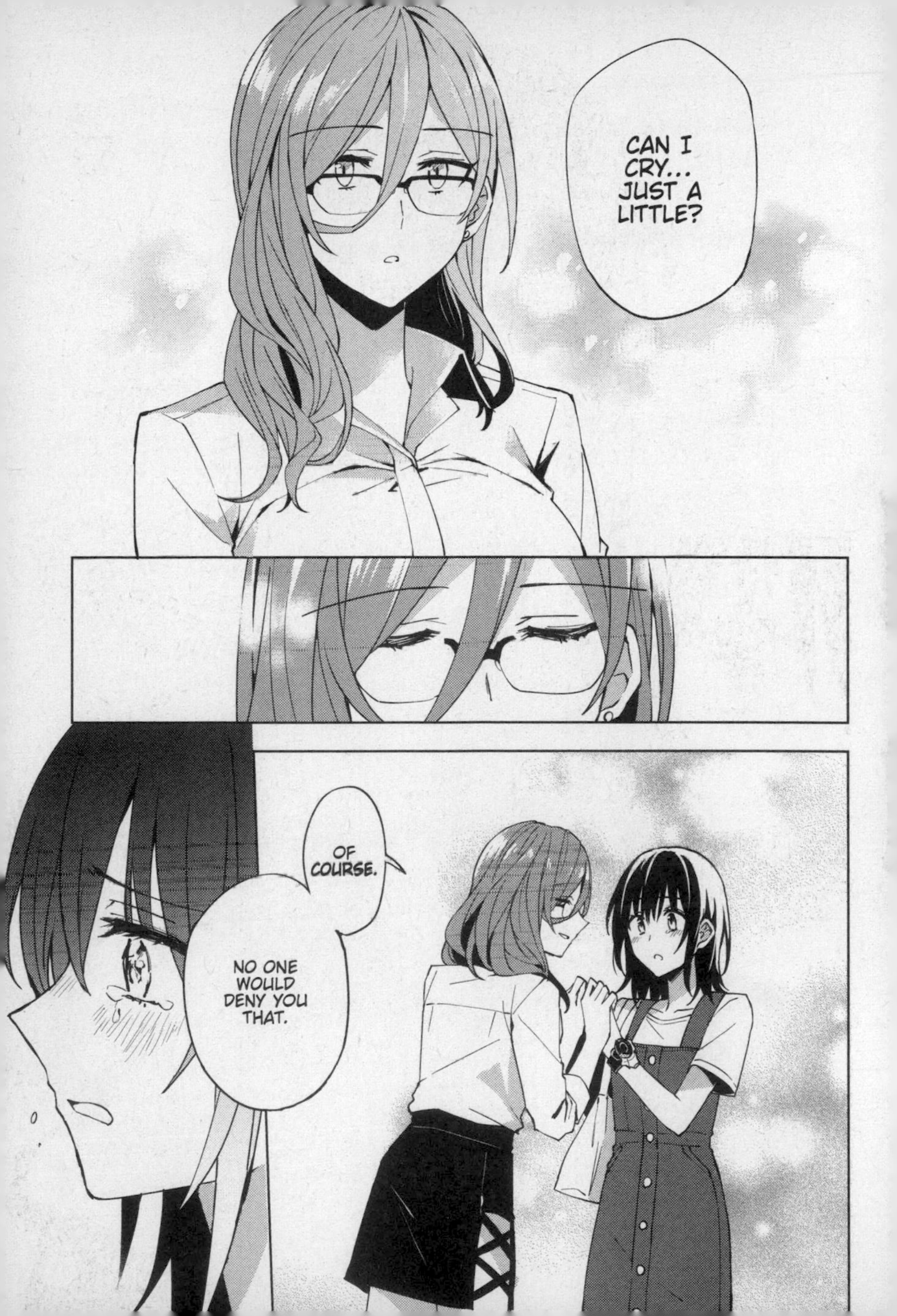
CAN I CRY... JUST A LITTLE?
OF COURSE.
NO ONE WOULD DENY YOU THAT.

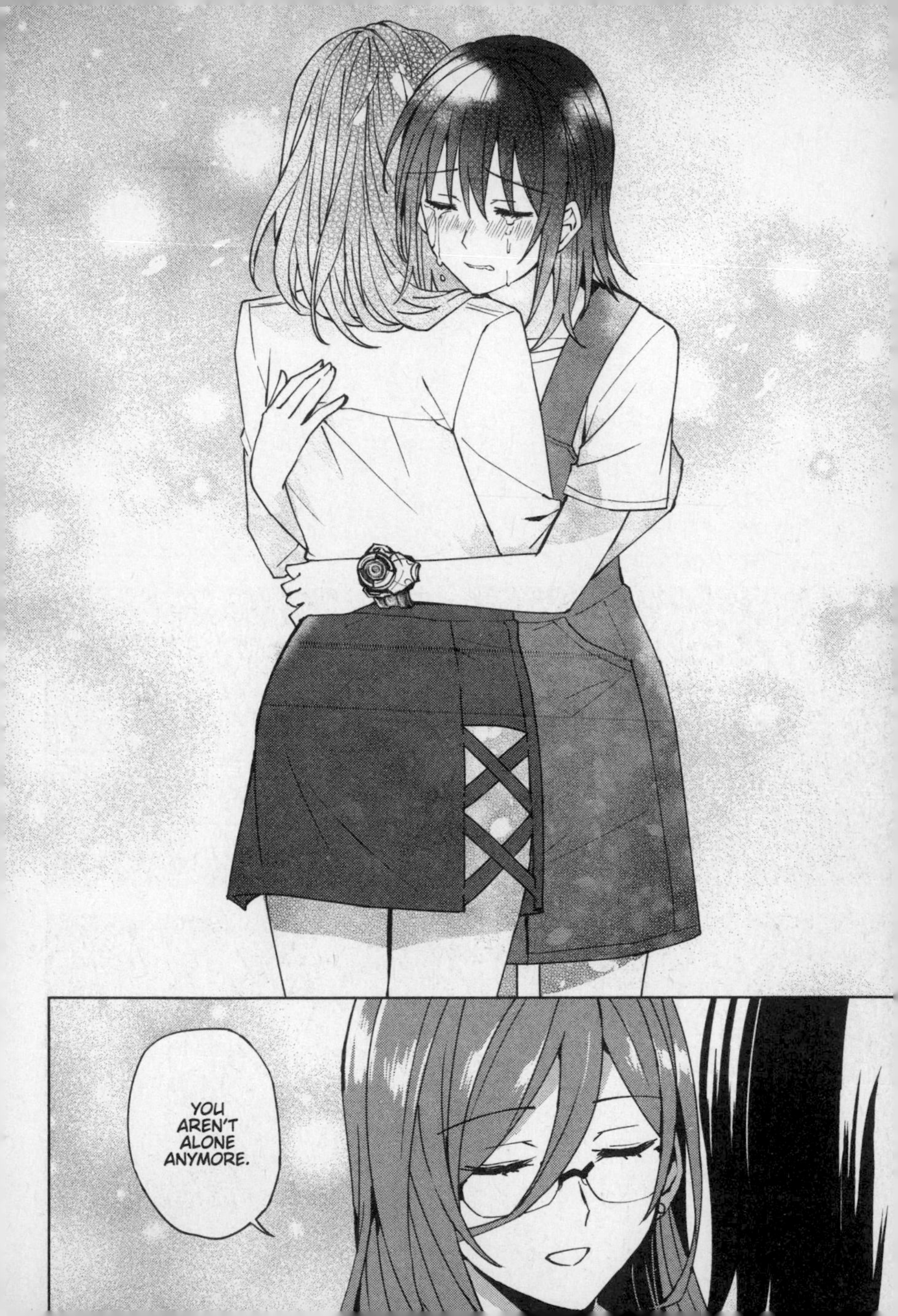
YOU AREN'T ALONE ANYMORE.

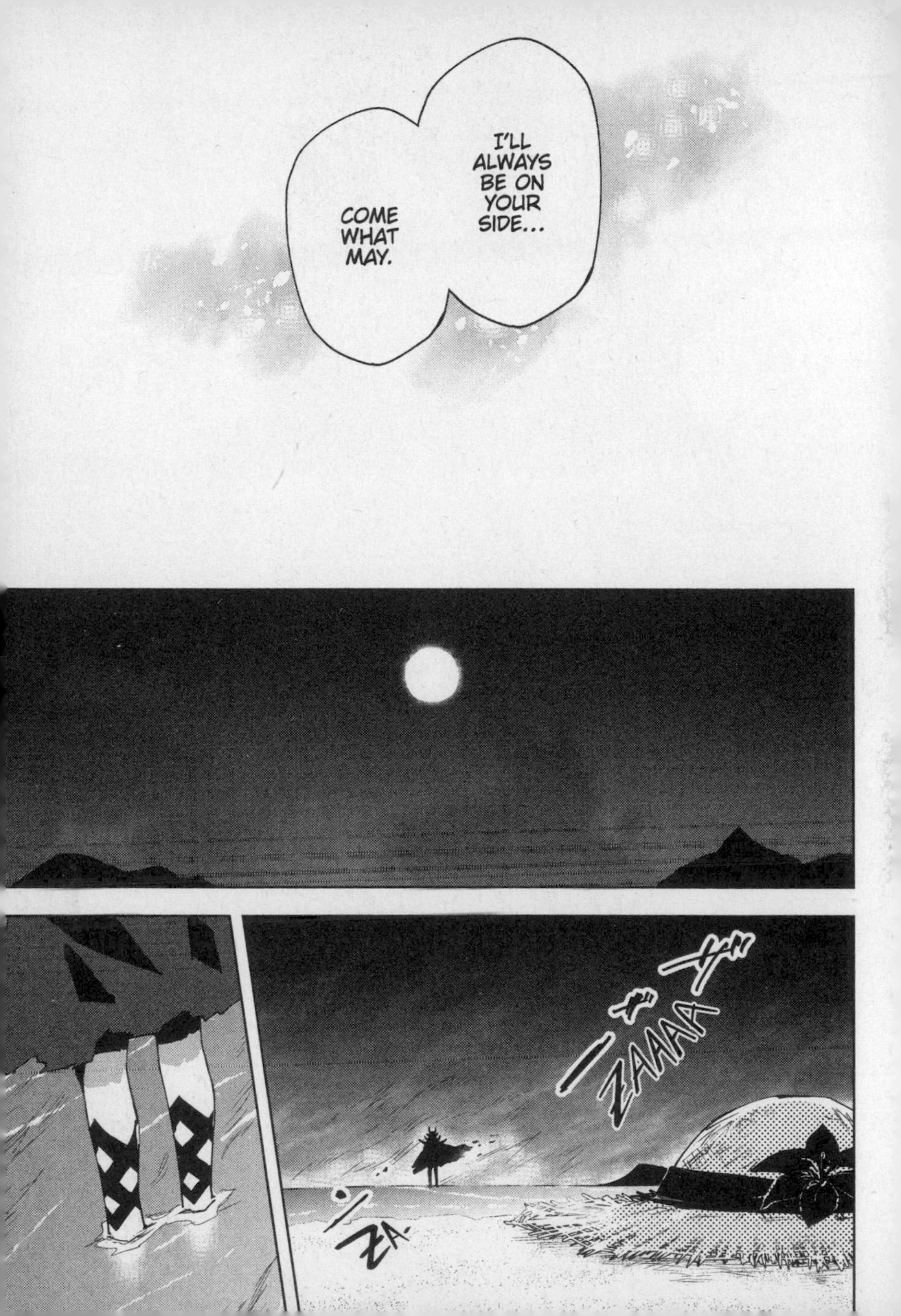
I'LL ALWAYS BE ON YOUR SIDE...
COME WHAT MAY.
ZAAAA
ZA

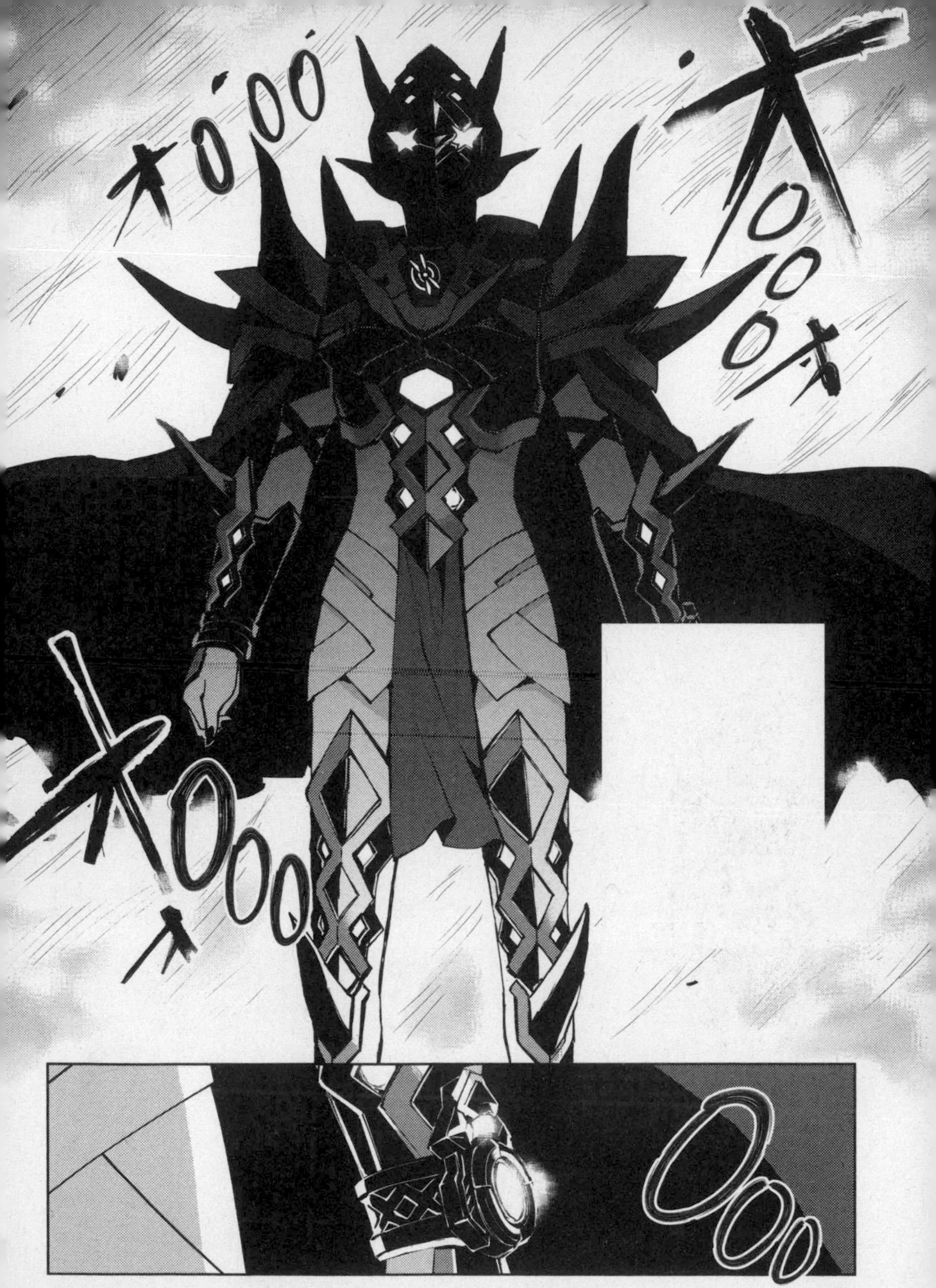

Destroy Antinoid (Kaijin)
Superwomen in Love!
Honey Trap & Rapid Rabbit
Character Data

SUPERWOMEN IN LOVE!

HONEY TRAP & RAPID RABBIT

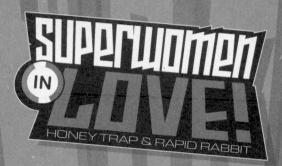

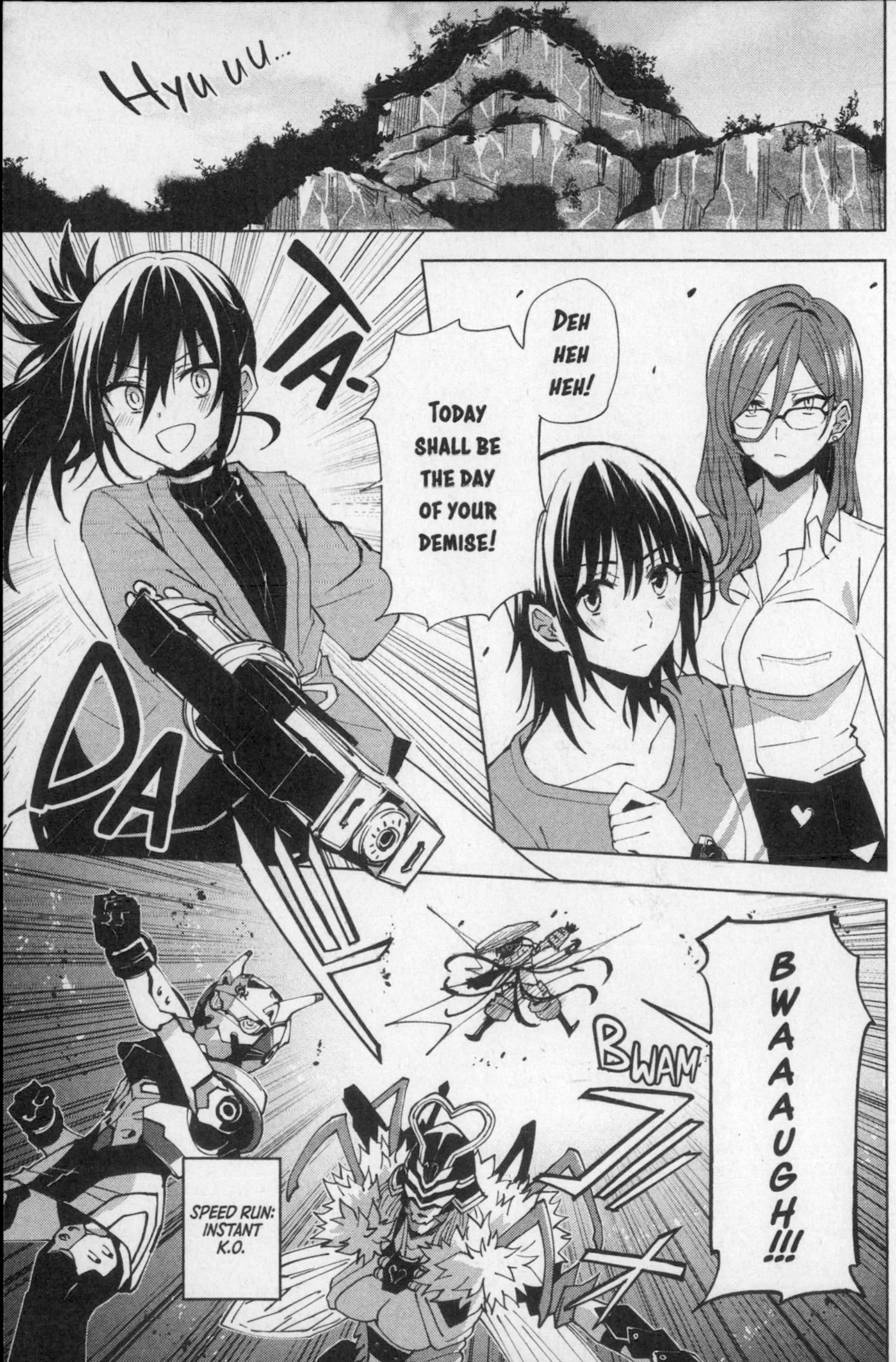
Hyu uu...
DEH HEH HEH!
TODAY SHALL BE THE DAY OF YOUR DEMISE!
TA-DA
BWAAAAUGH!!!
BWAM
SPEED RUN: INSTANT K.O.

CHAPTER 13 X-DAY

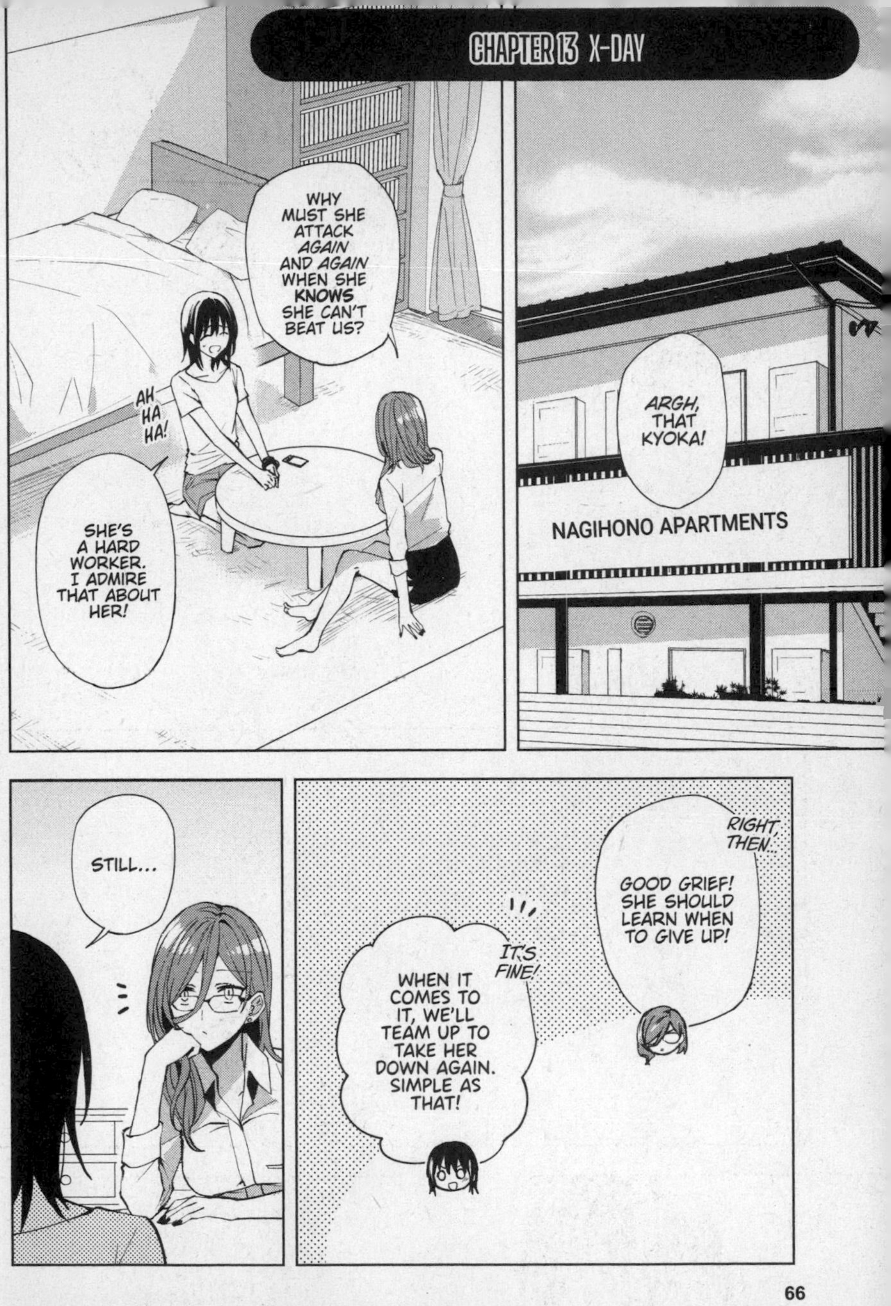

ARGH, THAT KYOKA!
NAGIHONO APARTMENTS
WHY MUST SHE ATTACK *AGAIN* AND *AGAIN* WHEN SHE **KNOWS** SHE CAN'T BEAT US?
AH HA HA!
SHE'S A HARD WORKER. I ADMIRE THAT ABOUT HER!
RIGHT, THEN...
GOOD GRIEF! SHE SHOULD LEARN WHEN TO GIVE UP!
IT'S FINE!
WHEN IT COMES TO IT, WE'LL TEAM UP TO TAKE HER DOWN AGAIN. SIMPLE AS THAT!
STILL...

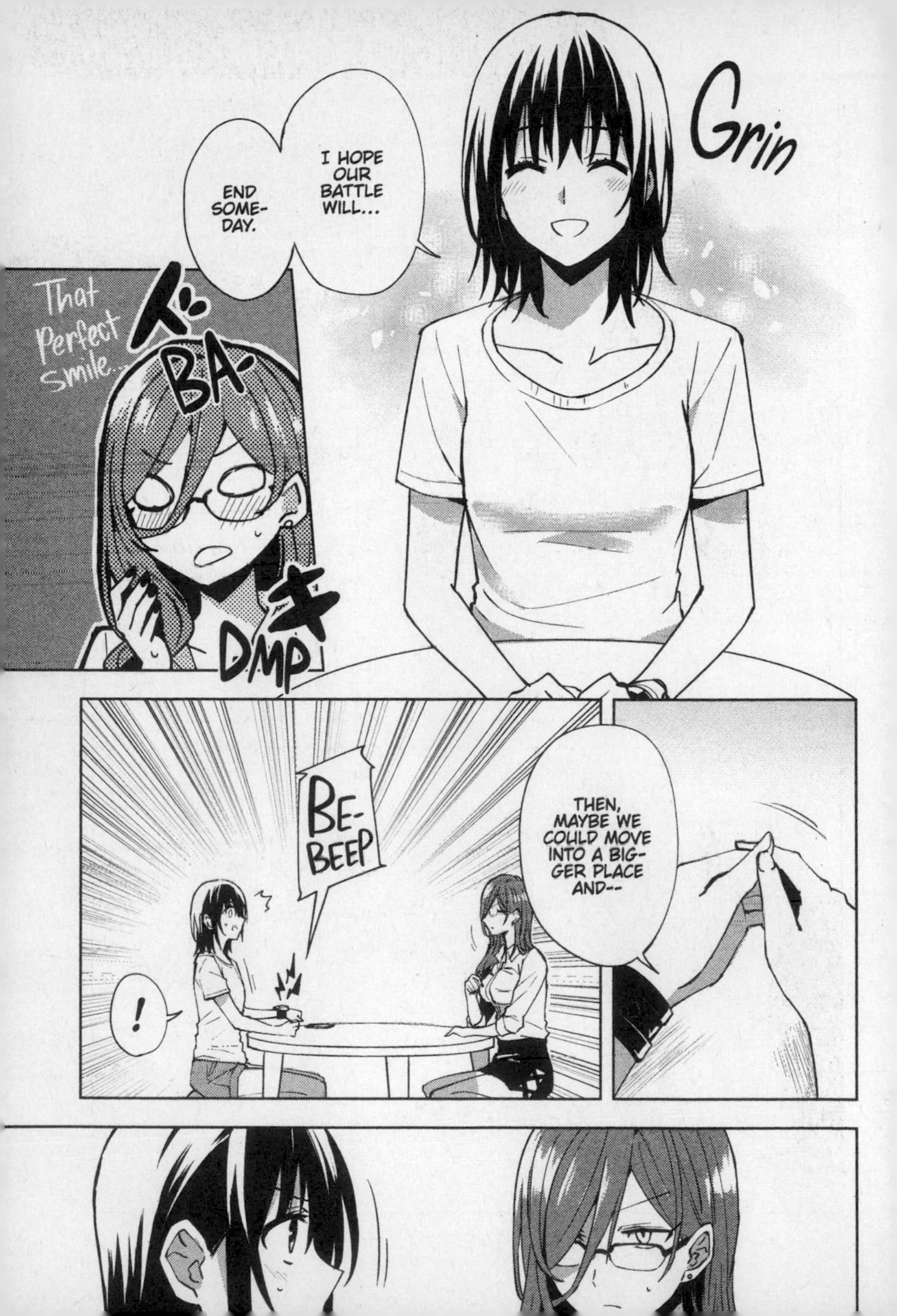
Grin
I HOPE OUR BATTLE WILL...
END SOME-DAY.
That Perfect smile...
BA-
DMP
THEN, MAYBE WE COULD MOVE INTO A BIG-GER PLACE AND--
BE-BEEP
!

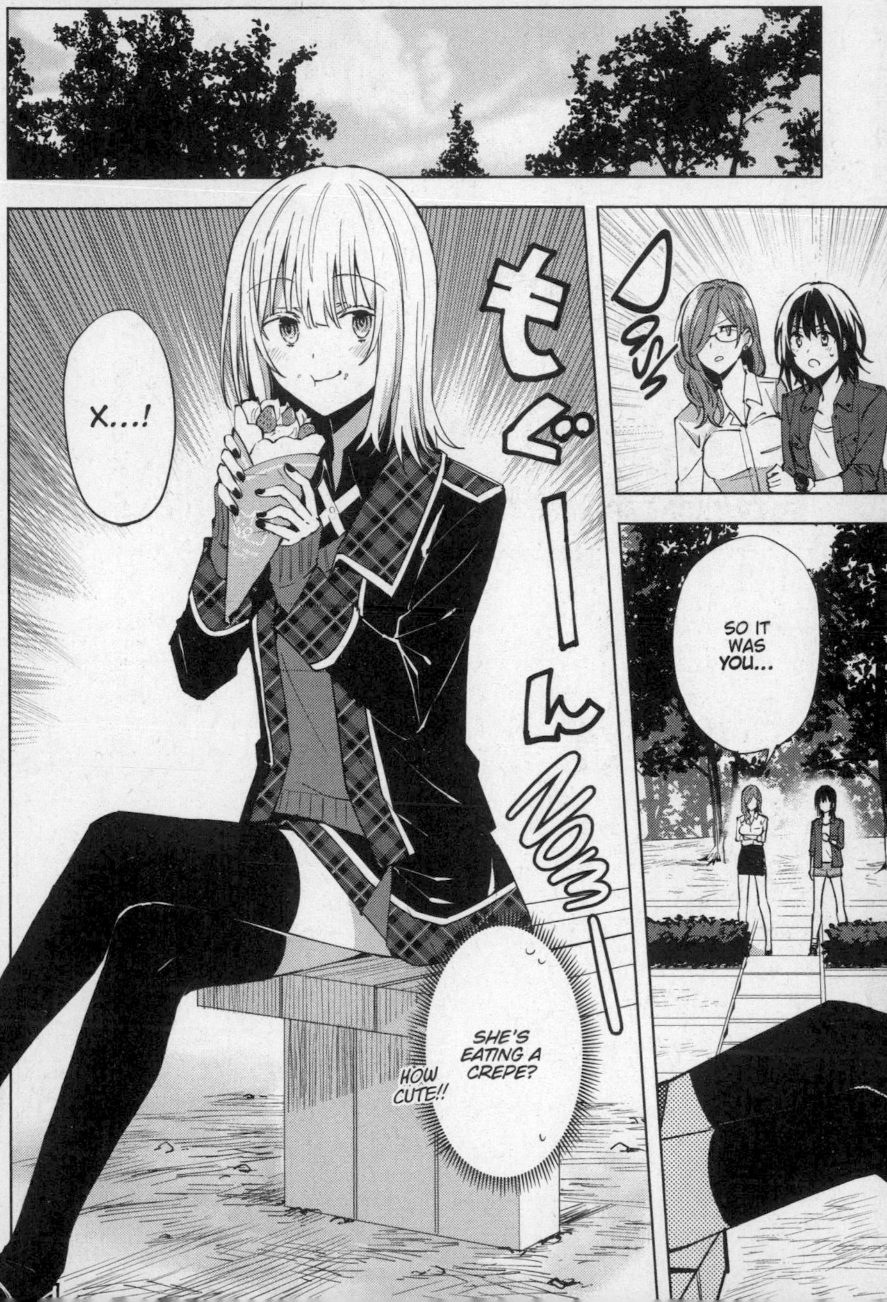
Dash
SO IT WAS YOU...
もぐーん
Nom—
X...!
SHE'S EATING A CREPE?
HOW CUTE!!

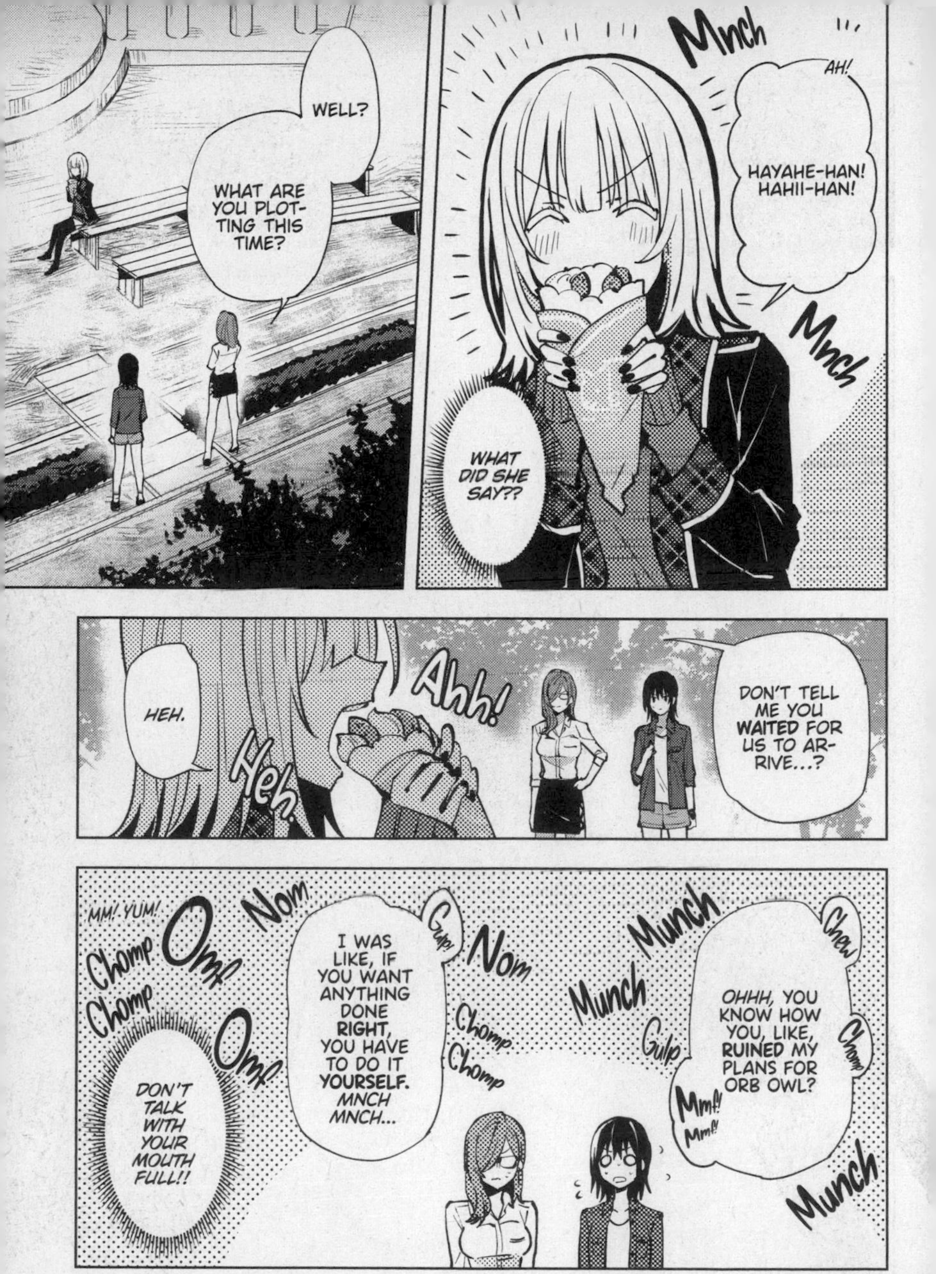
Mnch
AH!
HAYAHE-HAN! HAHII-HAN!
Mnch
WHAT DID SHE SAY??
WELL?
WHAT ARE YOU PLOTTING THIS TIME?
DON'T TELL ME YOU WAITED FOR US TO ARRIVE...?
Ahh!
Heh.
HEH.
Chew
OHHH, YOU KNOW HOW YOU, LIKE, RUINED MY PLANS FOR ORB OWL?
Chomp
Munch
Munch
Munch
Gulp
Mmf! Mmf!
Nom
Gulp!
I WAS LIKE, IF YOU WANT ANYTHING DONE RIGHT, YOU HAVE TO DO IT YOURSELF. MNCH MNCH...
Chomp Chomp
Nom
Omf
MM! YUM!
Chomp Chomp
Omf
DON'T TALK WITH YOUR MOUTH FULL!!

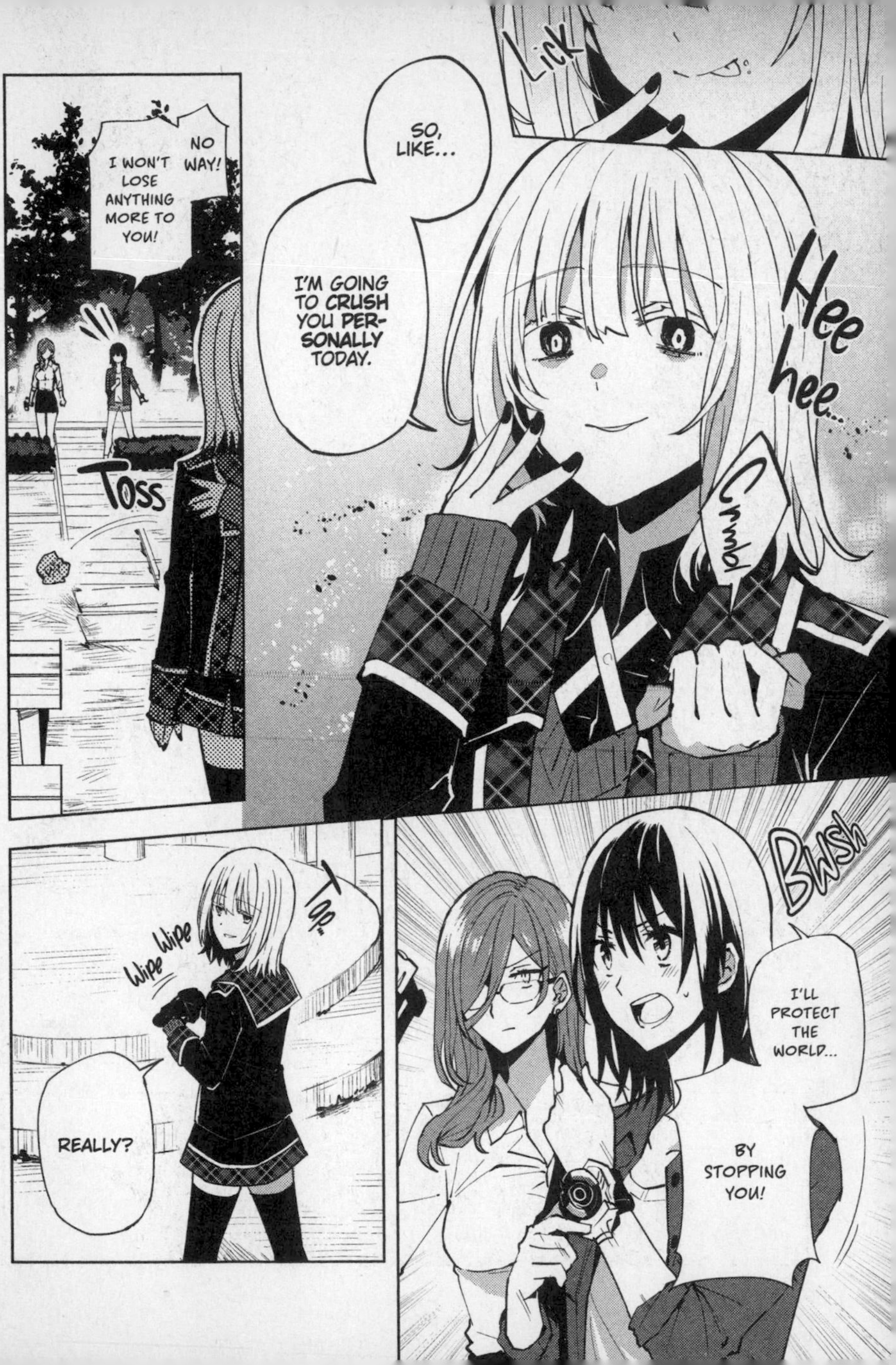
Lick
SO, LIKE...
I'M GOING TO CRUSH YOU PERSONALLY TODAY.
Hee hee...
Crmbl
NO WAY!
I WON'T LOSE ANYTHING MORE TO YOU!
Toss
Bwsh
I'LL PROTECT THE WORLD...
BY STOPPING YOU!
Tap..
Wipe Wipe
REALLY?

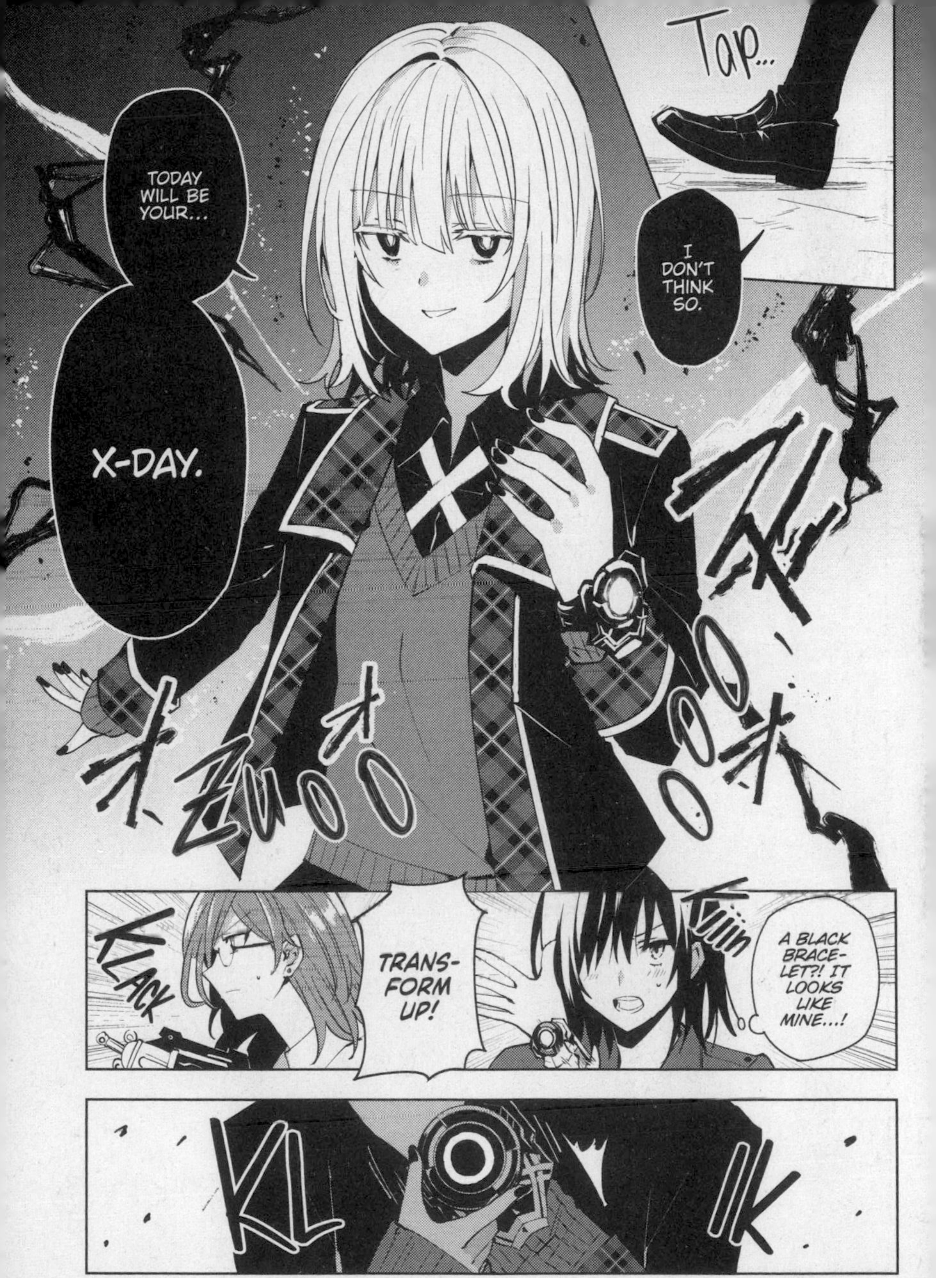
Tap...
I DON'T THINK SO.
TODAY WILL BE YOUR...
X-DAY.
ZUOOO
A BLACK BRACELET?! IT LOOKS LIKE MINE...!
TRANS-FORM UP!
KLACK
KL IK

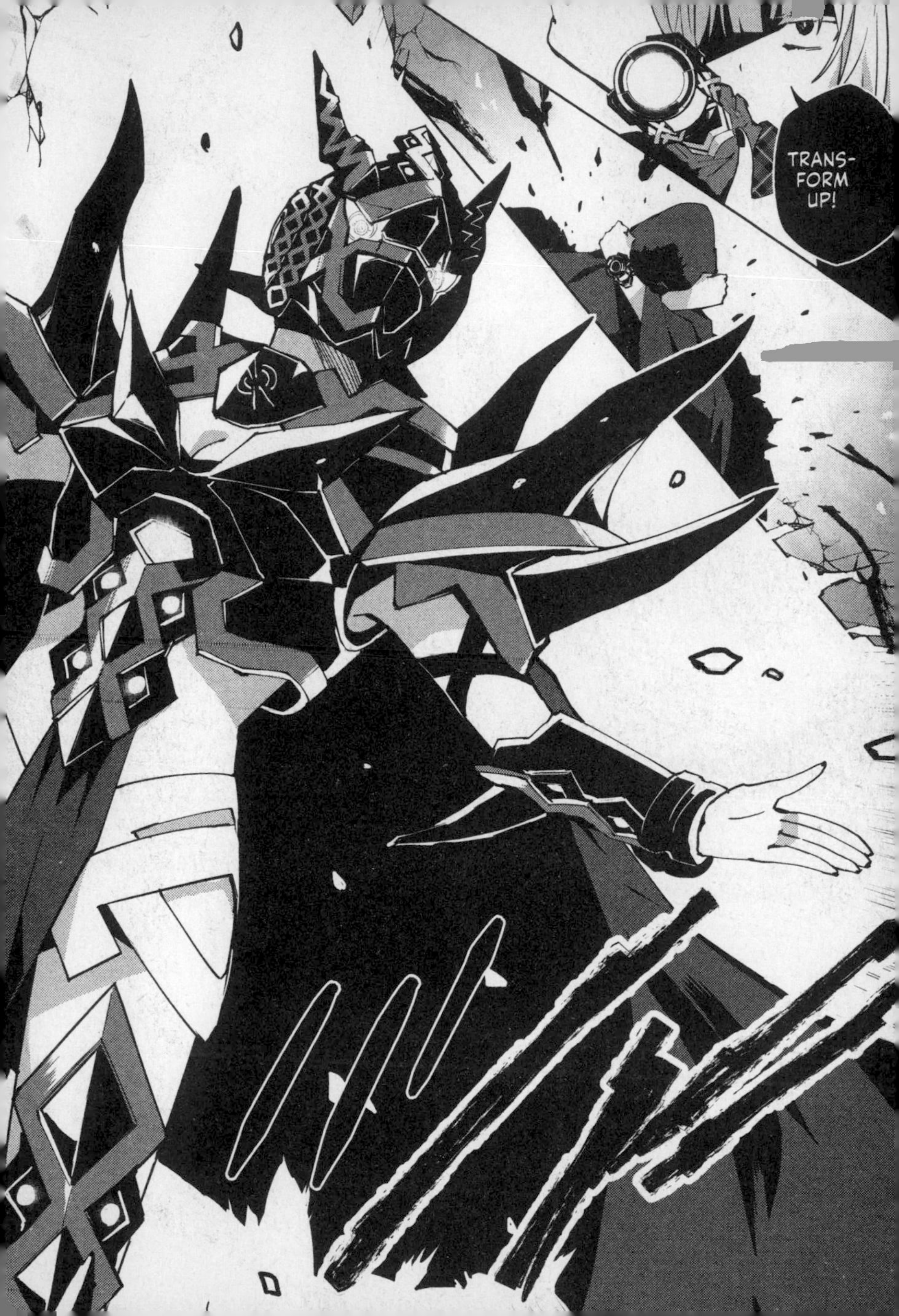
TRANS-FORM UP!

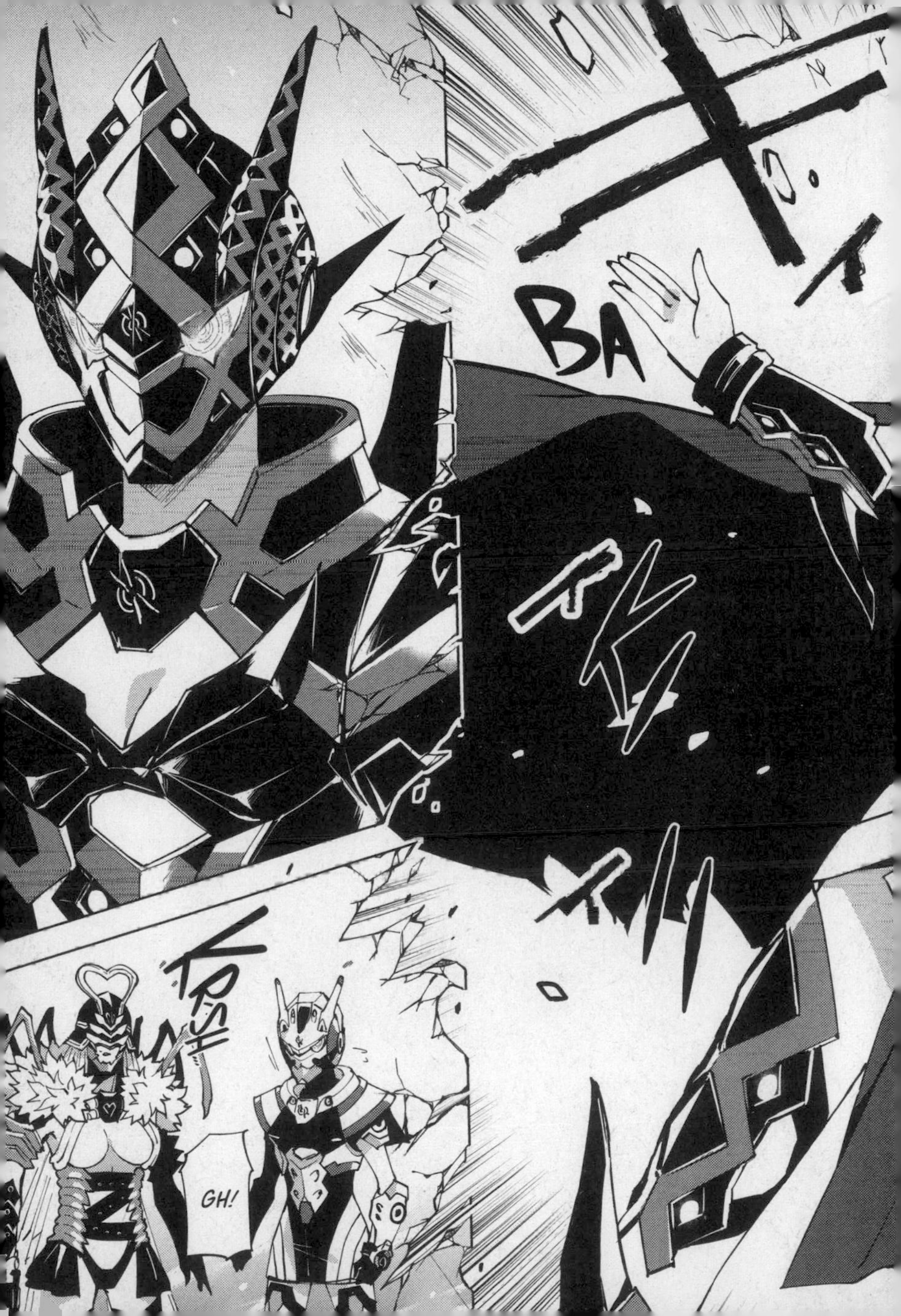
BA
KRSH...
GH!

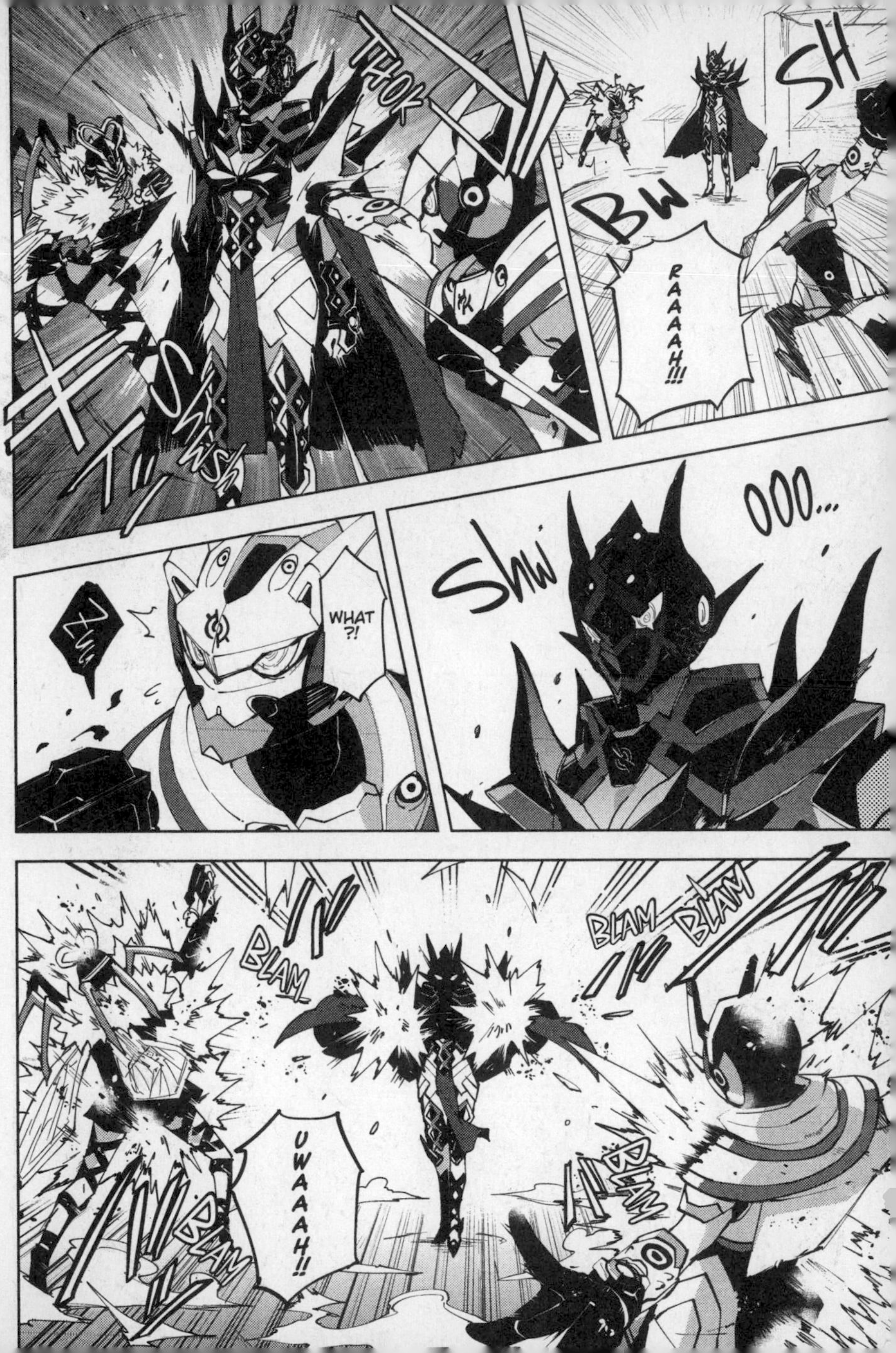
SH
Bw
RAAAAAH!!!
THOK
Shwish
OOO...
Shw
WHAT?!
Zu
BLAM
BLAM
BLAM
UWAAAAH!!
BLAM
BLAM

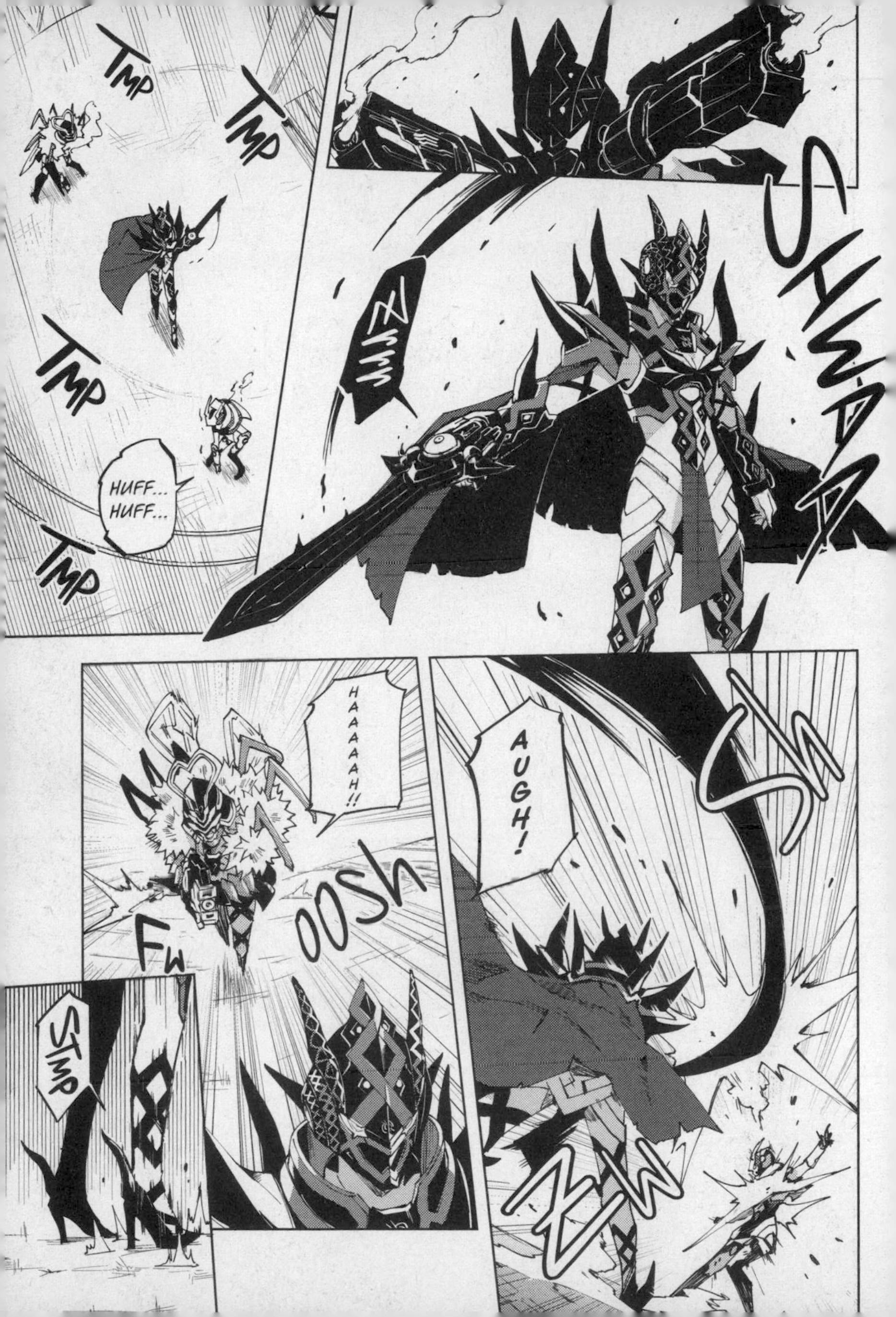
SHWAP
Zrrrr
TMP
TMP
TMP
TMP
HUFF... HUFF...
AUGH!
Sh
HAAAAAAH!!
Fw
OOSh
STMP

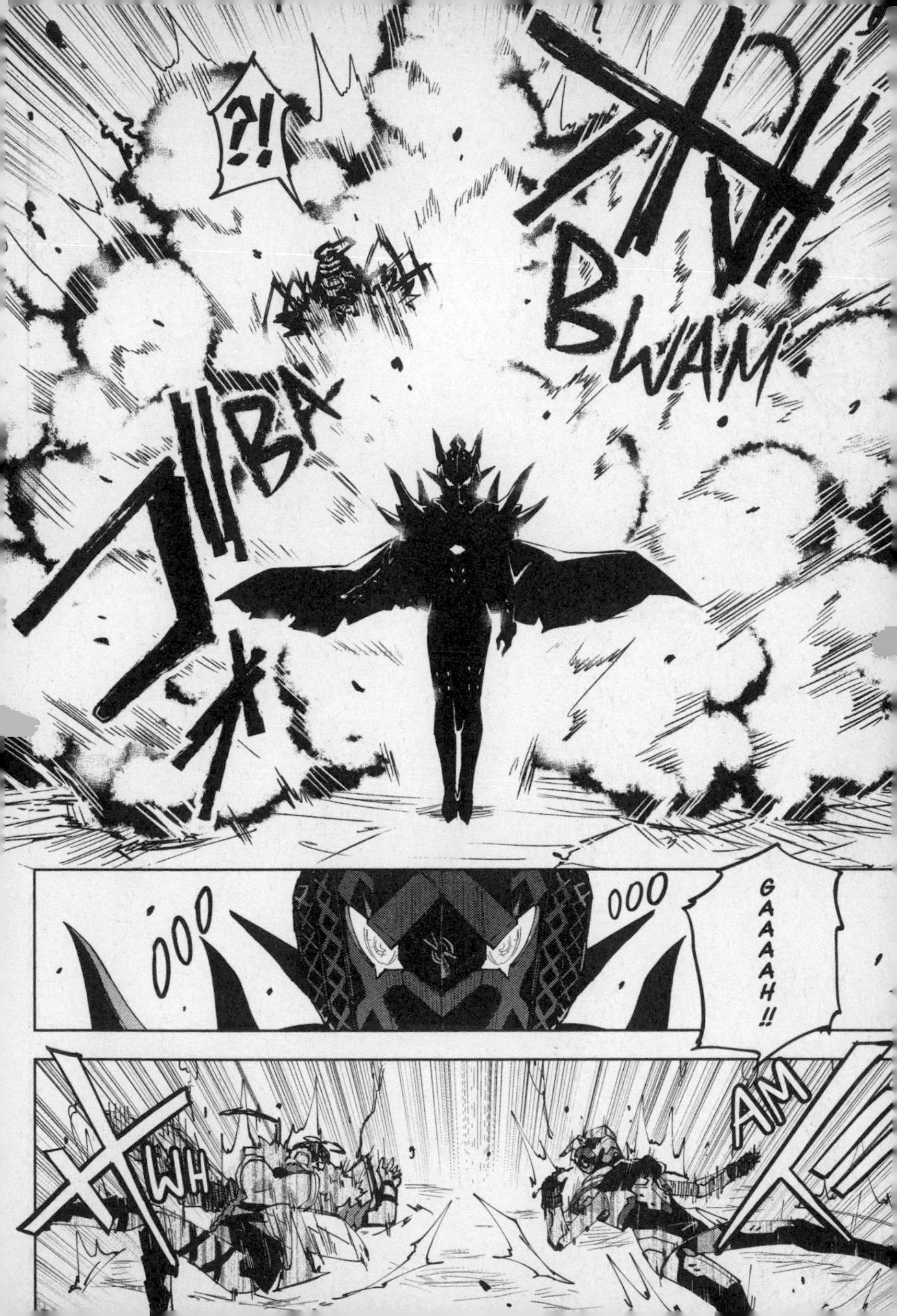
BWAM
?!
BA
GAAAAAH!!
OOO
OOO
AM
WH

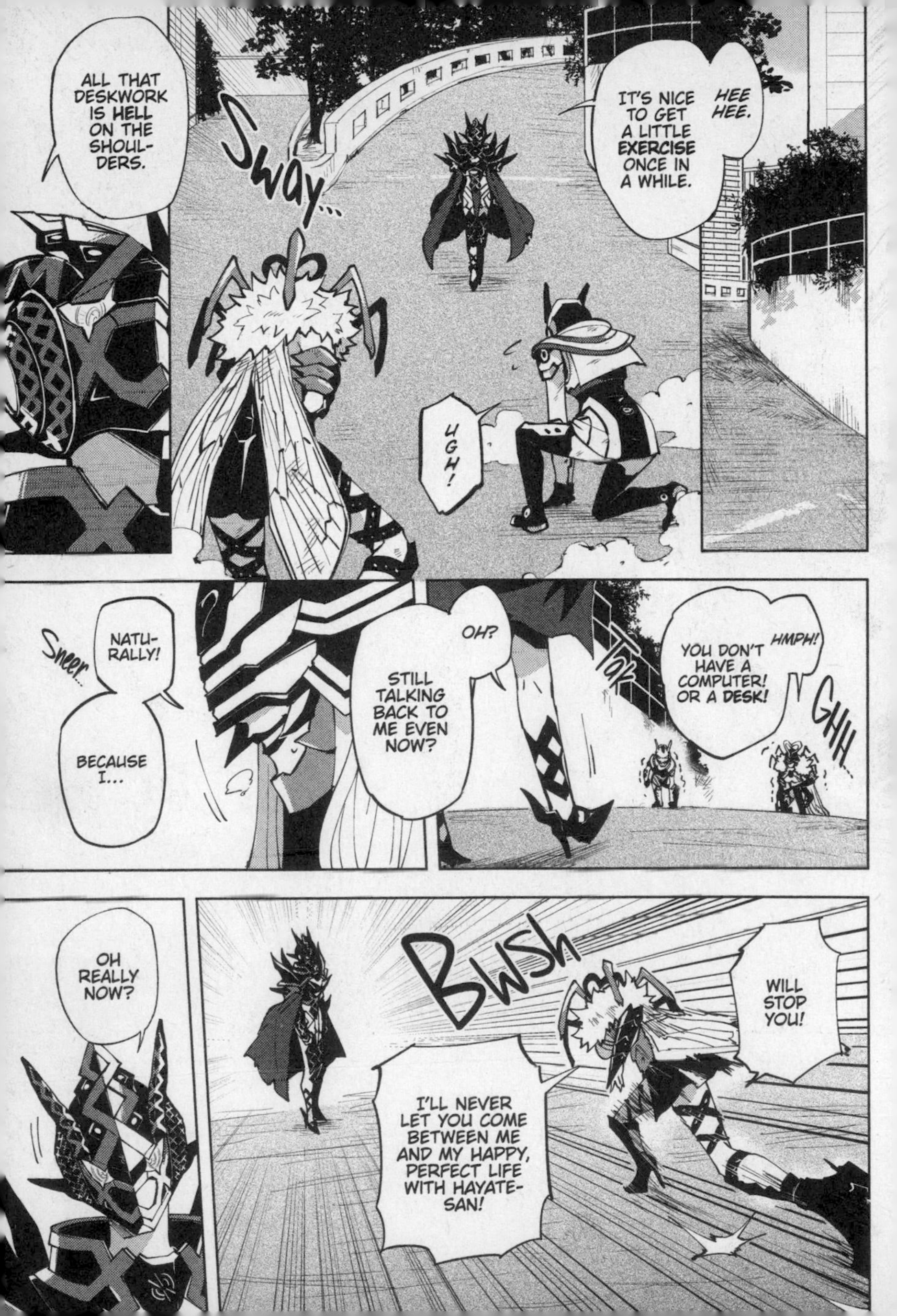
HEE HEE.
IT'S NICE TO GET A LITTLE EXERCISE ONCE IN A WHILE.
Sway...
UGH!
ALL THAT DESKWORK IS HELL ON THE SHOULDERS.
HMPH!
YOU DON'T HAVE A COMPUTER! OR A DESK!
GHH
Tak
OH?
STILL TALKING BACK TO ME EVEN NOW?
Sneer...
NATURALLY!
BECAUSE I...
WILL STOP YOU!
Bwsh
I'LL NEVER LET YOU COME BETWEEN ME AND MY HAPPY, PERFECT LIFE WITH HAYATE-SAN!
OH REALLY NOW?

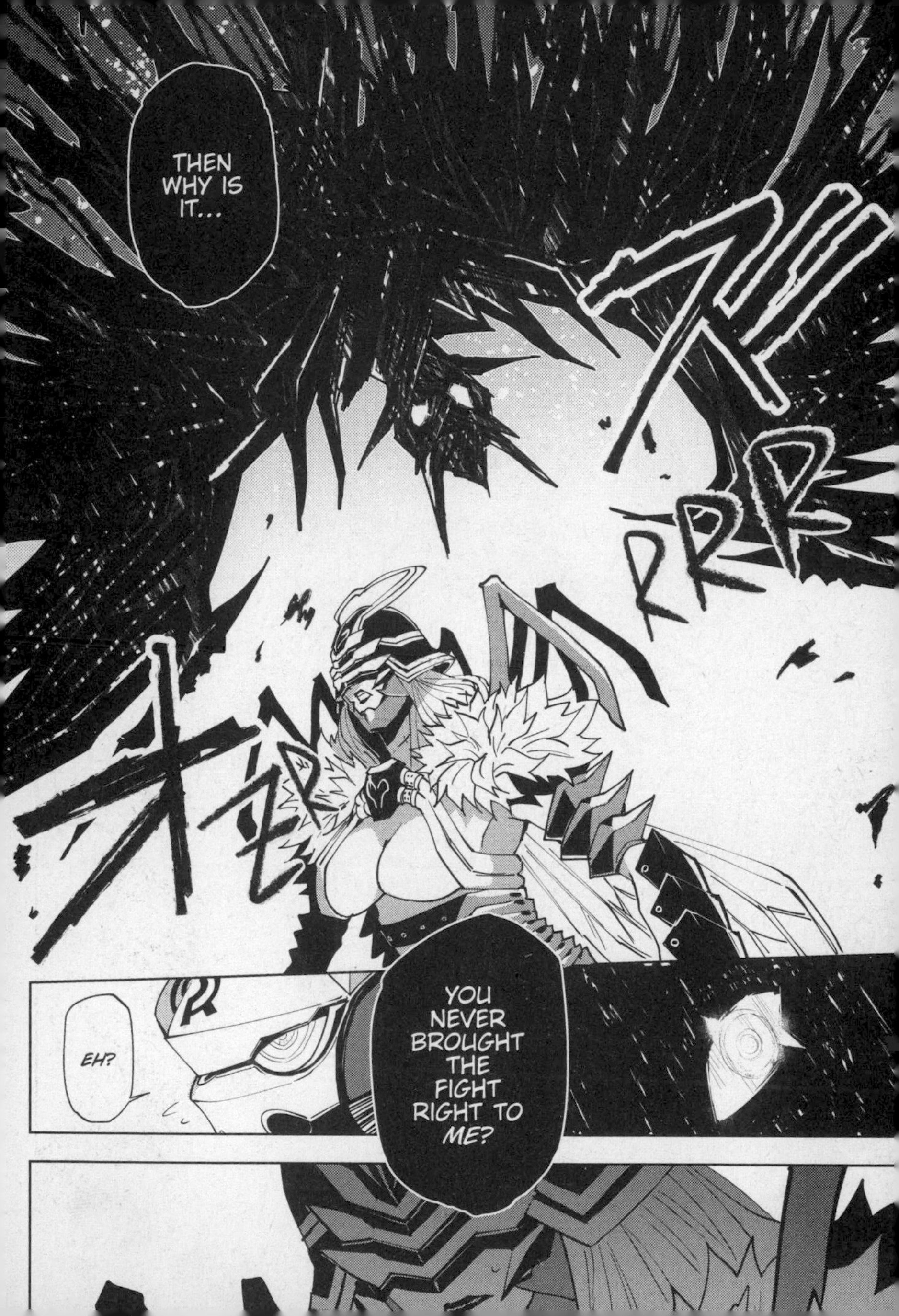
THEN WHY IS IT...
YOU NEVER BROUGHT THE FIGHT RIGHT TO ME?
EH?

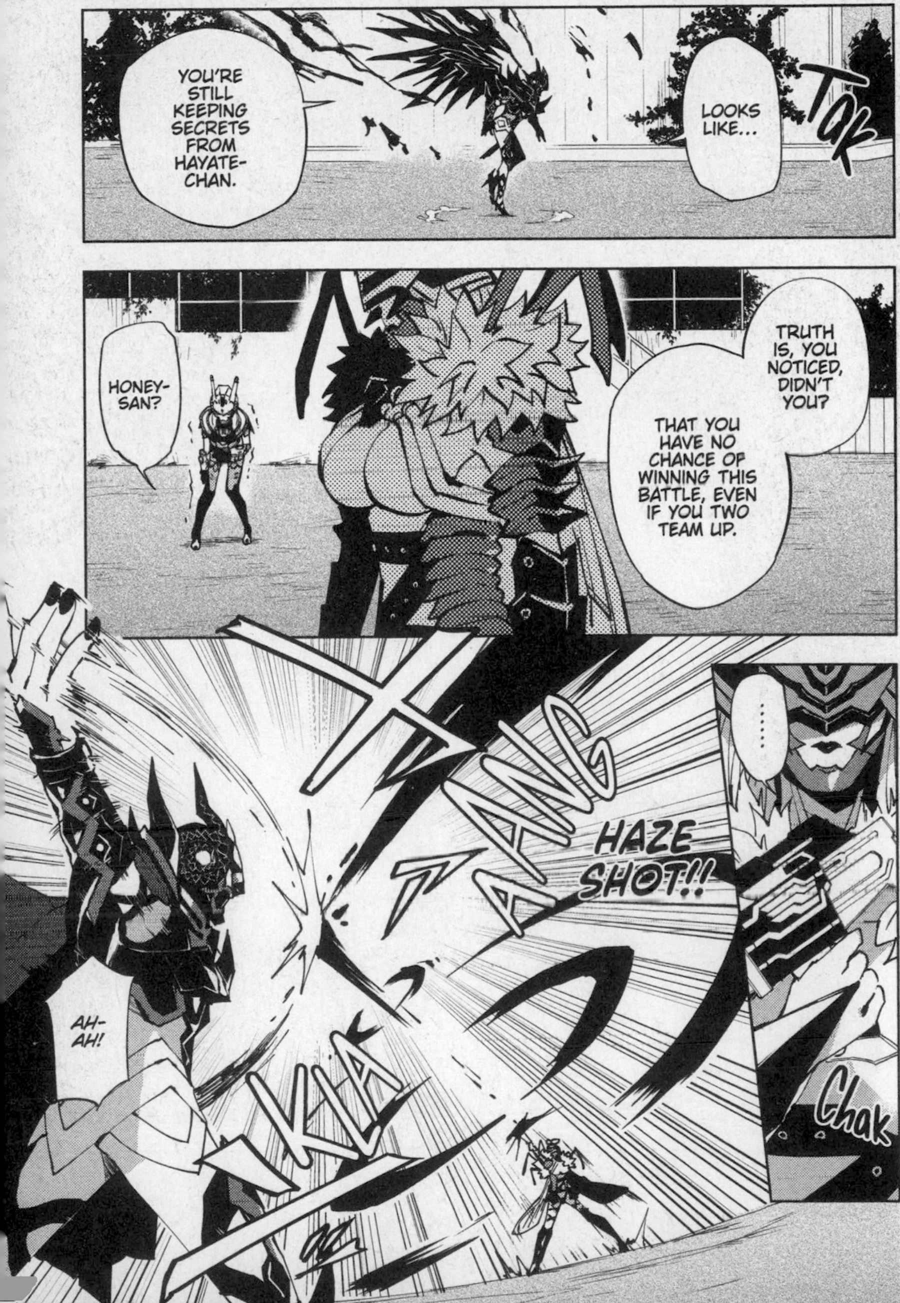

LOOKS LIKE...
TAK
YOU'RE STILL KEEPING SECRETS FROM HAYATE-CHAN.
TRUTH IS, YOU NOTICED, DIDN'T YOU?
THAT YOU HAVE NO CHANCE OF WINNING THIS BATTLE, EVEN IF YOU TWO TEAM UP.
HONEY-SAN?
......
Chak
HAZE SHOT!!
AH-AH!

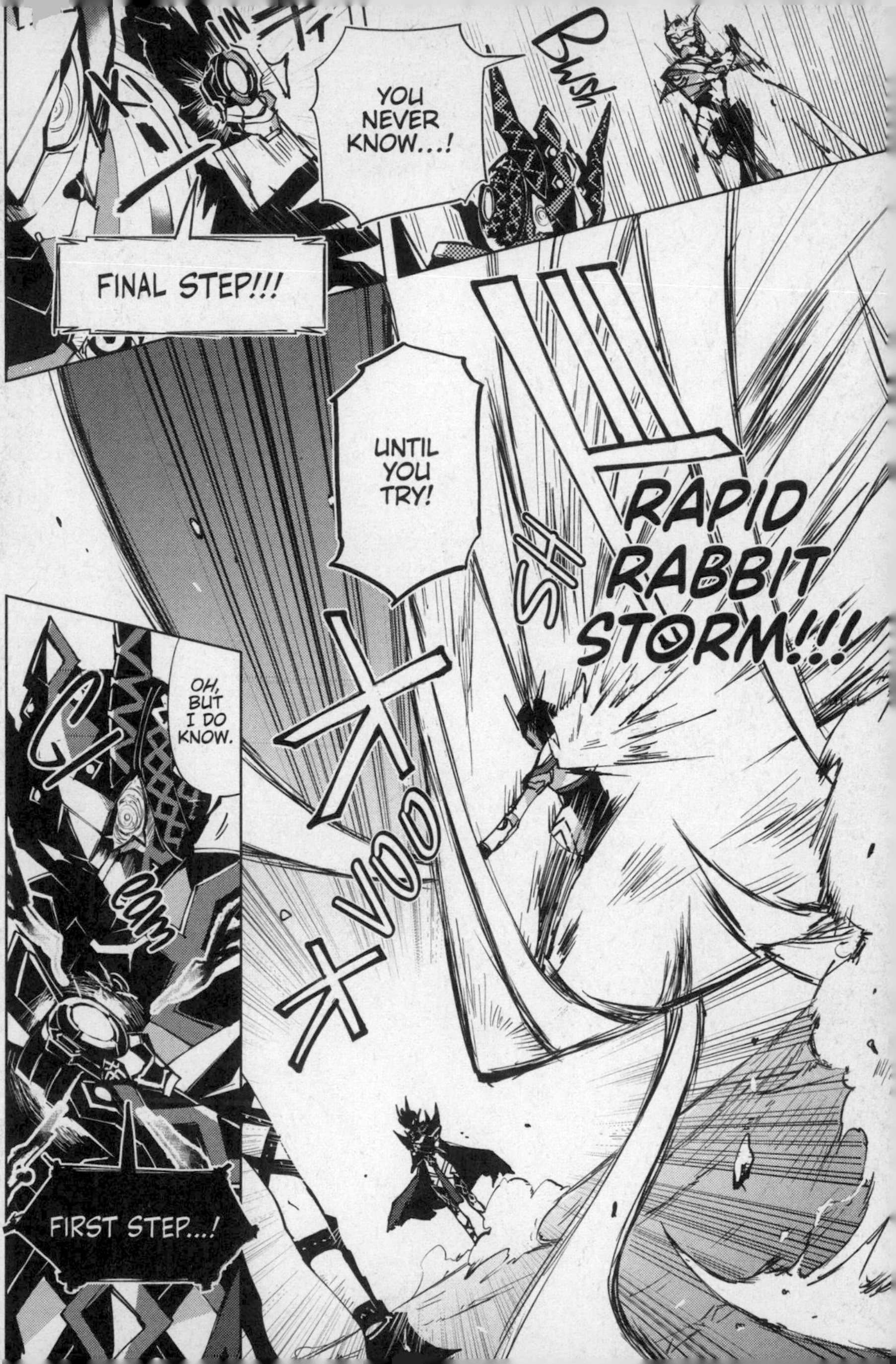

Bwsh
YOU NEVER KNOW...!
FINAL STEP!!!
UNTIL YOU TRY!
SHH
RAPID RABBIT STORM!!!
VOOO
OH, BUT I DO KNOW.
Gleam
FIRST STEP...!

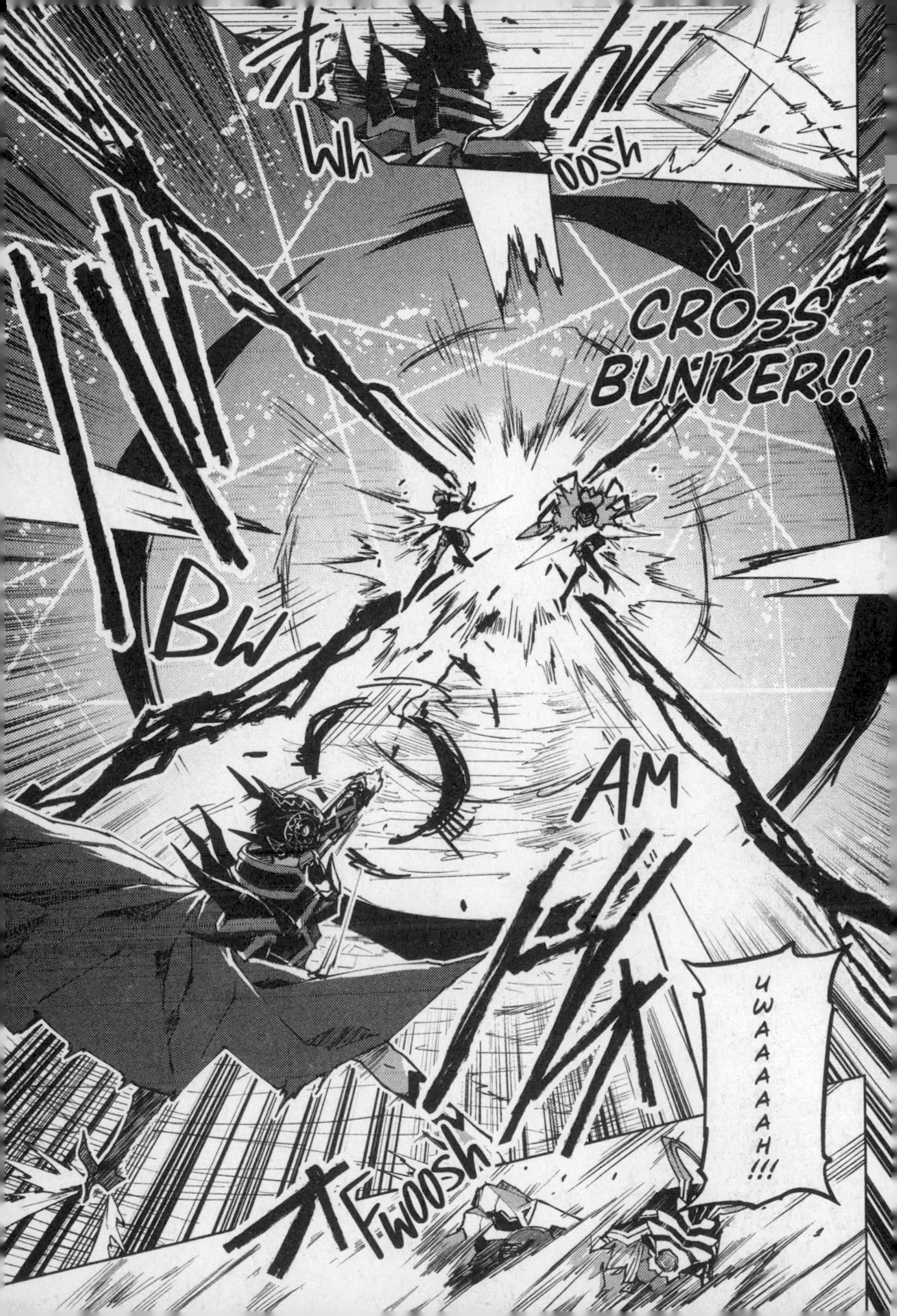
Wh
oosh
X CROSS BUNKER!!
Bw
AM
UWAAAAAAH!!!
FWOOSH

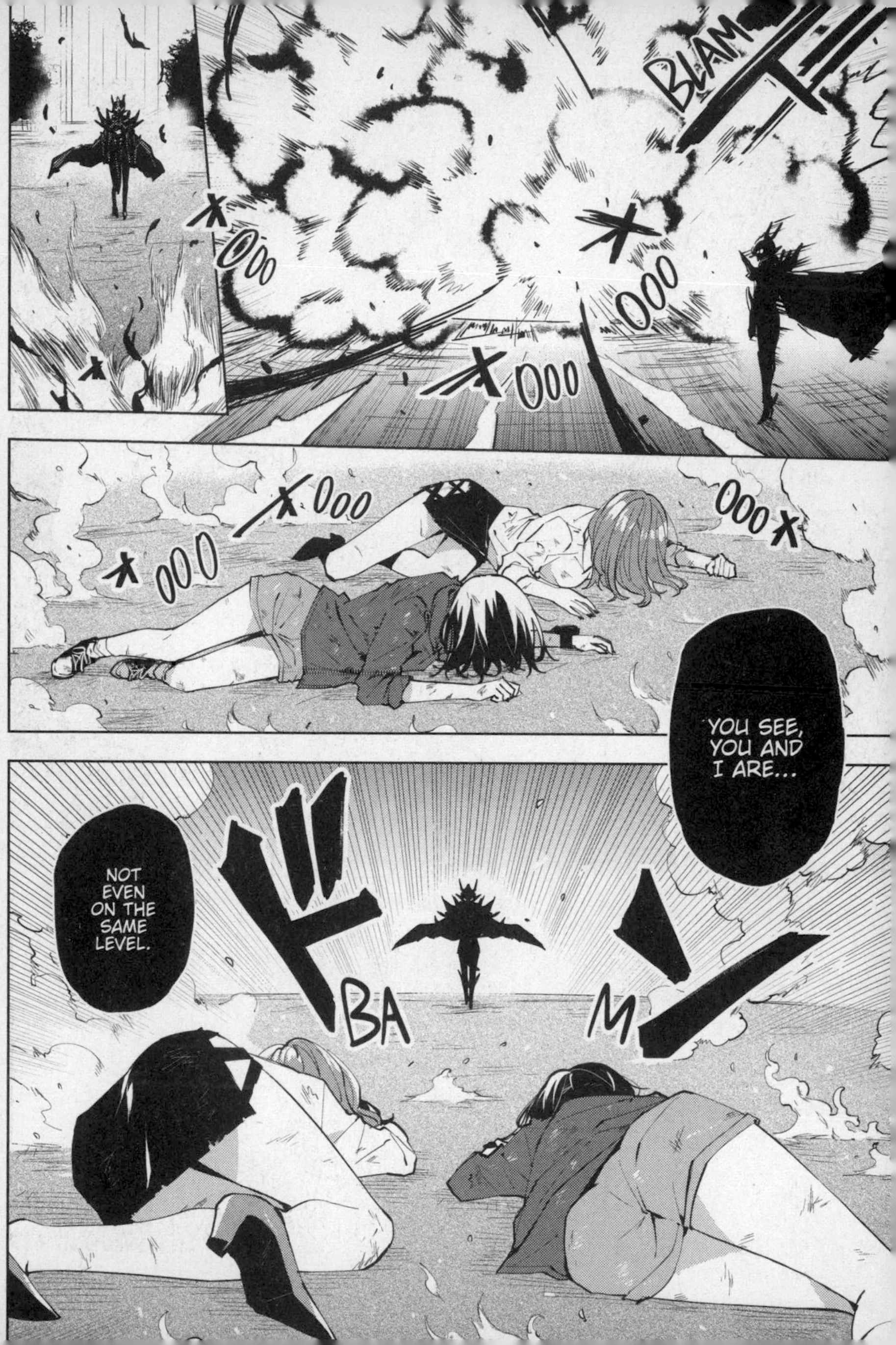
BLAM
YOU SEE, YOU AND I ARE...
BAM
NOT EVEN ON THE SAME LEVEL.

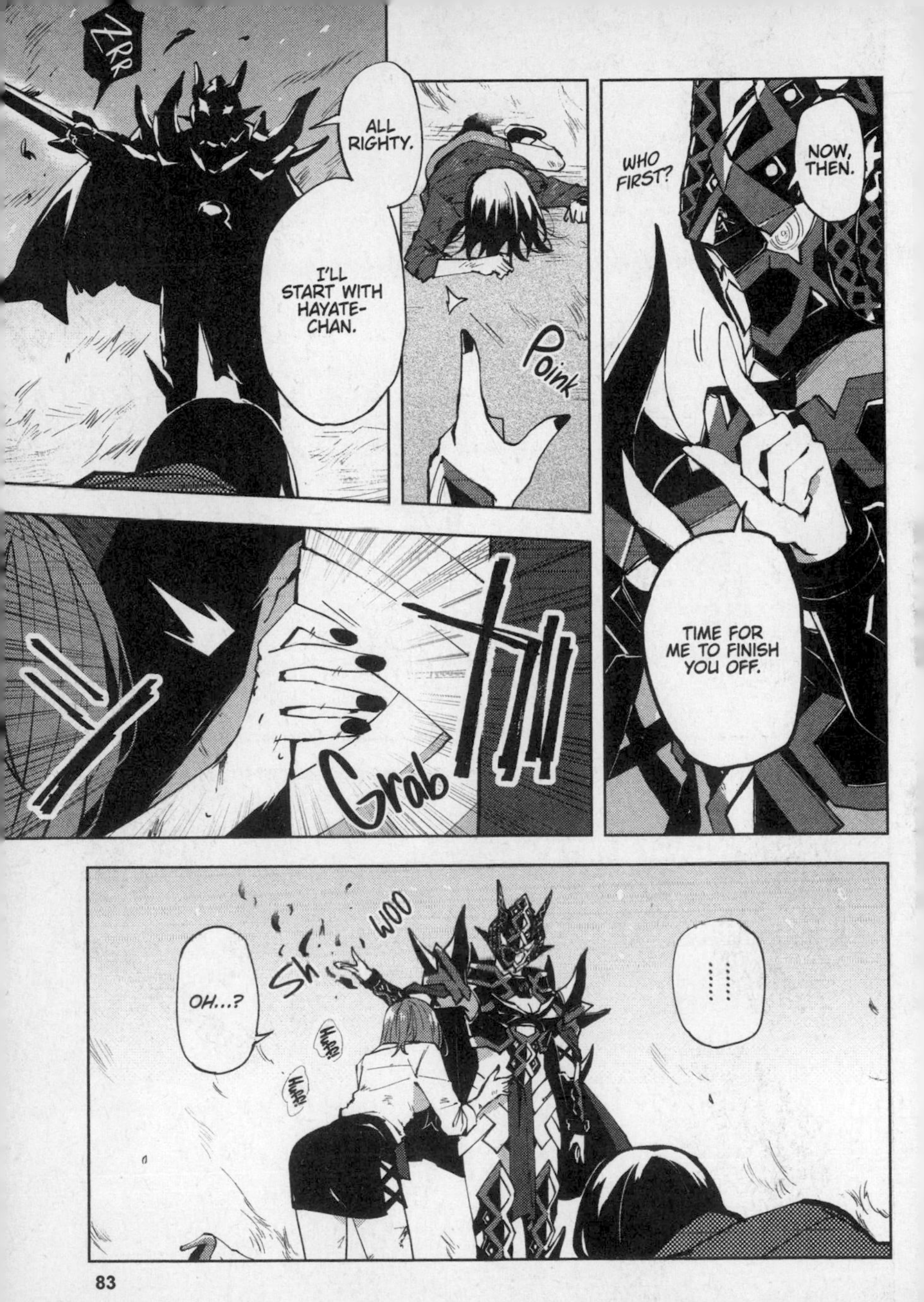
NOW, THEN.
WHO FIRST?
TIME FOR ME TO FINISH YOU OFF.
Poink
ZRR
ALL RIGHTY.
I'LL START WITH HAYATE-CHAN.
Grab
......
Sh WOO
Huff!
Huff!
OH...?

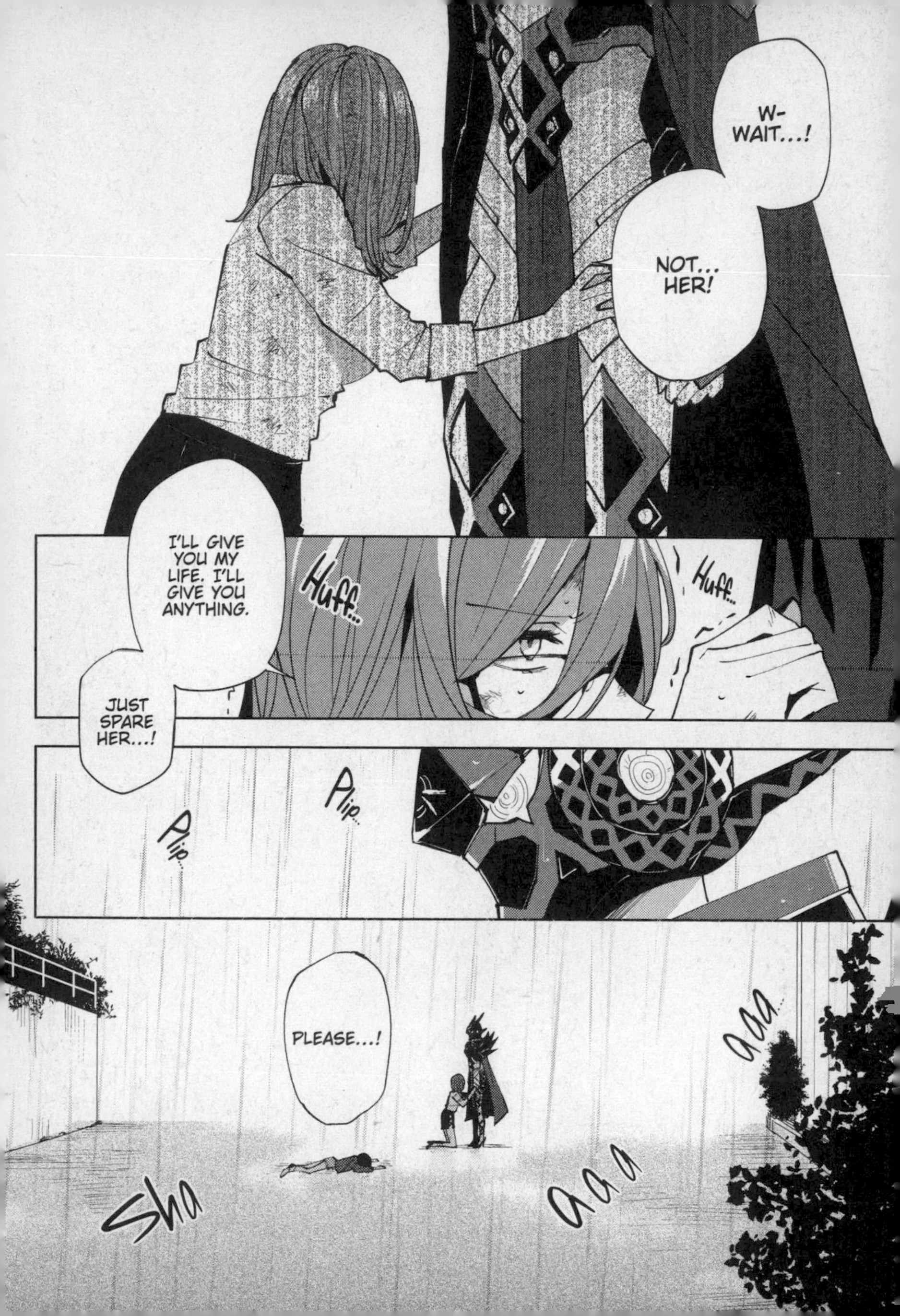
W-WAIT...!
NOT... HER!
Huff...
Huff...
I'LL GIVE YOU MY LIFE. I'LL GIVE YOU ANYTHING.
JUST SPARE HER...!
Plip...
Plip...
aaa...
PLEASE...!
aaa
Sha

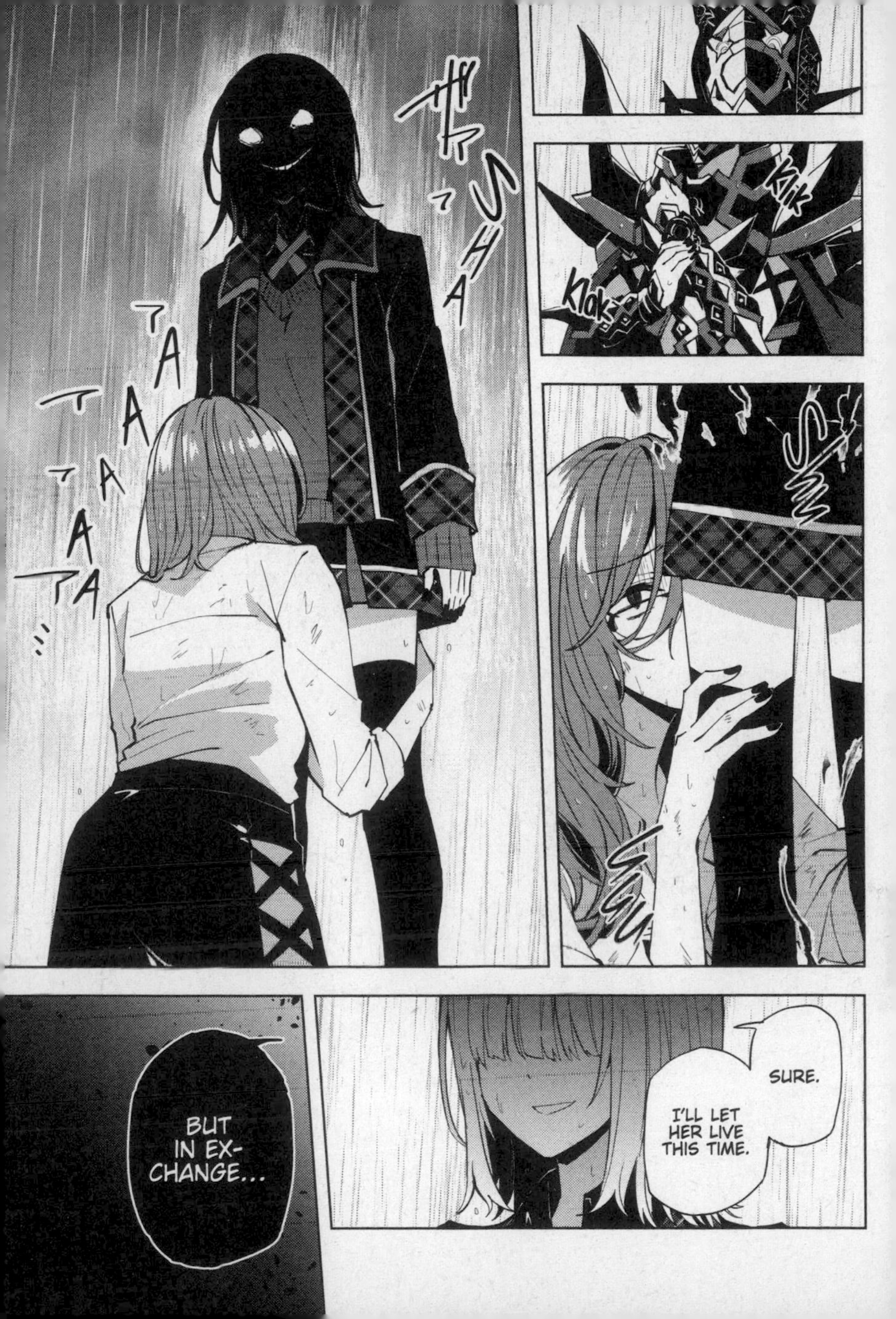
Klik
Klak
SHA
SURE.
I'LL LET HER LIVE THIS TIME.
BUT IN EX-CHANGE...

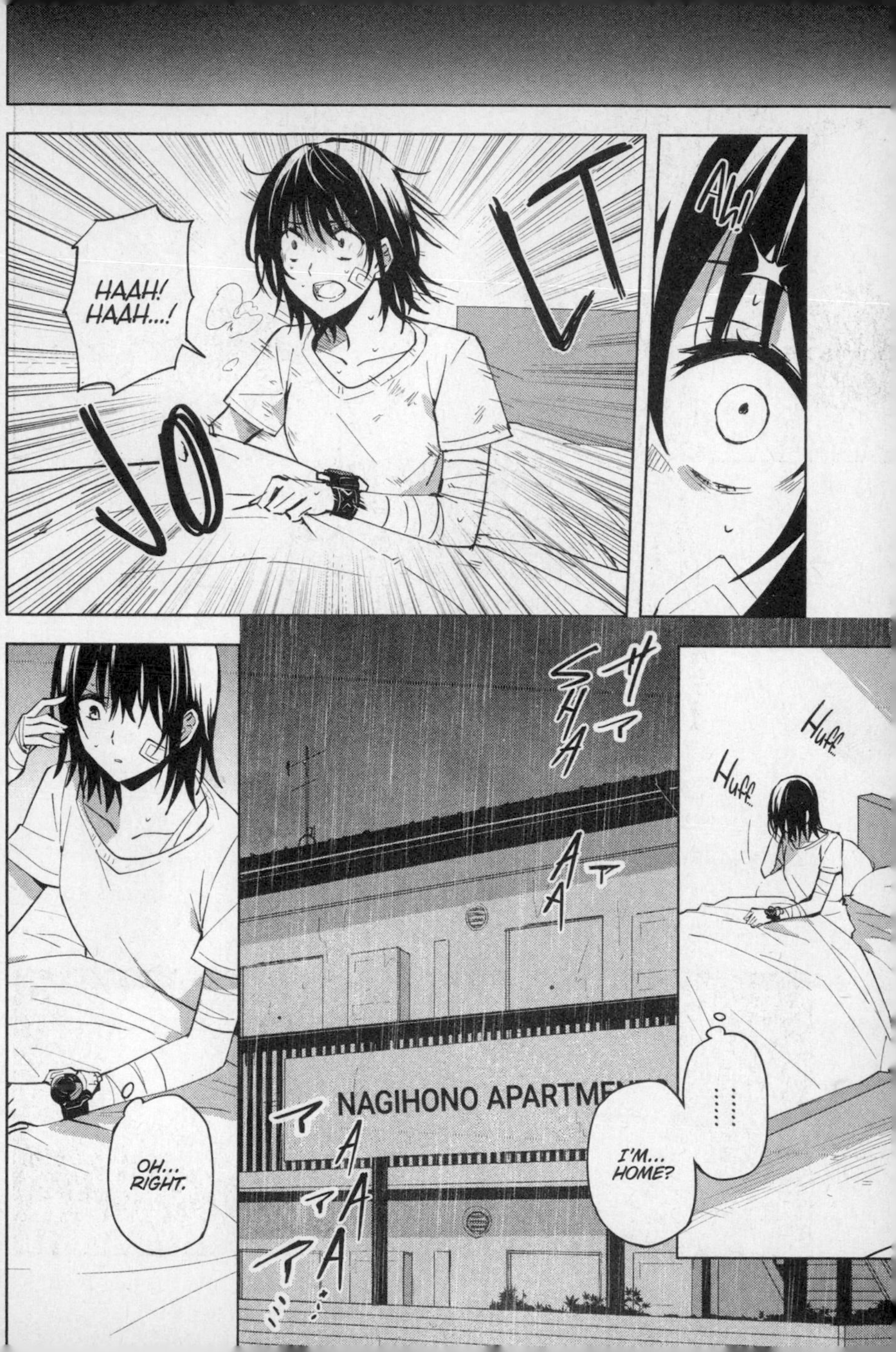
Ah!
HAAH! HAAH...!
JOLT
Huff...
Huff...
......
I'M... HOME?
NAGIHONO APARTMENTS
SHAAAAA サァァァァ...
OH... RIGHT.

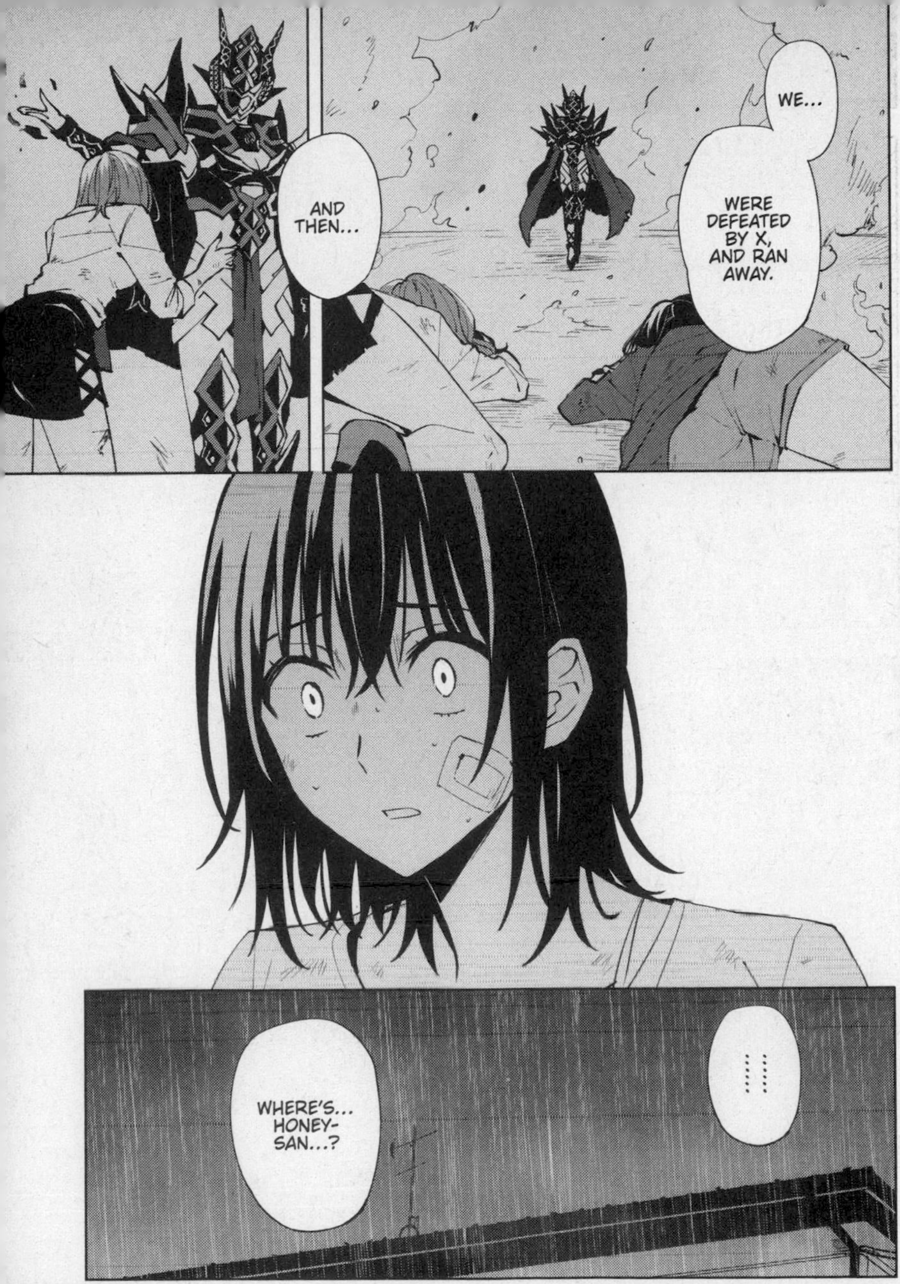
WE...
WERE DEFEATED BY X, AND RAN AWAY.
AND THEN...
......
WHERE'S... HONEY-SAN...?

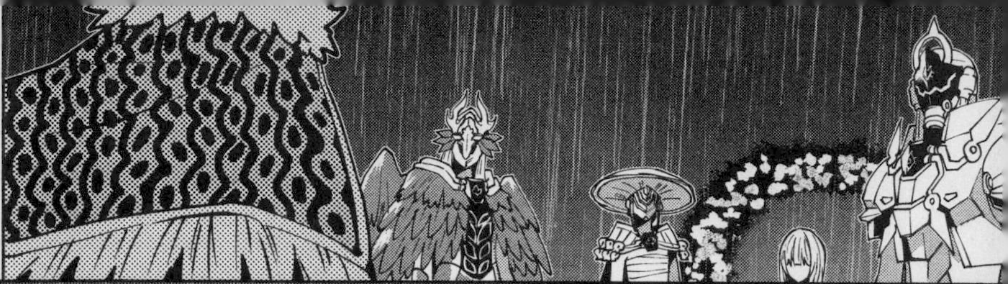

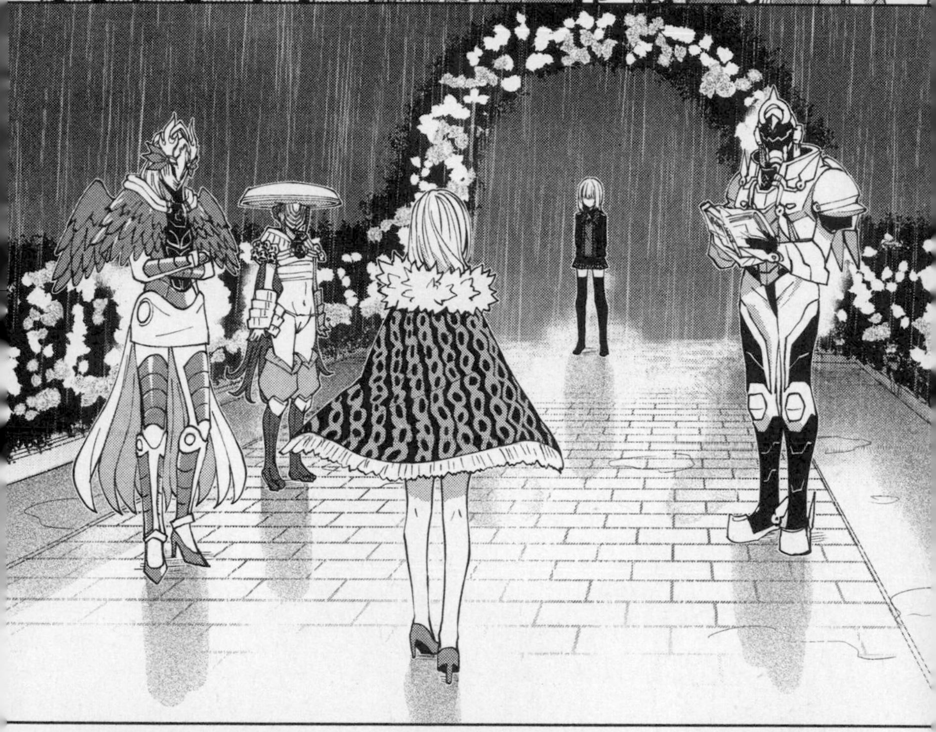

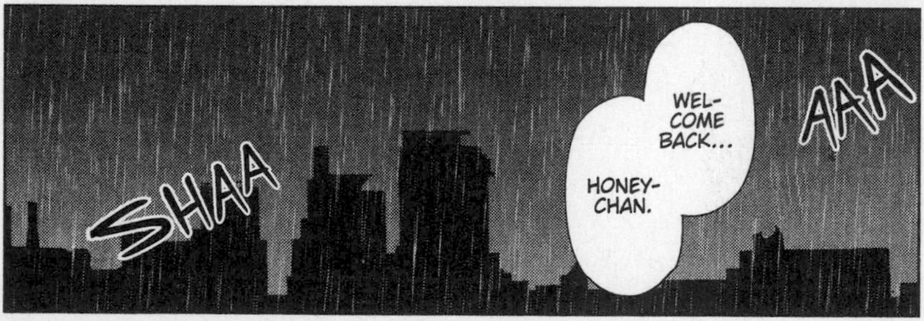
AAA
SHAA
WEL-
COME
BACK...
HONEY-
CHAN.

NOW EVERYTHING'S LIKE BEFORE... RIGHT?

SUPERWOMEN IN LOVE!

HONEY TRAP & RAPID RABBIT

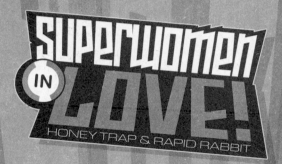

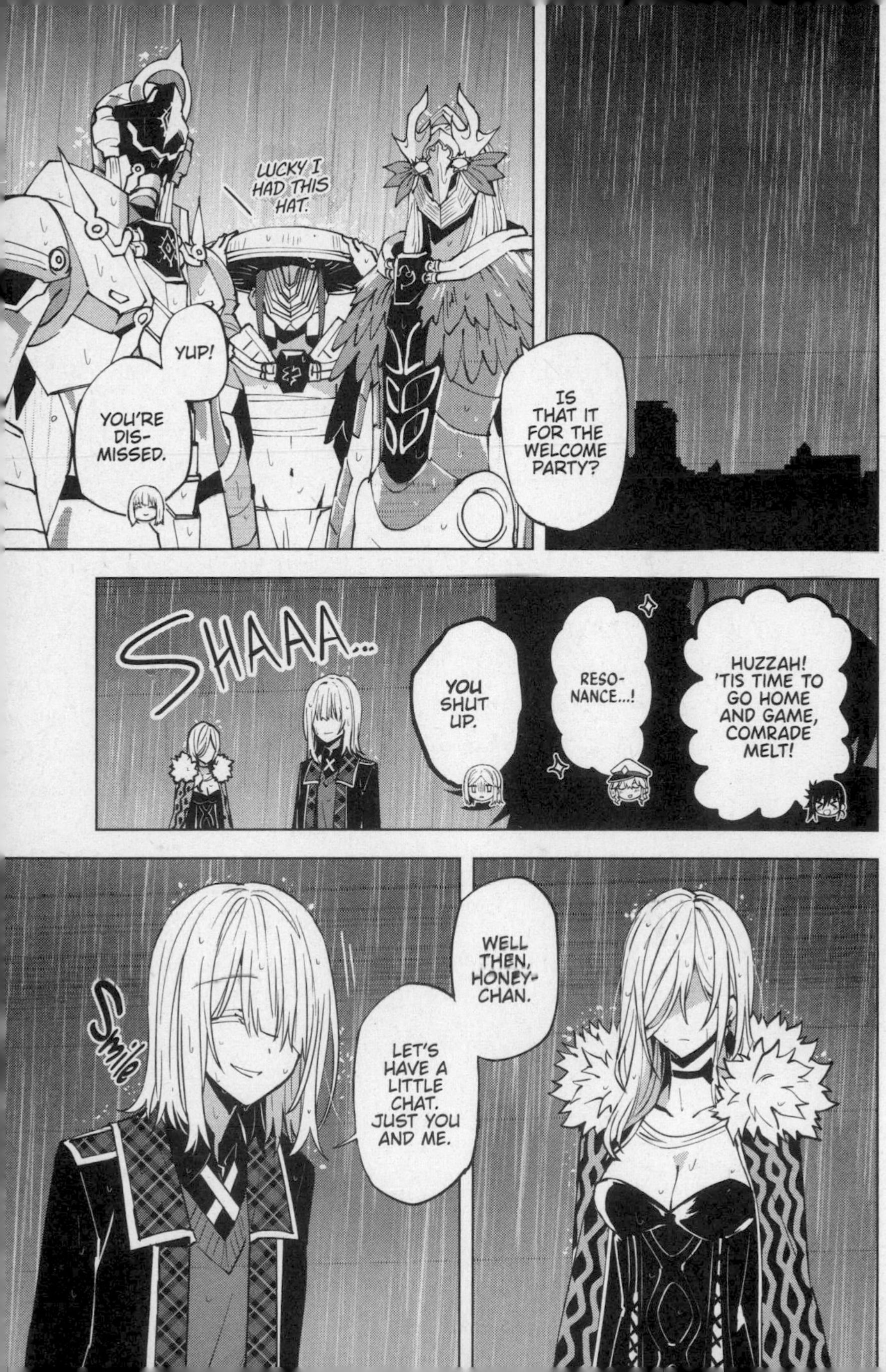
IS THAT IT FOR THE WELCOME PARTY?
LUCKY I HAD THIS HAT.
YUP!
YOU'RE DIS-MISSED.
HUZZAH! 'TIS TIME TO GO HOME AND GAME, COMRADE MELT!
RESO-NANCE...!
YOU SHUT UP.
SHAAA...
WELL THEN, HONEY-CHAN.
LET'S HAVE A LITTLE CHAT. JUST YOU AND ME.
Smile

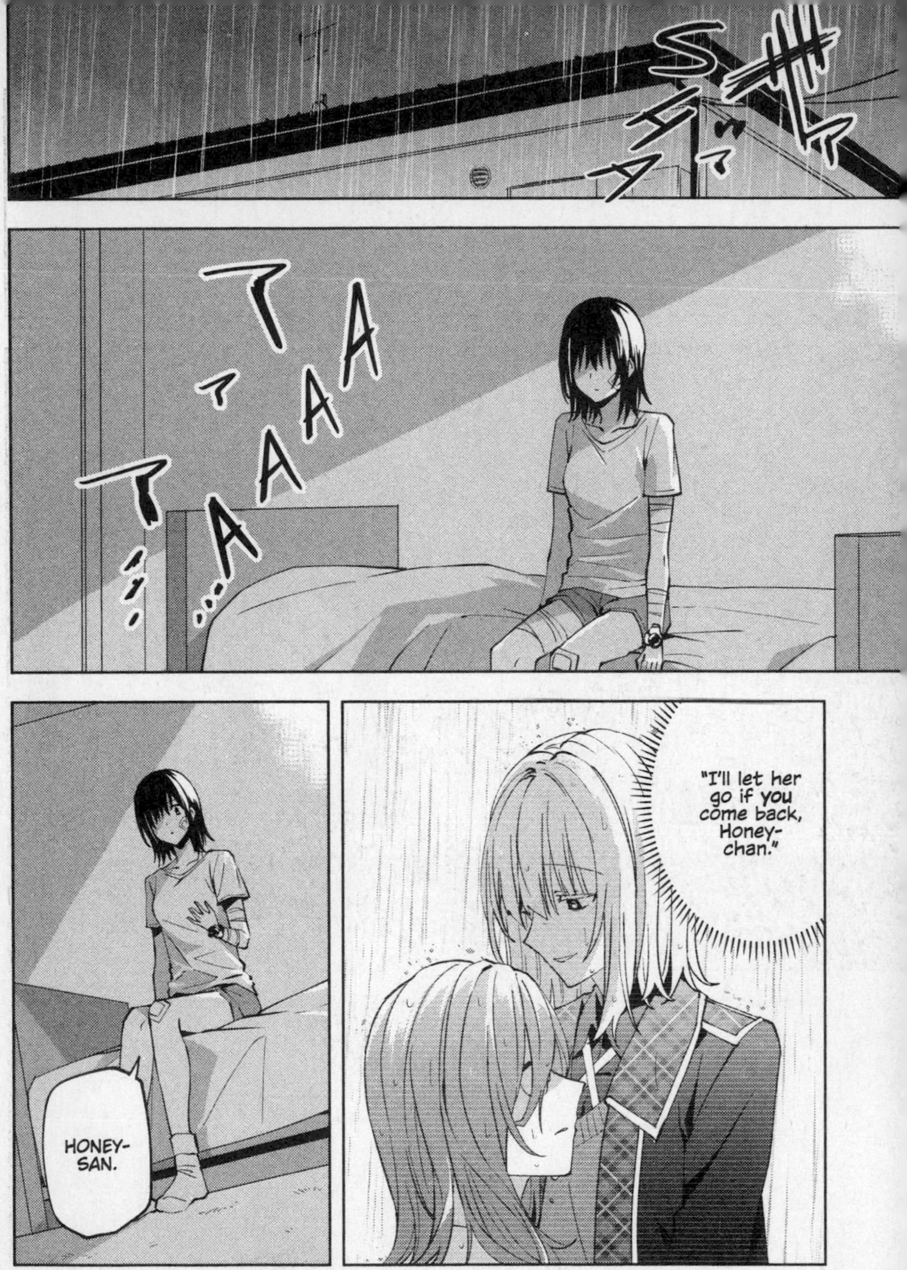
SHA
AAAA...
"I'll let her go if you come back, Honey-chan."
HONEY-SAN.

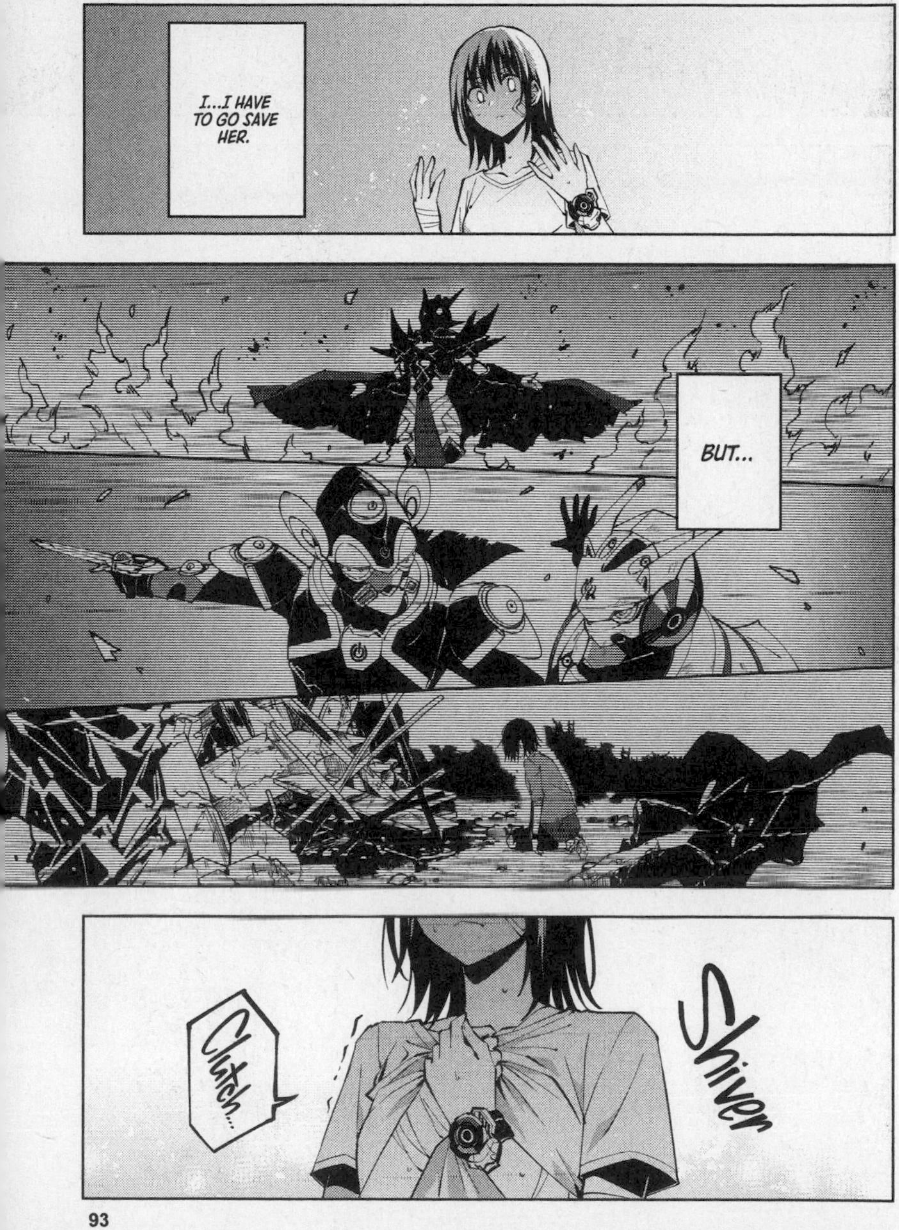
I...I HAVE TO GO SAVE HER.
BUT...
Shiver
Clutch...

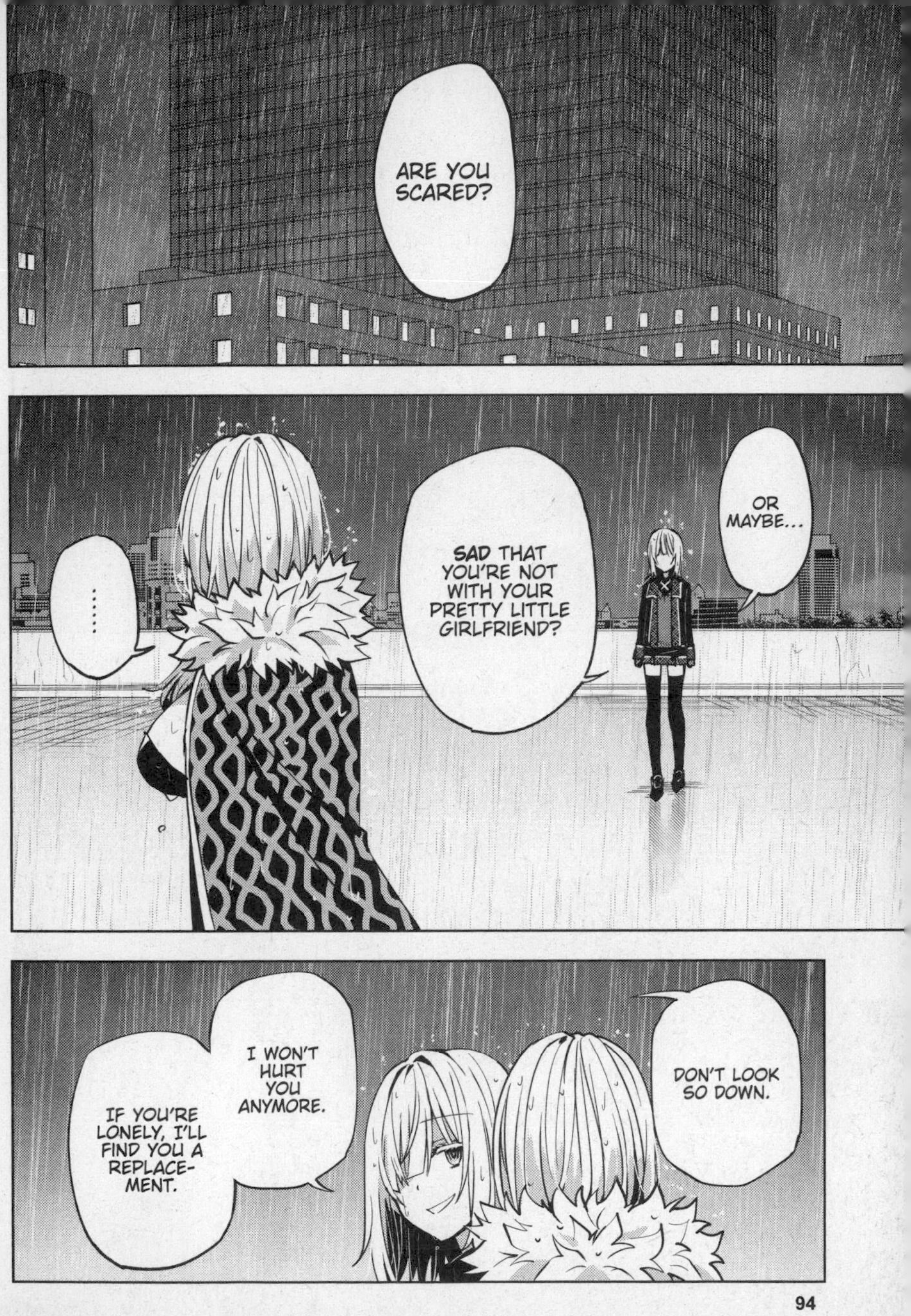
ARE YOU SCARED?
OR MAYBE...
SAD THAT YOU'RE NOT WITH YOUR PRETTY LITTLE GIRLFRIEND?
......
DON'T LOOK SO DOWN.
I WON'T HURT YOU ANYMORE.
IF YOU'RE LONELY, I'LL FIND YOU A REPLACEMENT.

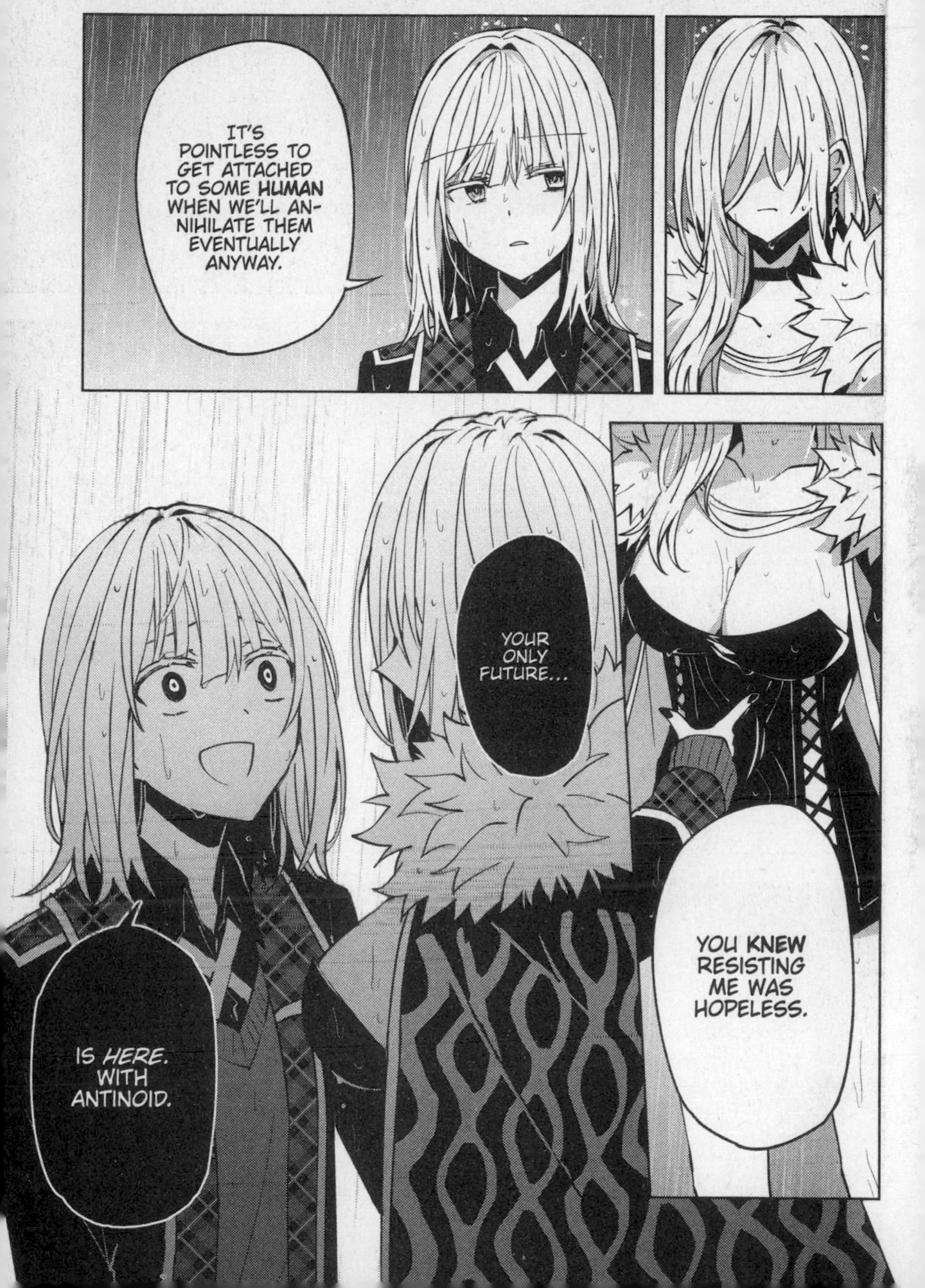
IT'S POINTLESS TO GET ATTACHED TO SOME HUMAN WHEN WE'LL AN-NIHILATE THEM EVENTUALLY ANYWAY.
YOU KNEW RESISTING ME WAS HOPELESS.
YOUR ONLY FUTURE...
IS *HERE.* WITH ANTINOID.

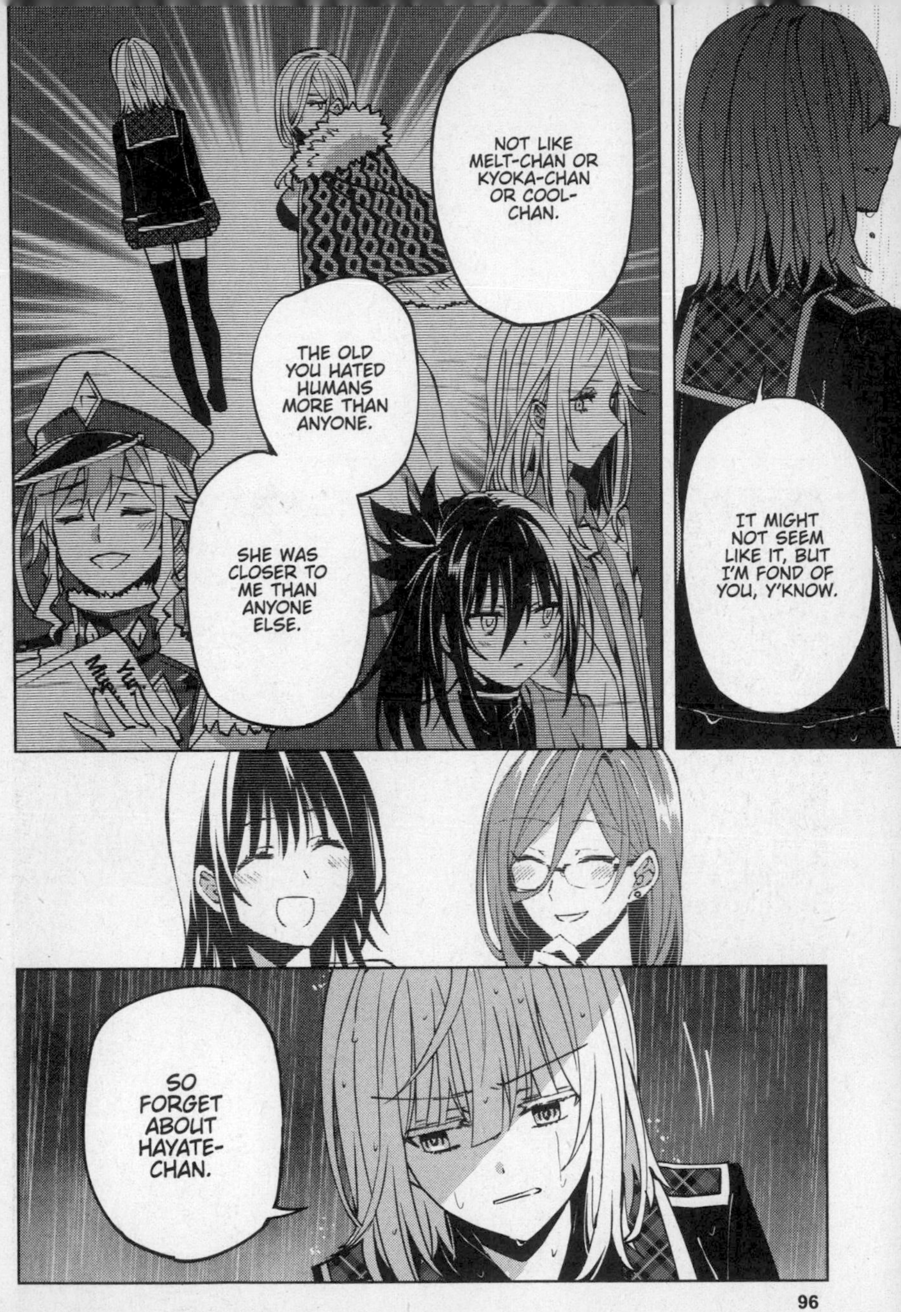
IT MIGHT NOT SEEM LIKE IT, BUT I'M FOND OF YOU, Y'KNOW.
NOT LIKE MELT-CHAN OR KYOKA-CHAN OR COOL-CHAN.
THE OLD YOU HATED HUMANS MORE THAN ANYONE.
SHE WAS CLOSER TO ME THAN ANYONE ELSE.
SO FORGET ABOUT HAYATE-CHAN.

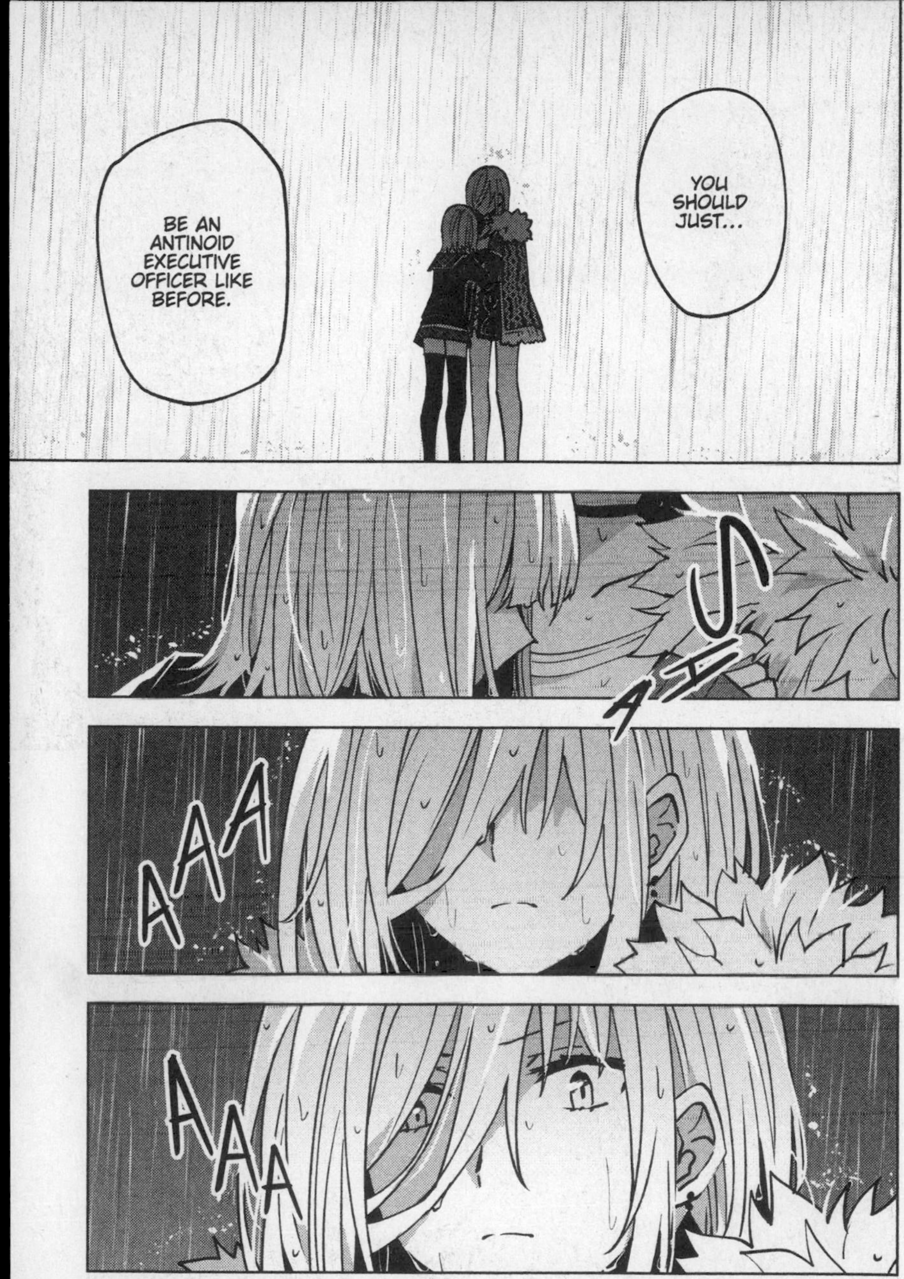
YOU SHOULD JUST...
BE AN ANTINOID EXECUTIVE OFFICER LIKE BEFORE.
SHA
AAA
AAA

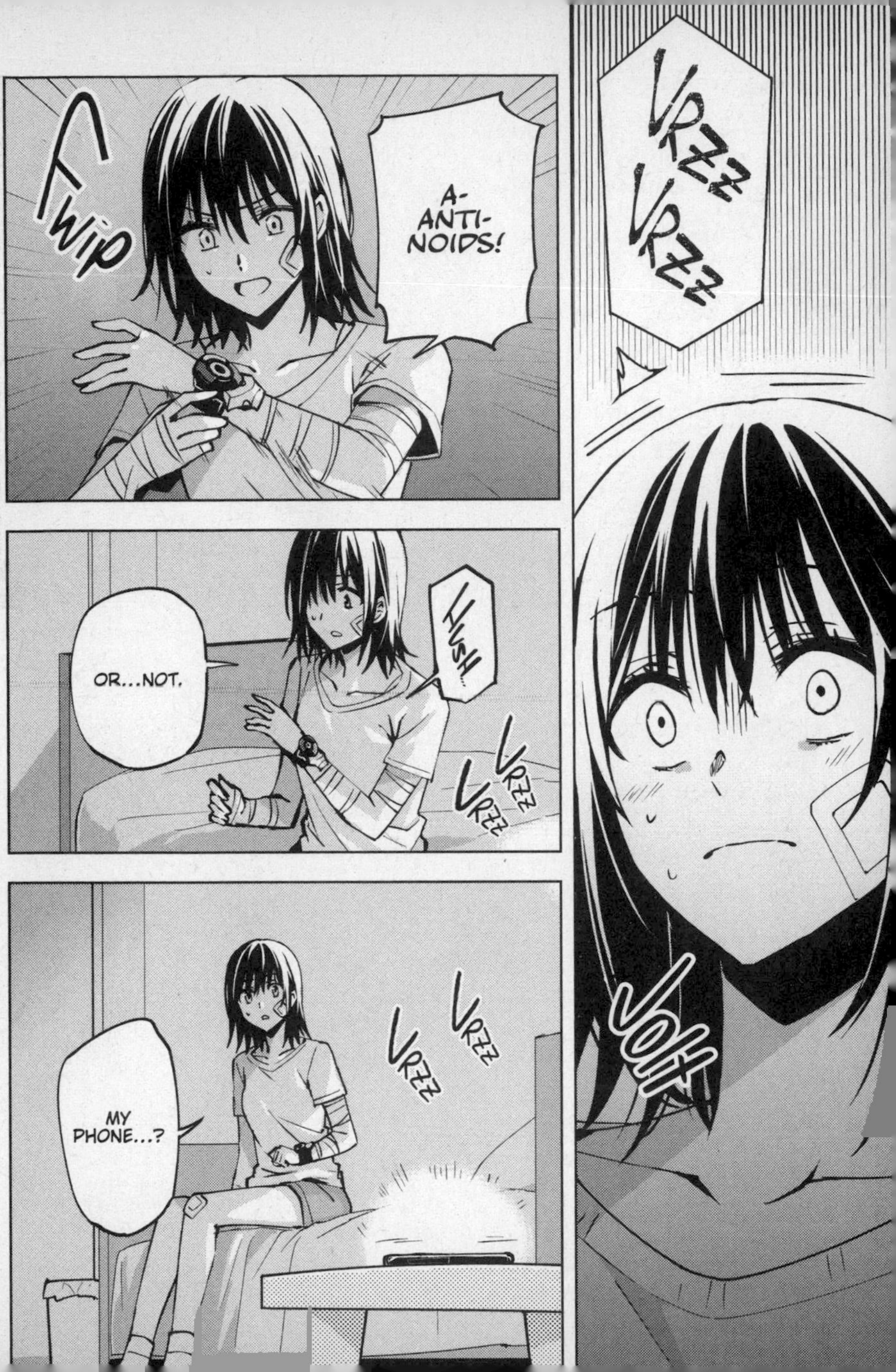
VRZZ VRZZ
JOLT
FWIP
A-ANTI-NOIDS!
HUSH...
VRZZ VRZZ
OR...NOT.
VRZZ VRZZ
MY PHONE...?

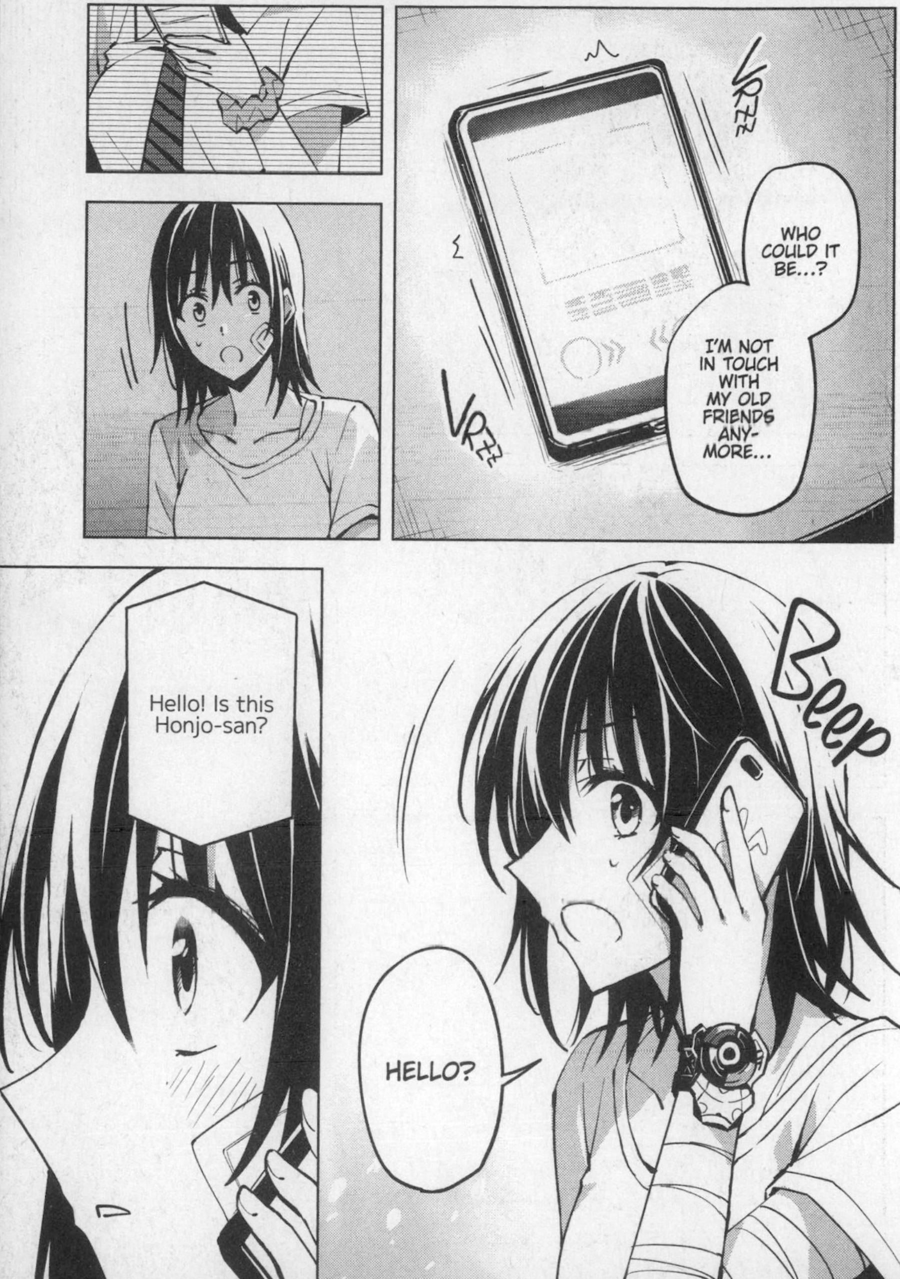
VRZZ
WHO COULD IT BE...?
I'M NOT IN TOUCH WITH MY OLD FRIENDS ANYMORE...
Beep
HELLO?
Hello! Is this Honjo-san?

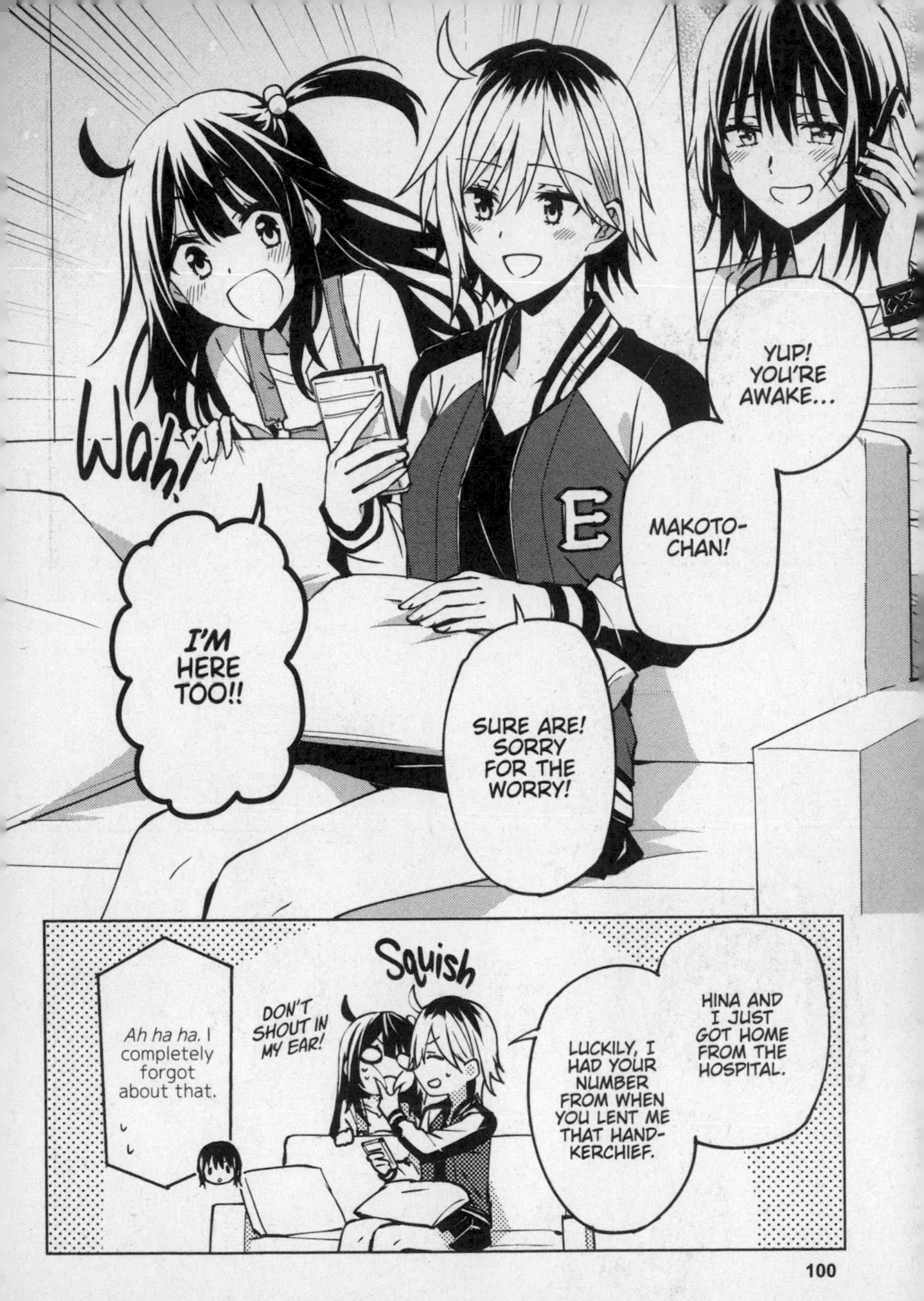
YUP! YOU'RE AWAKE...
MAKOTO-CHAN!
SURE ARE! SORRY FOR THE WORRY!
Wah!
I'M HERE TOO!!
HINA AND I JUST GOT HOME FROM THE HOSPITAL.
LUCKILY, I HAD YOUR NUMBER FROM WHEN YOU LENT ME THAT HAND-KERCHIEF.
Squish
DON'T SHOUT IN MY EAR!
Ah ha ha. I completely forgot about that.

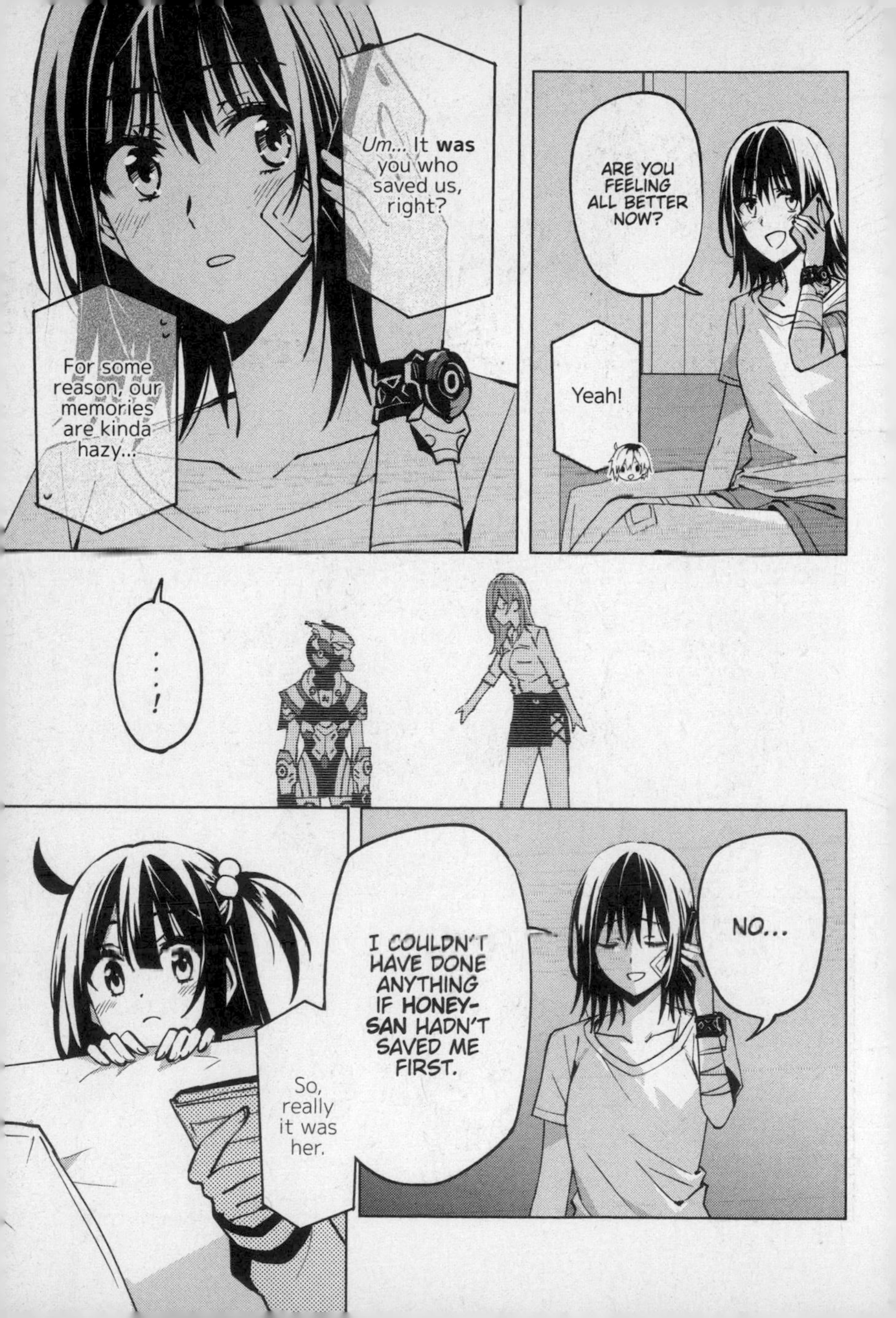
ARE YOU FEELING ALL BETTER NOW?
Yeah!
Um... It was you who saved us, right?
For some reason, our memories are kinda hazy...
...!
NO...
I COULDN'T HAVE DONE ANYTHING IF HONEY-SAN HADN'T SAVED ME FIRST.
So, really it was her.

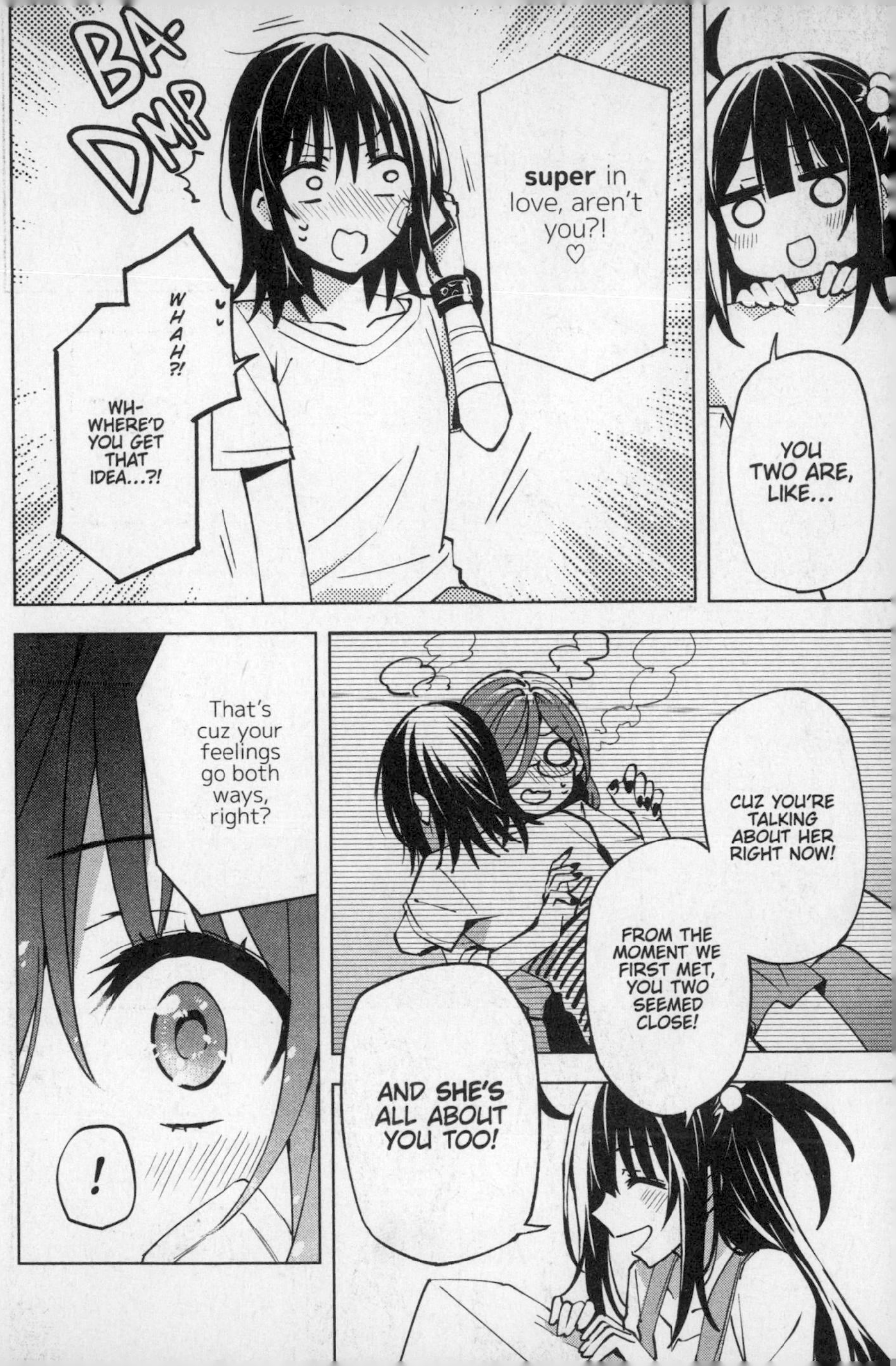
YOU TWO ARE, LIKE...
super in love, aren't you?! ♡
BA-DMP
WHAH?!
WH-WHERE'D YOU GET THAT IDEA...?!
CUZ YOU'RE TALKING ABOUT HER RIGHT NOW!
FROM THE MOMENT WE FIRST MET, YOU TWO SEEMED CLOSE!
AND SHE'S ALL ABOUT YOU TOO!
That's cuz your feelings go both ways, right?
!

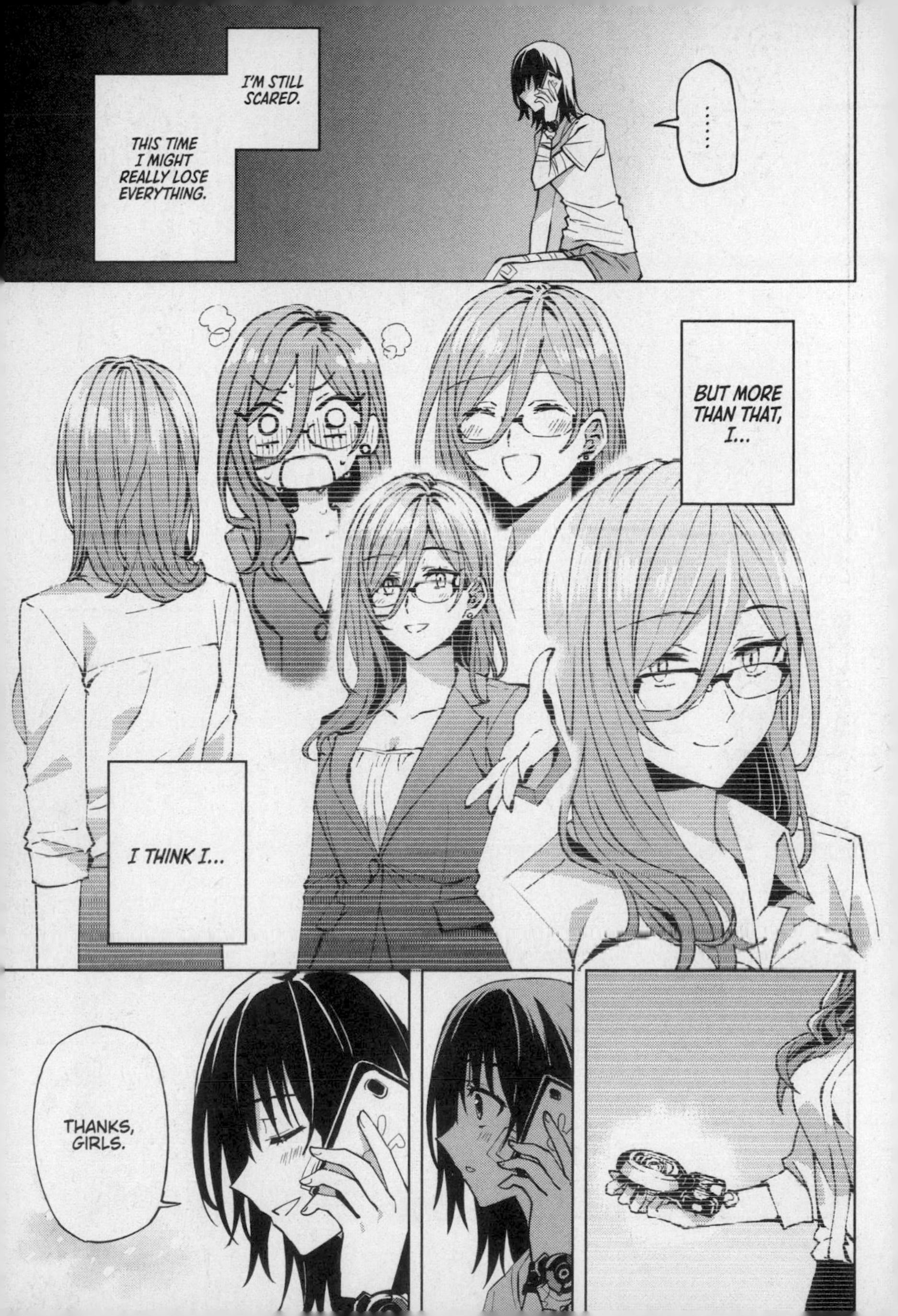
……
I'M STILL SCARED.
THIS TIME I MIGHT REALLY LOSE EVERYTHING.
BUT MORE THAN THAT, I...
I THINK I...
THANKS, GIRLS.

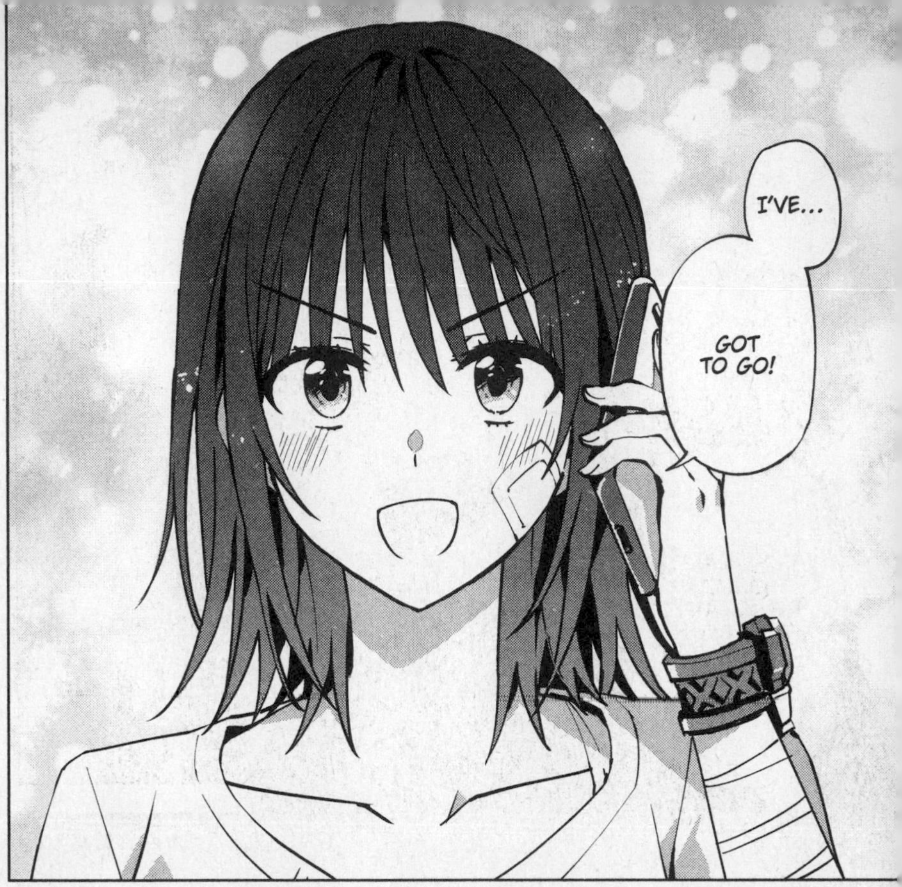
I'VE...
GOT TO GO!

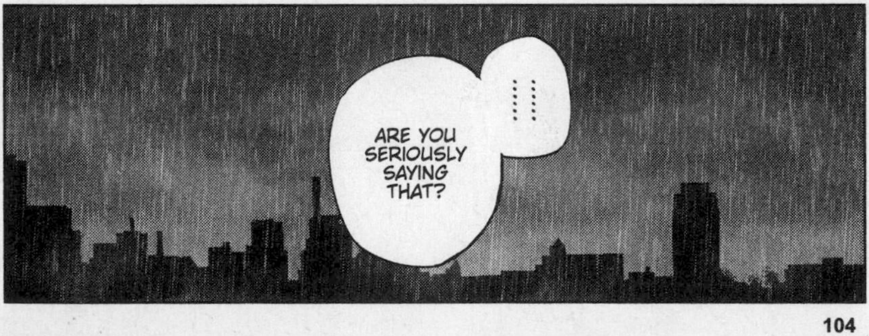
……
ARE YOU SERIOUSLY SAYING THAT?

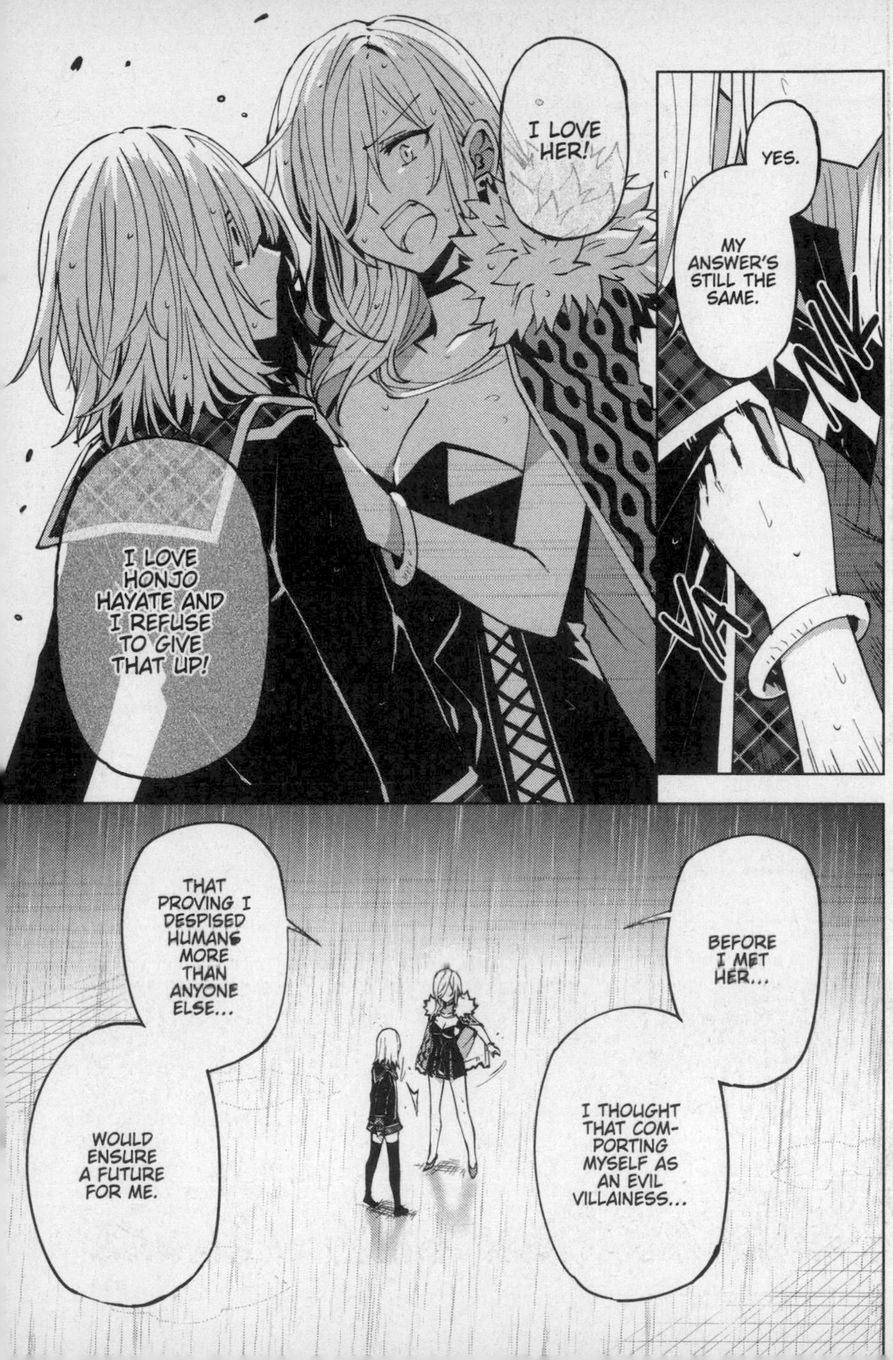
YES.
MY ANSWER'S STILL THE SAME.
I LOVE HER!
I LOVE HONJO HAYATE AND I REFUSE TO GIVE THAT UP!
BEFORE I MET HER...
I THOUGHT THAT COM-PORTING MYSELF AS AN EVIL VILLAINESS...
THAT PROVING I DESPISED HUMANS MORE THAN ANYONE ELSE...
WOULD ENSURE A FUTURE FOR ME.

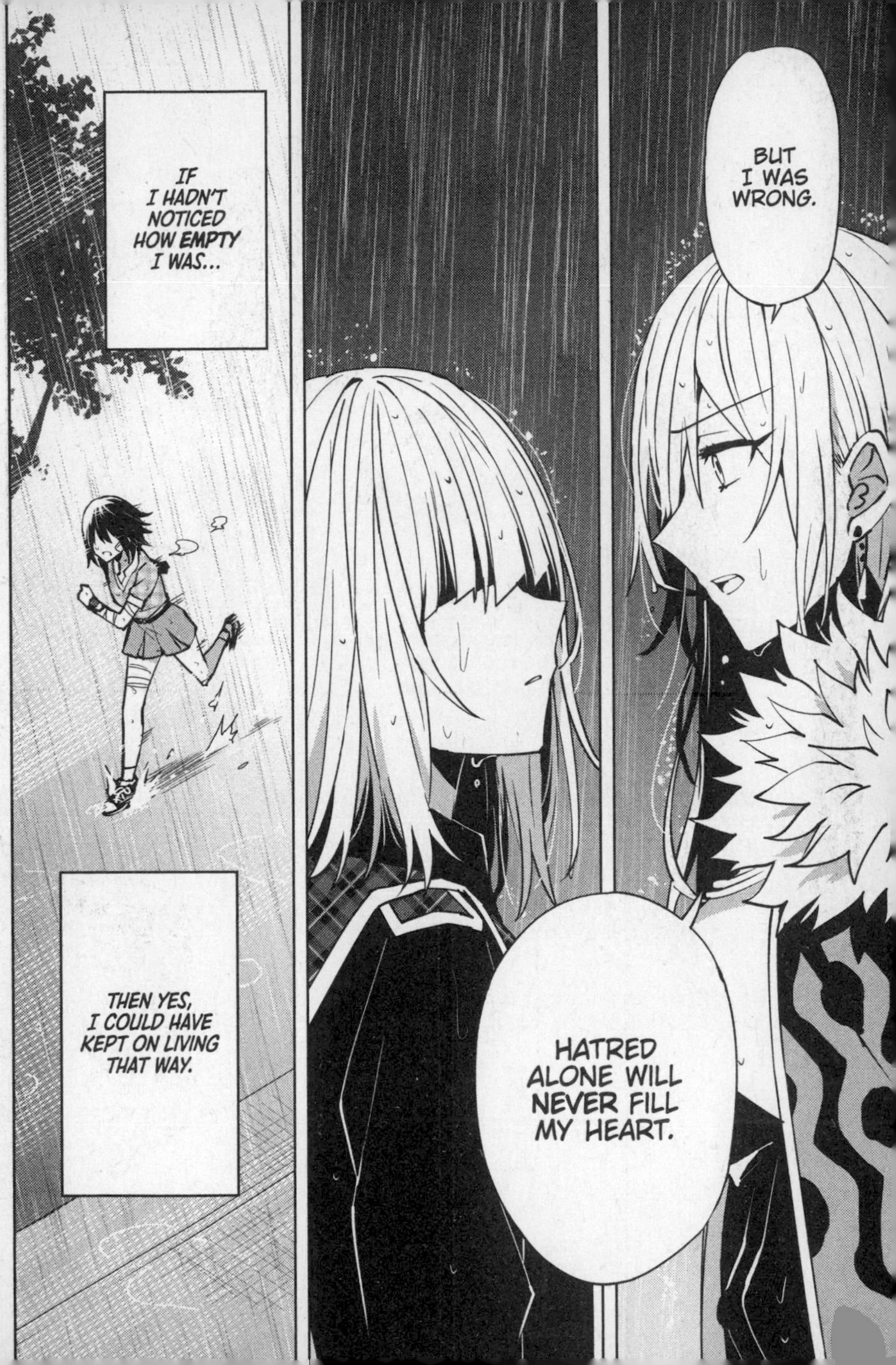
BUT I WAS WRONG.
HATRED ALONE WILL NEVER FILL MY HEART.
IF I HADN'T NOTICED HOW EMPTY I WAS...
THEN YES, I COULD HAVE KEPT ON LIVING THAT WAY.

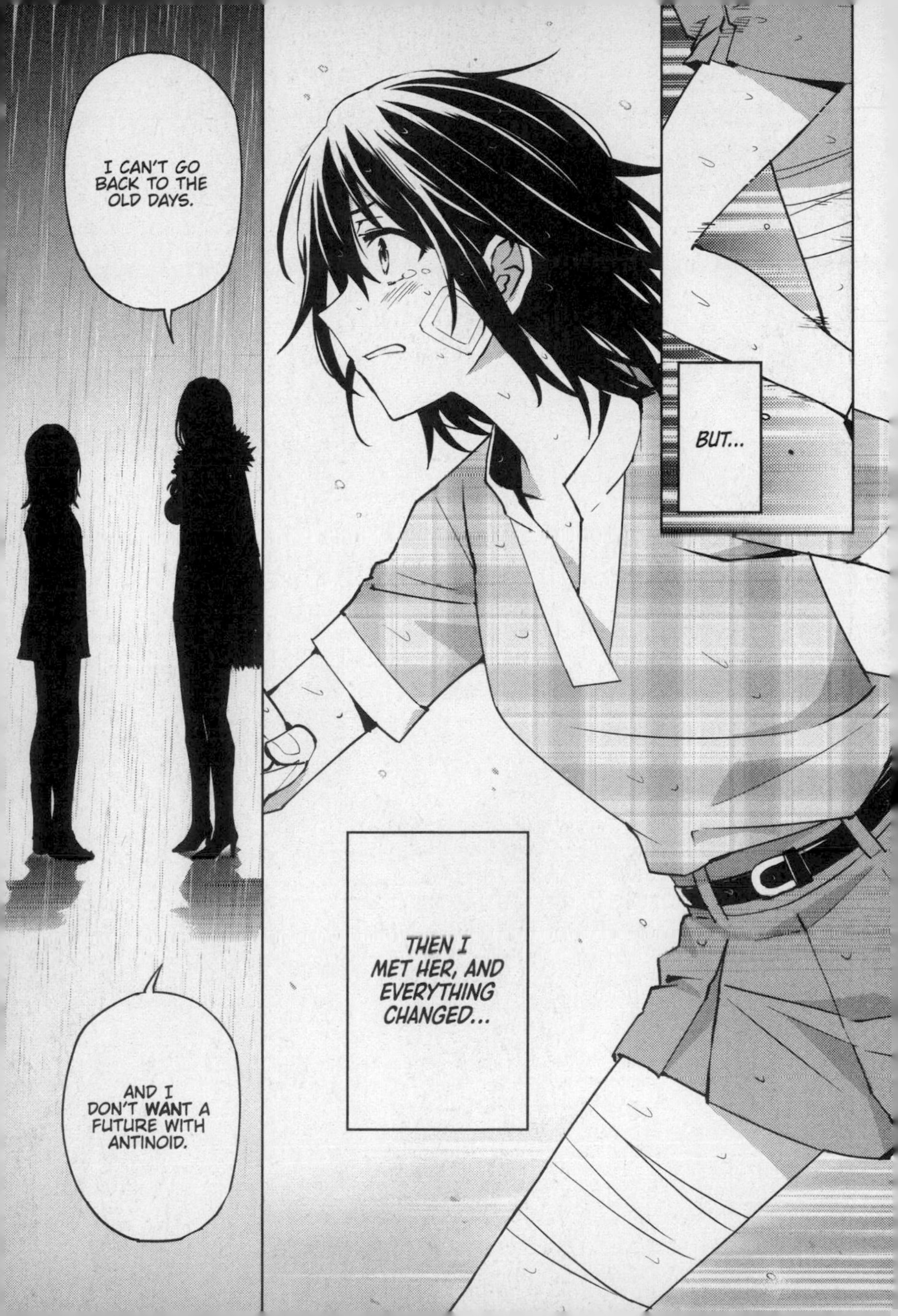
BUT...
THEN I MET HER, AND EVERYTHING CHANGED...
I CAN'T GO BACK TO THE OLD DAYS.
AND I DON'T WANT A FUTURE WITH ANTINOID.

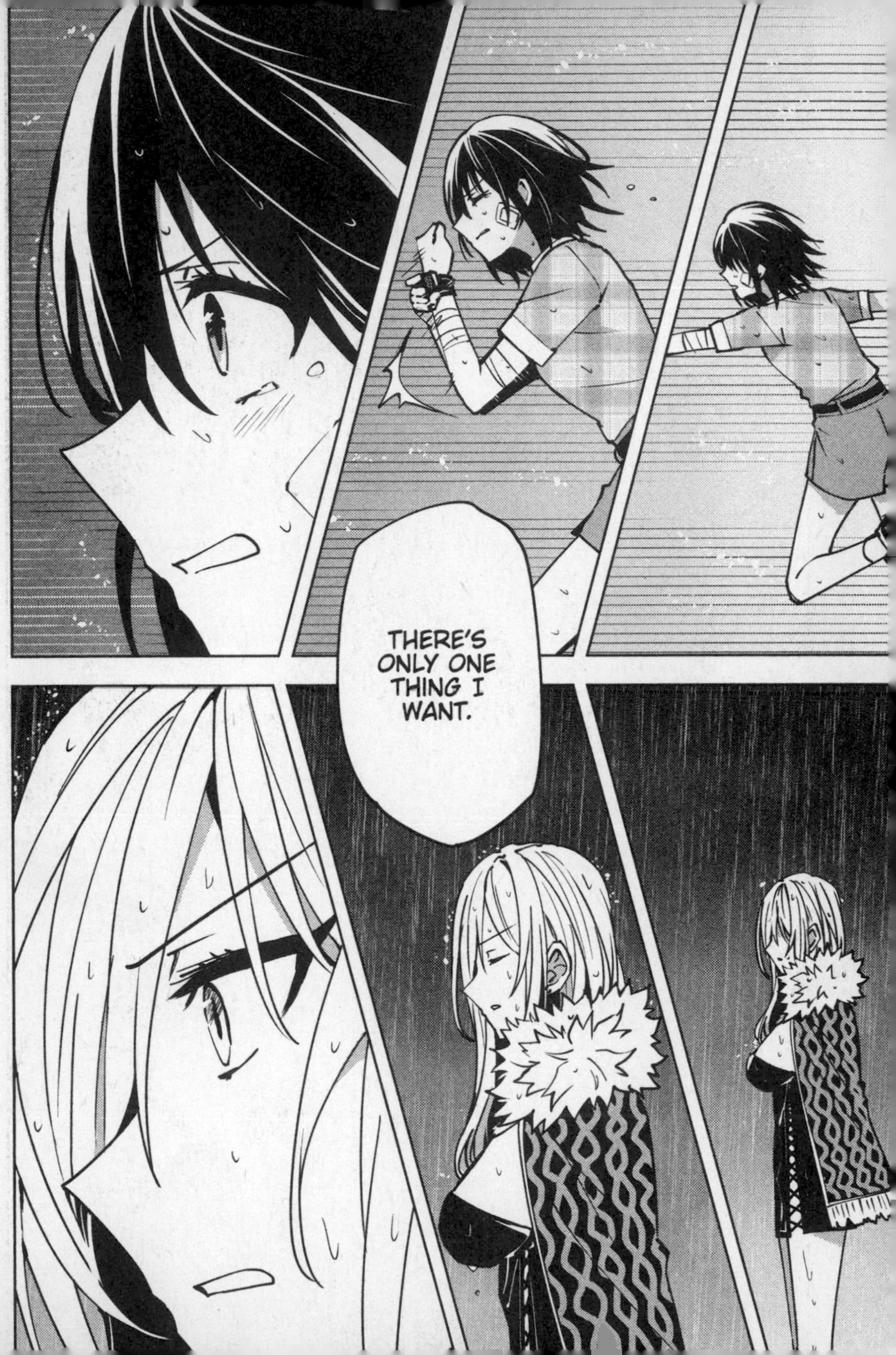
THERE'S ONLY ONE THING I WANT.

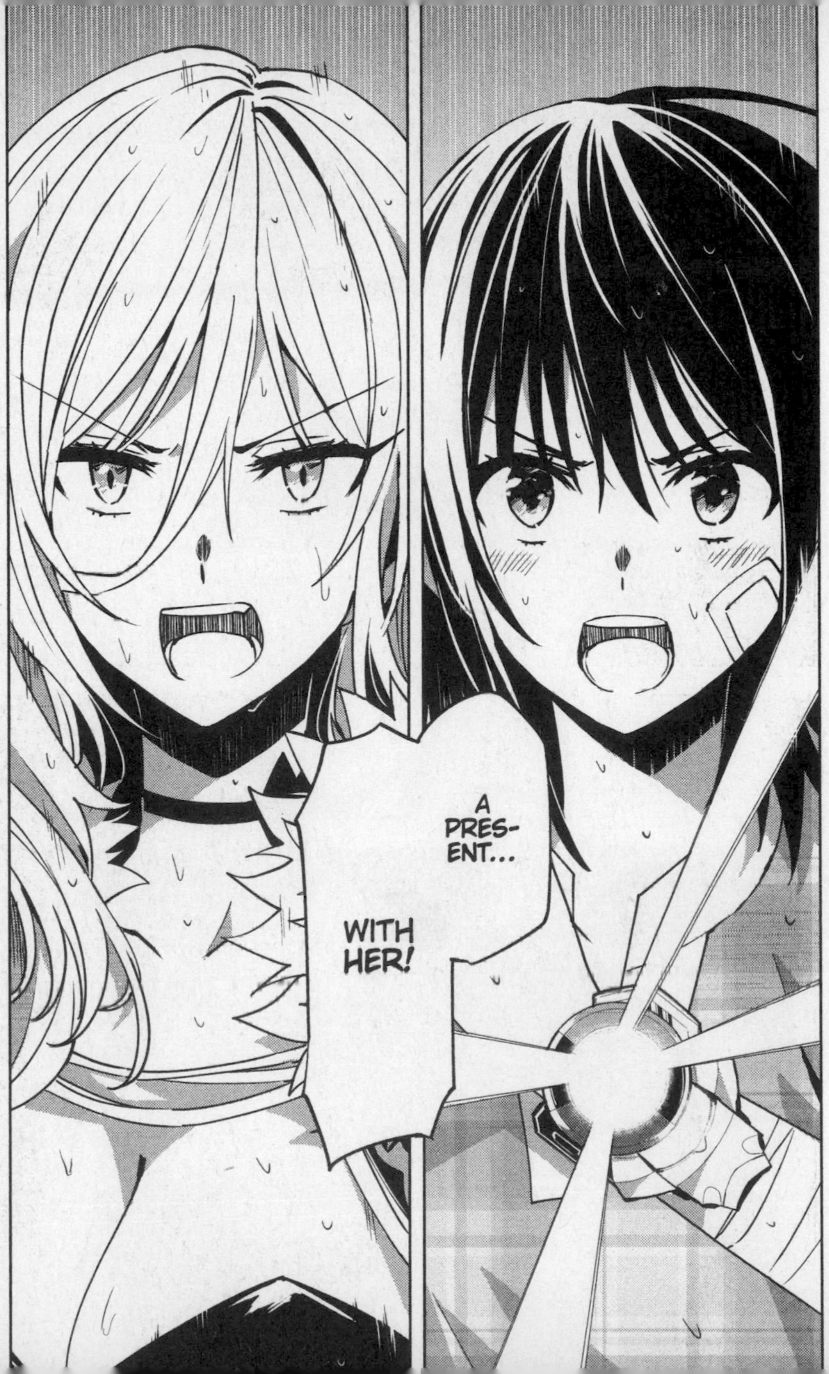
A PRES-ENT...
WITH HER!

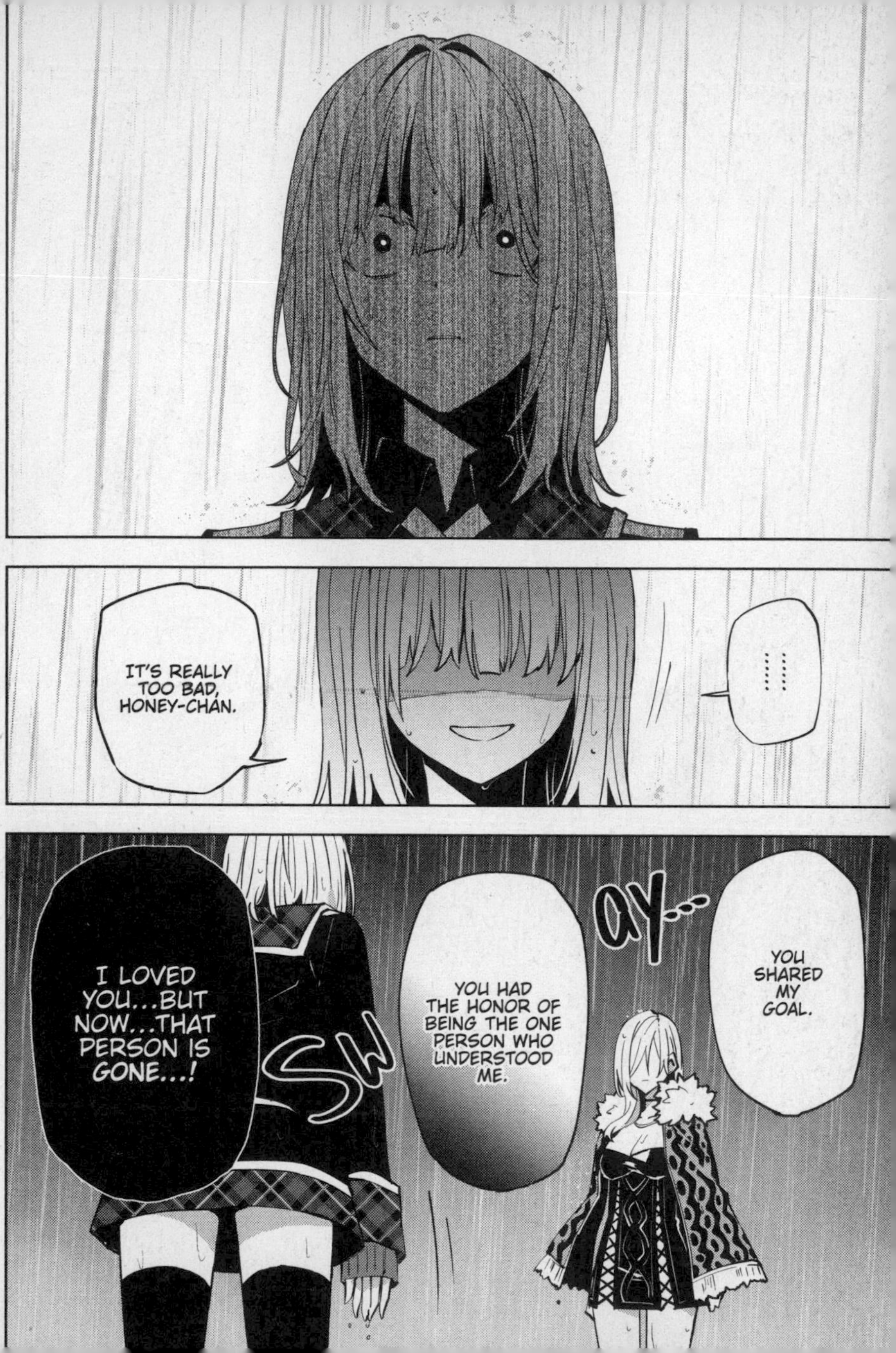
……
IT'S REALLY TOO BAD, HONEY-CHAN.
YOU SHARED MY GOAL.
AY…
YOU HAD THE HONOR OF BEING THE ONE PERSON WHO UNDERSTOOD ME.
SW
I LOVED YOU…BUT NOW…THAT PERSON IS GONE…!

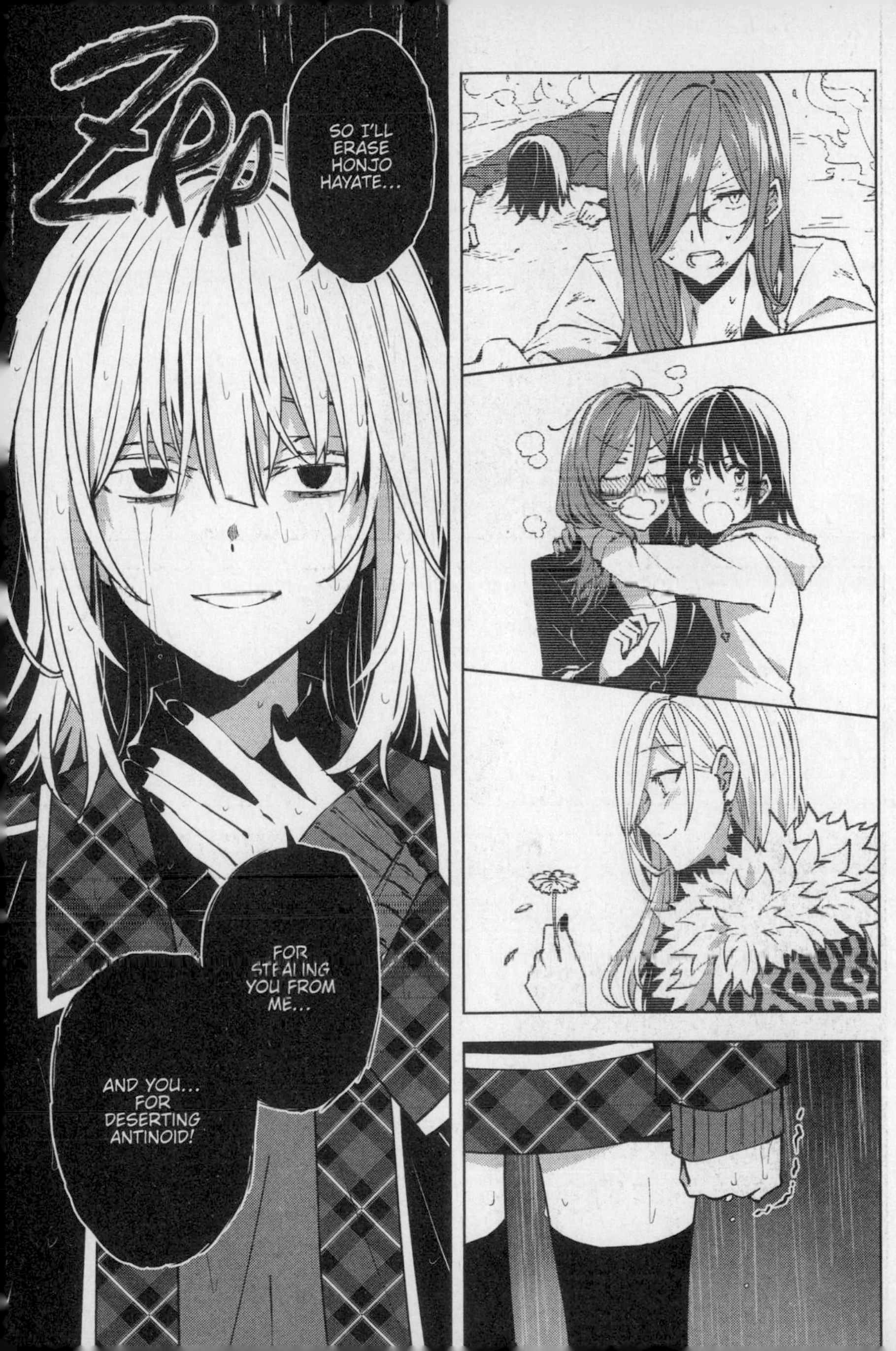
ZRR
SO I'LL ERASE HONJO HAYATE...
FOR STEALING YOU FROM ME...
AND YOU... FOR DESERTING ANTINOID!

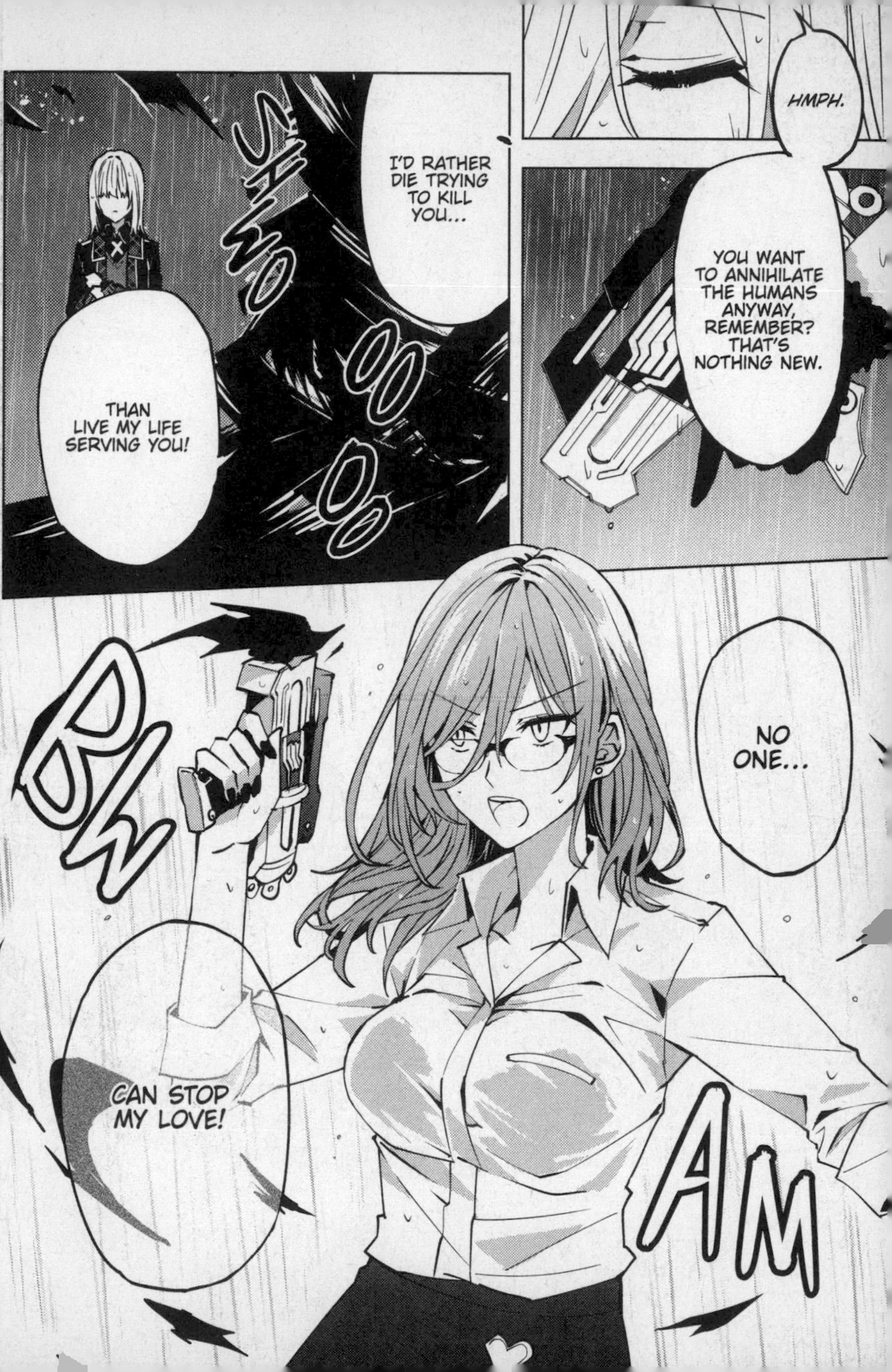
HMPH.
YOU WANT TO ANNIHILATE THE HUMANS ANYWAY, REMEMBER? THAT'S NOTHING NEW.
I'D RATHER DIE TRYING TO KILL YOU...
THAN LIVE MY LIFE SERVING YOU!
SHWOOOOOOOO
NO ONE...
CAN STOP MY LOVE!
BLAM

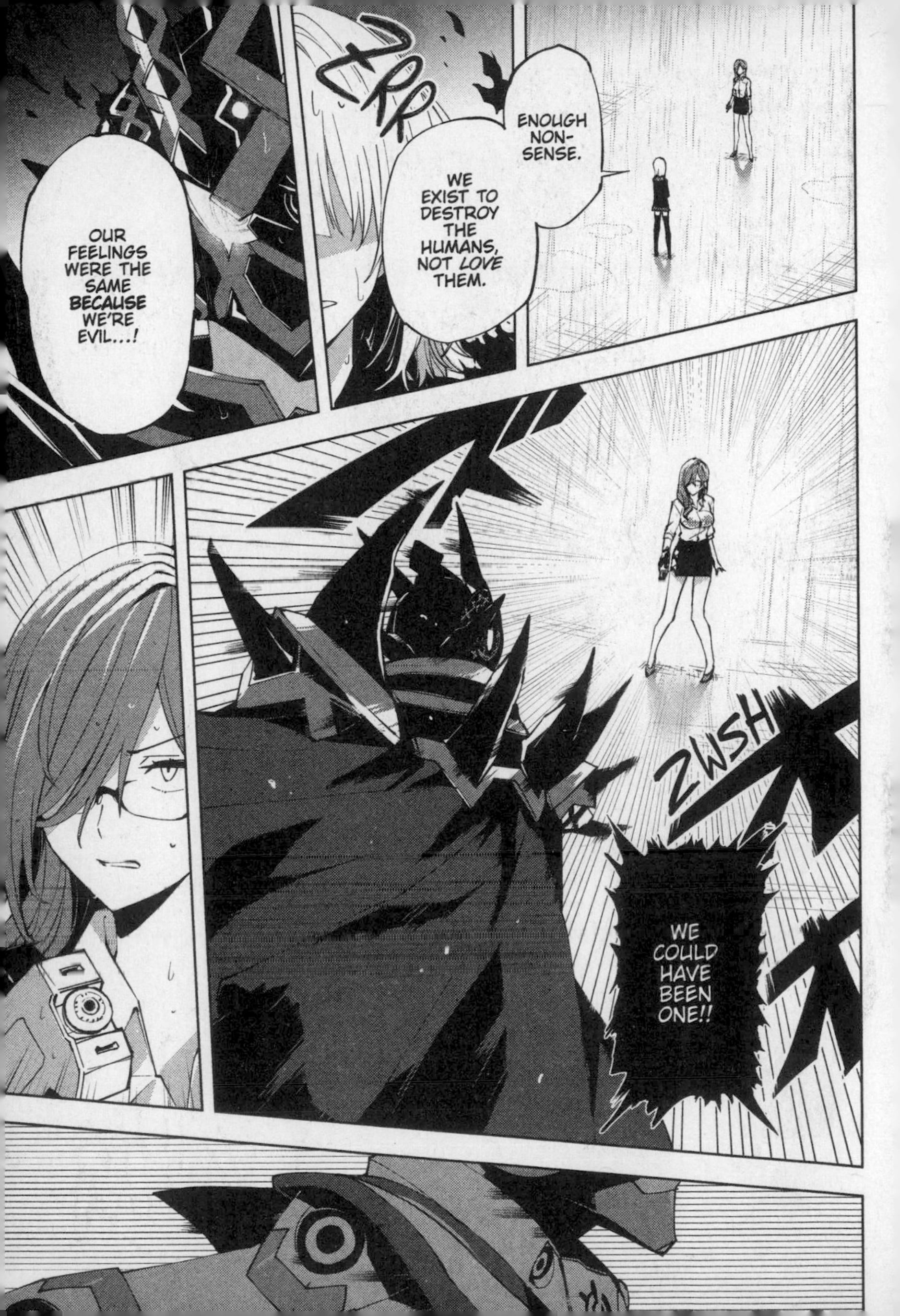
ZRR
ENOUGH NON-SENSE.
WE EXIST TO DESTROY THE HUMANS, NOT *LOVE* THEM.
OUR FEELINGS WERE THE SAME BECAUSE WE'RE EVIL...!
ZWSH
WE COULD HAVE BEEN ONE!!

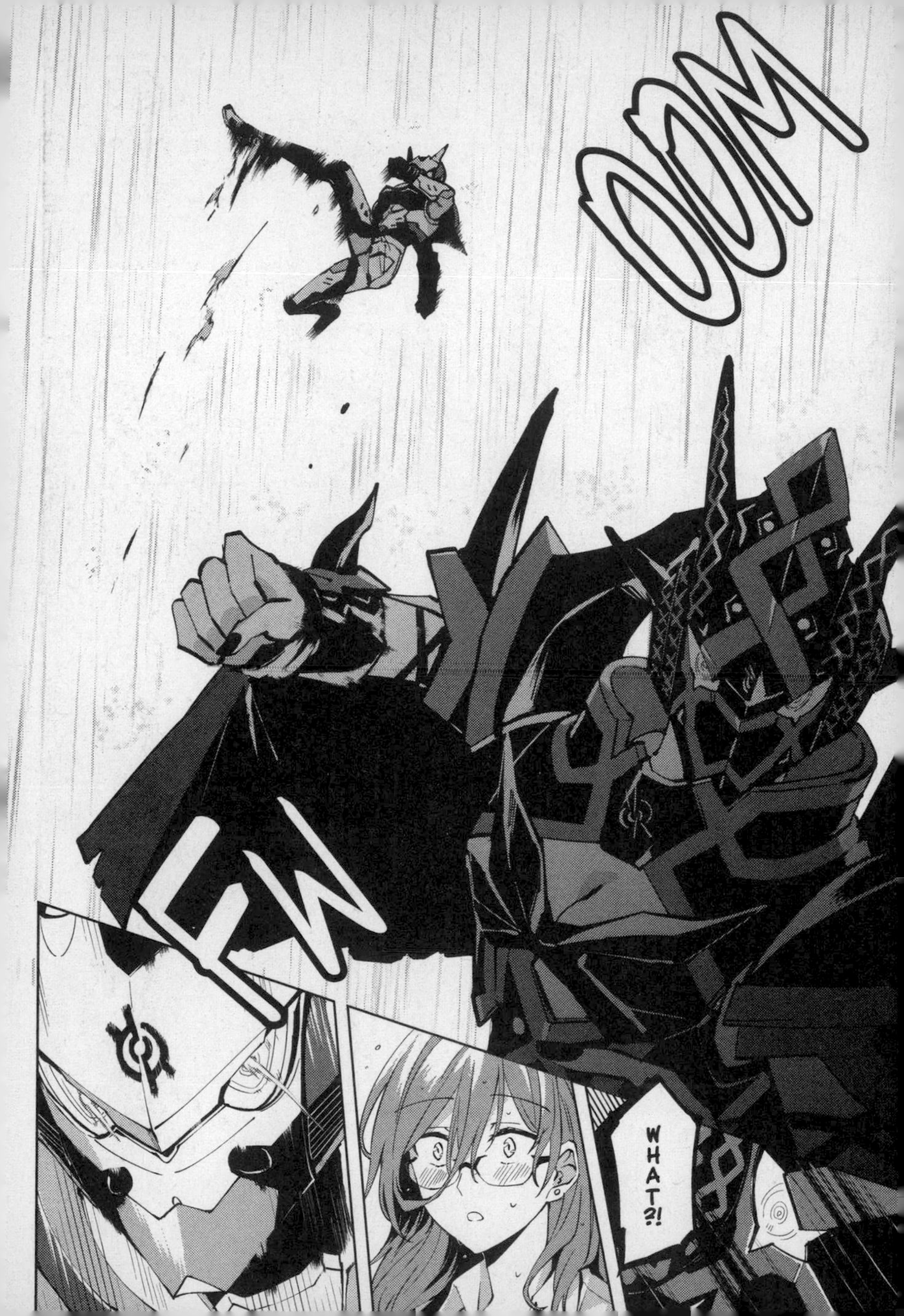
WHAT?!

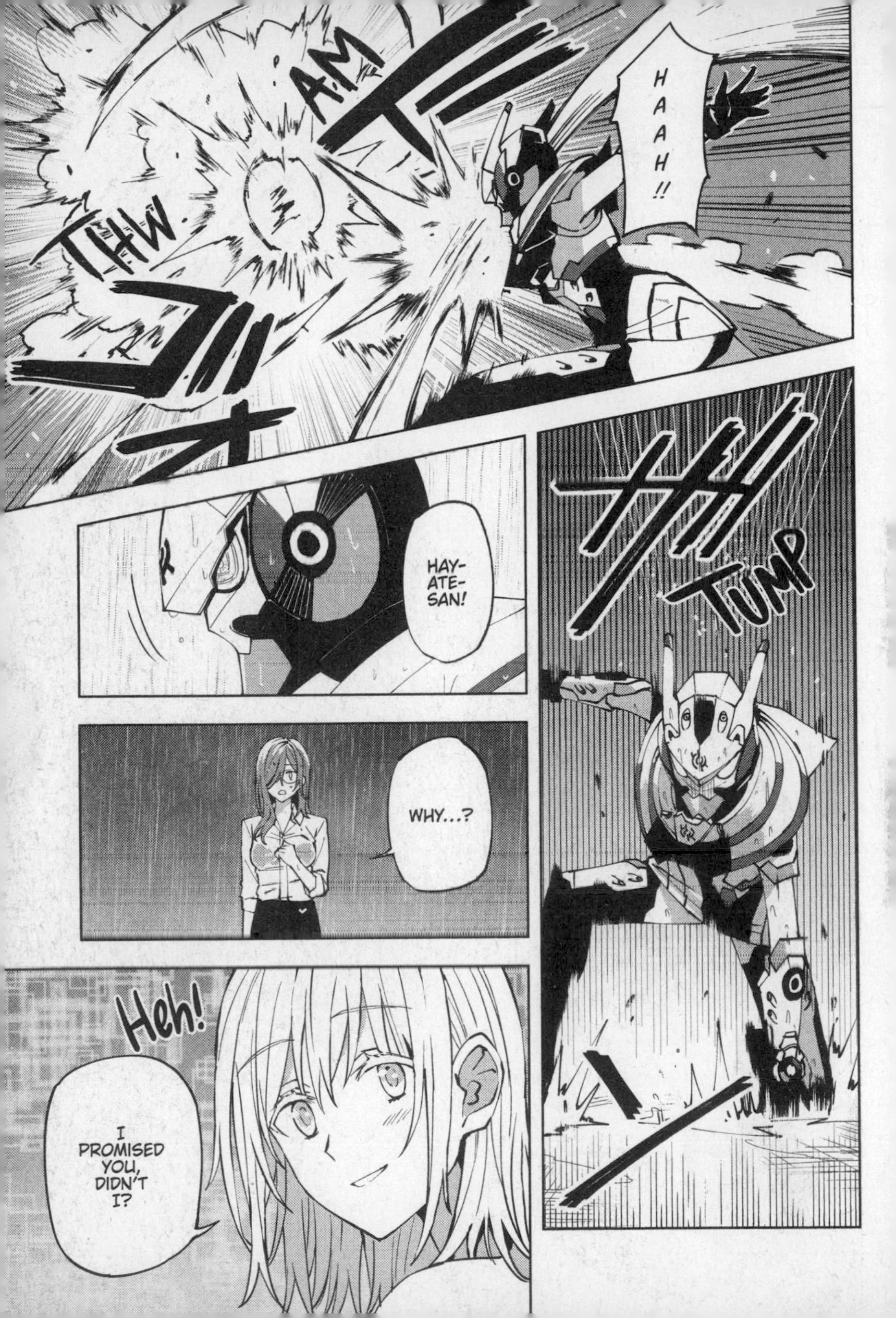
HAAAH!!
THWAM
TUMP
HAY-ATE-SAN!
WHY...?
Heh!
I PROMISED YOU, DIDN'T I?

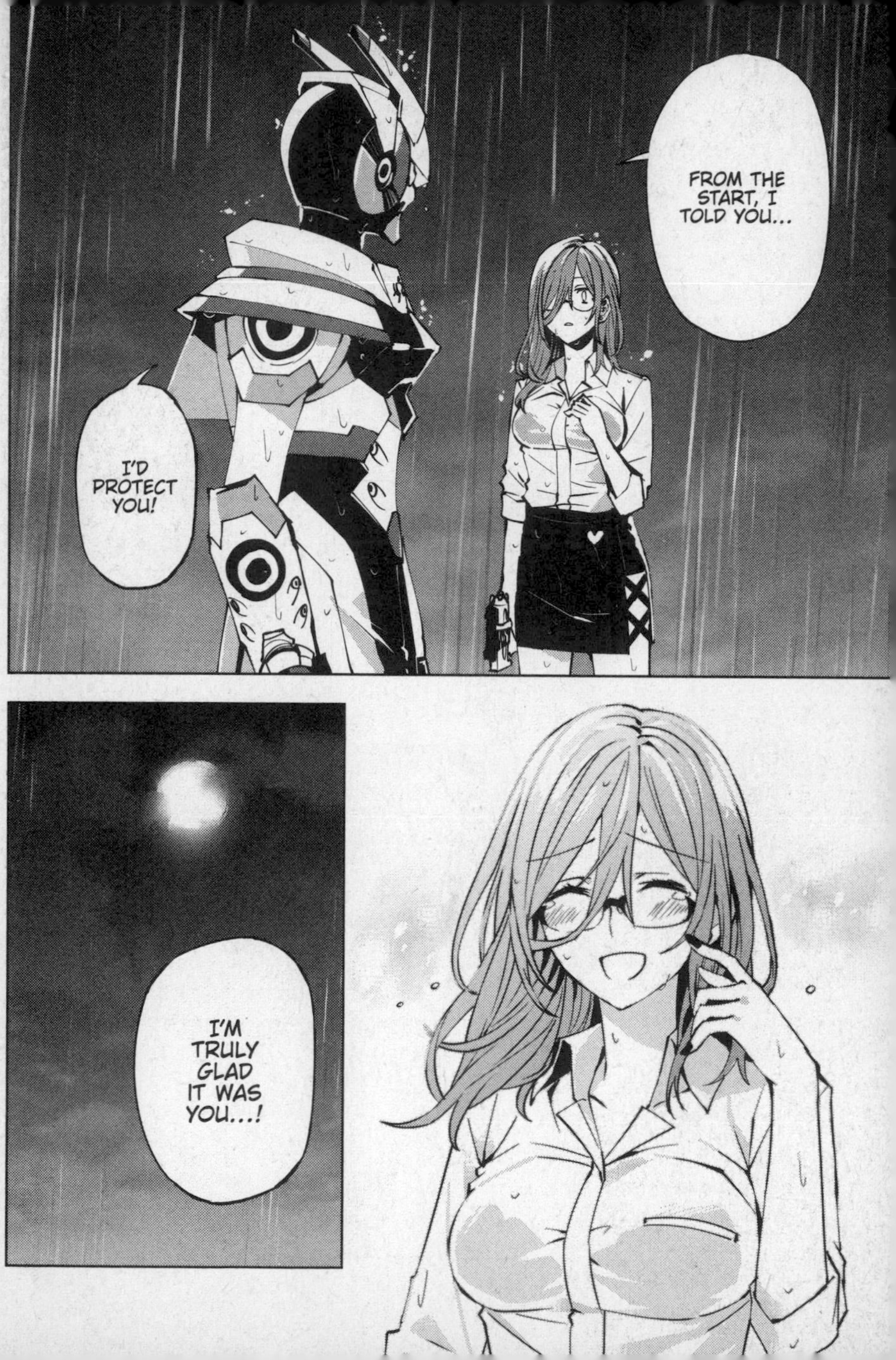
FROM THE START, I TOLD YOU...
I'D PROTECT YOU!
I'M TRULY GLAD IT WAS YOU...!

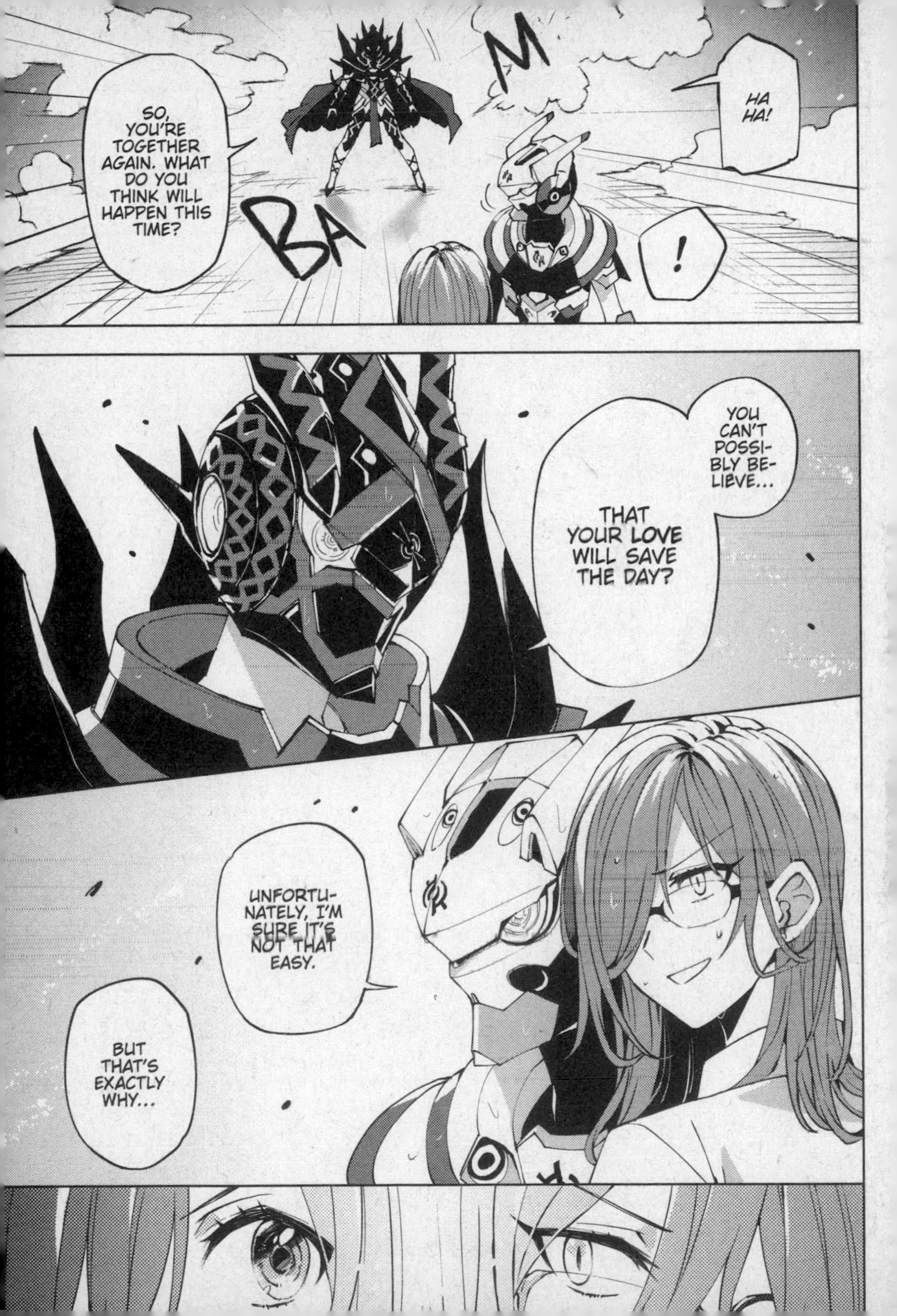
HA HA!
BAM
!
SO, YOU'RE TOGETHER AGAIN. WHAT DO YOU THINK WILL HAPPEN THIS TIME?
YOU CAN'T POSSIBLY BELIEVE...
THAT YOUR LOVE WILL SAVE THE DAY?
UNFORTUNATELY, I'M SURE IT'S NOT THAT EASY.
BUT THAT'S EXACTLY WHY...

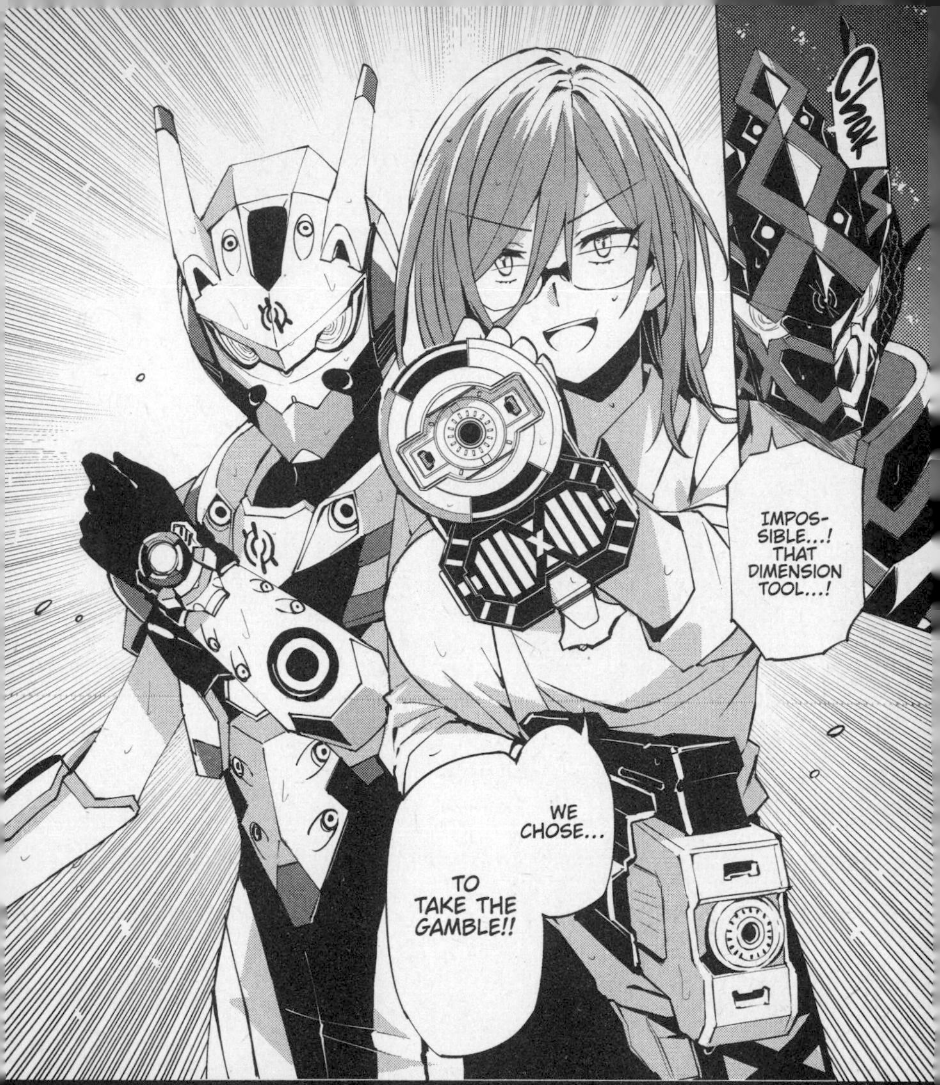
Clack
IMPOSSIBLE...! THAT DIMENSION TOOL...!
WE CHOSE...
TO TAKE THE GAMBLE!!

CHAPTER 14 BETTING ON HOPE

INCIDENTALLY, I GOT MY HANKY BACK SOON AFTER WE MET ORB OWL.

I DELIVERED IT MYSELF!

EH HEH HEH!

SUPERWOMEN IN LOVE!
HONEY TRAP & RAPID RABBIT

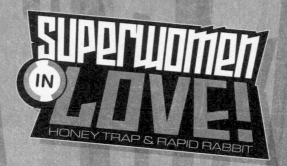

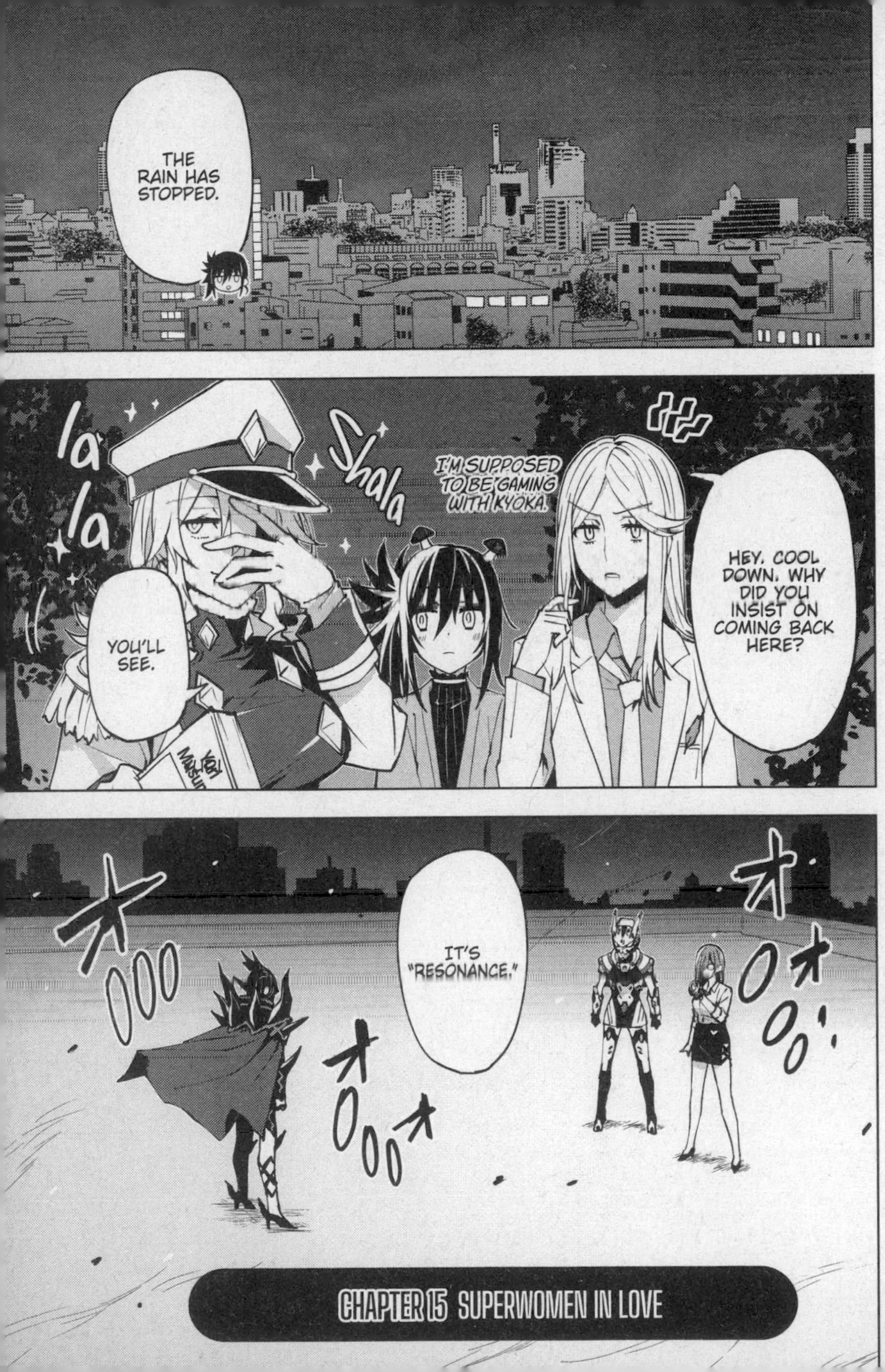
THE RAIN HAS STOPPED.
HEY. COOL DOWN. WHY DID YOU INSIST ON COMING BACK HERE?
I'M SUPPOSED TO BE GAMING WITH KYOKA.
Shala
YOU'LL SEE.
la la la
IT'S "RESONANCE."
CHAPTER 15 SUPERWOMEN IN LOVE

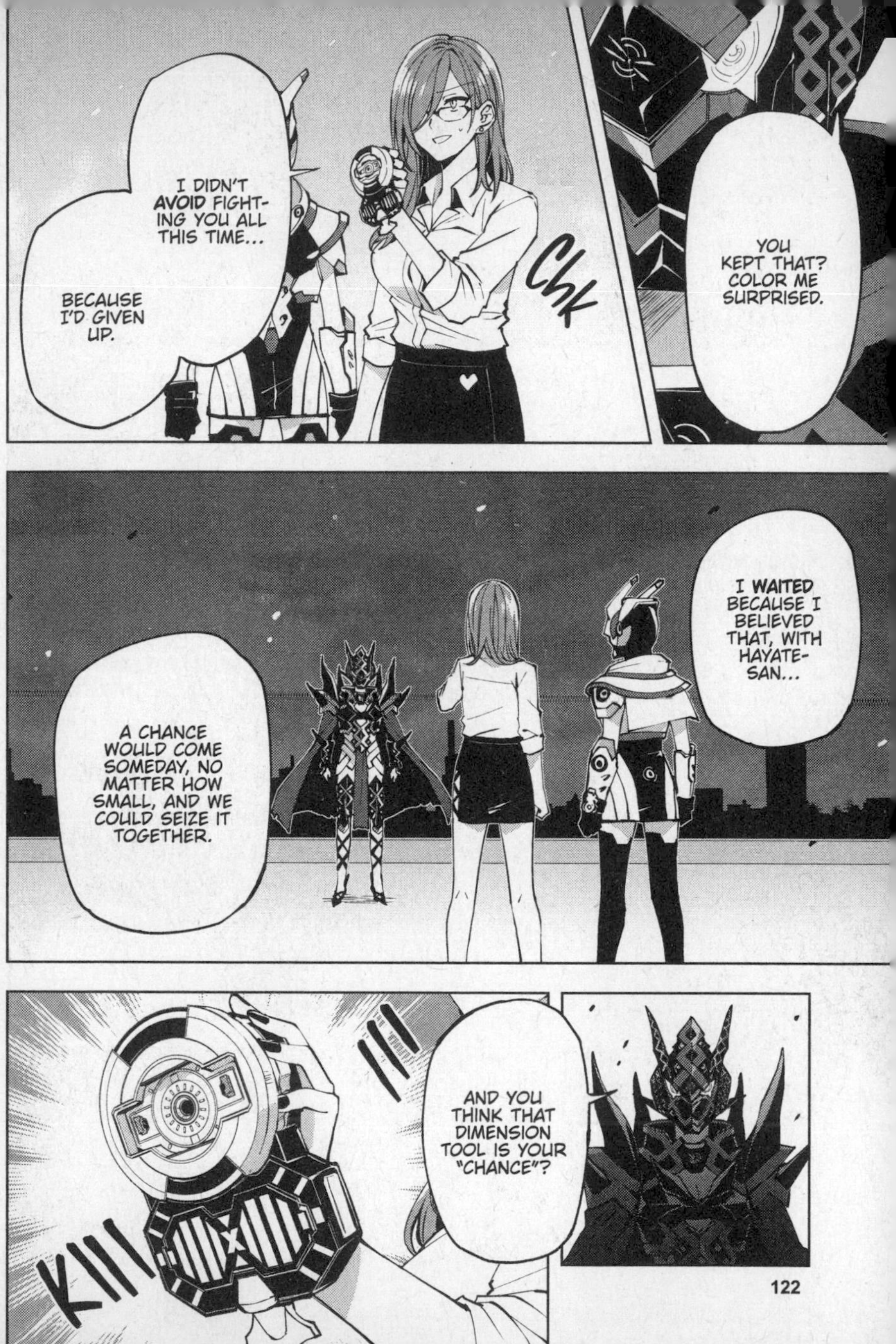
YOU KEPT THAT? COLOR ME SURPRISED.
Chk
I DIDN'T AVOID FIGHTING YOU ALL THIS TIME...
BECAUSE I'D GIVEN UP.
I WAITED BECAUSE I BELIEVED THAT, WITH HAYATE-SAN...
A CHANCE WOULD COME SOMEDAY, NO MATTER HOW SMALL, AND WE COULD SEIZE IT TOGETHER.
AND YOU THINK THAT DIMENSION TOOL IS YOUR "CHANCE"?
KIII

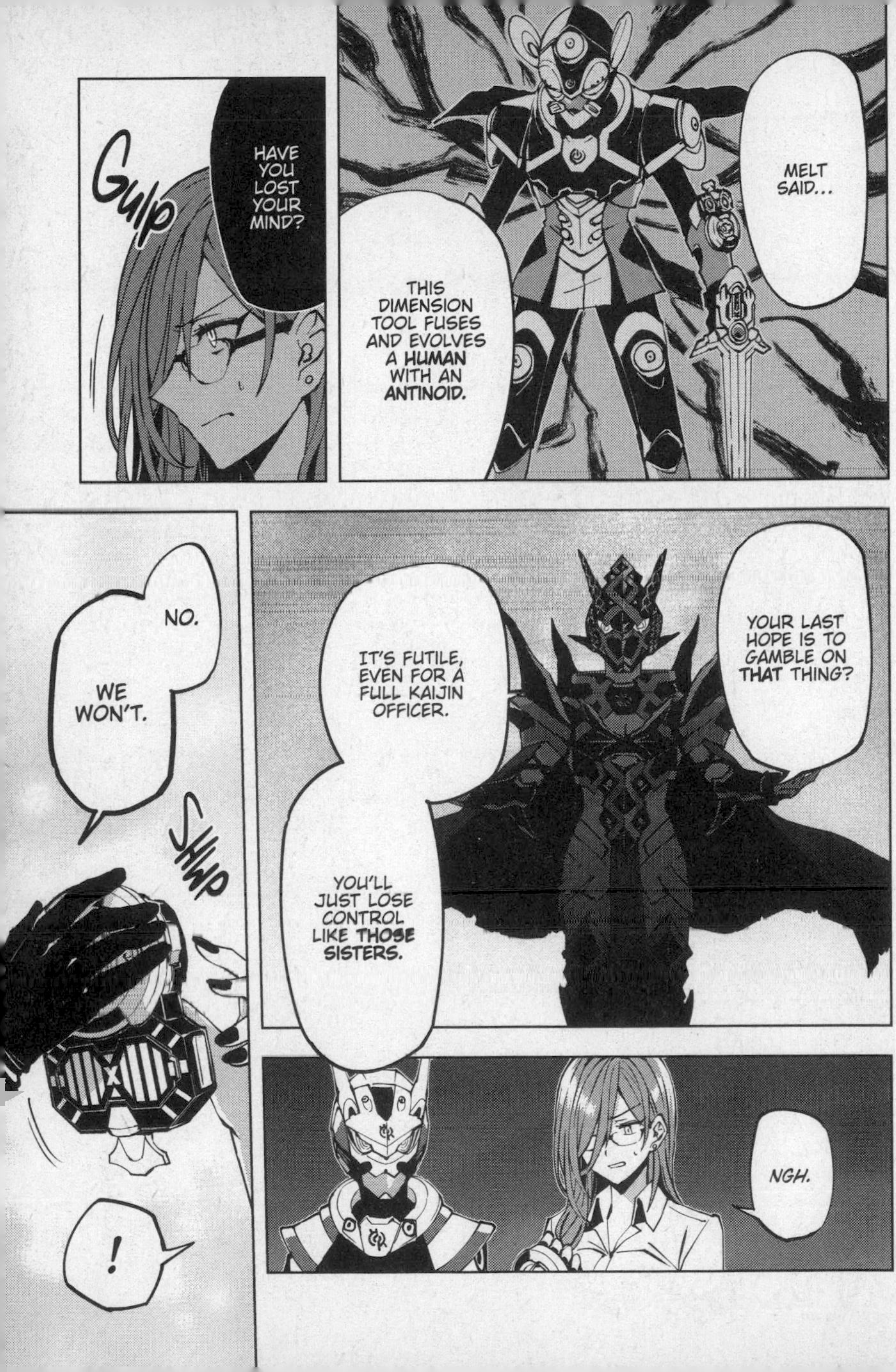
MELT SAID...
THIS DIMENSION TOOL FUSES AND EVOLVES A HUMAN WITH AN ANTINOID.
HAVE YOU LOST YOUR MIND?
Gulp
YOUR LAST HOPE IS TO GAMBLE ON THAT THING?
IT'S FUTILE, EVEN FOR A FULL KAIJIN OFFICER.
YOU'LL JUST LOSE CONTROL LIKE THOSE SISTERS.
NGH.
NO.
WE WON'T.
SHWP
!

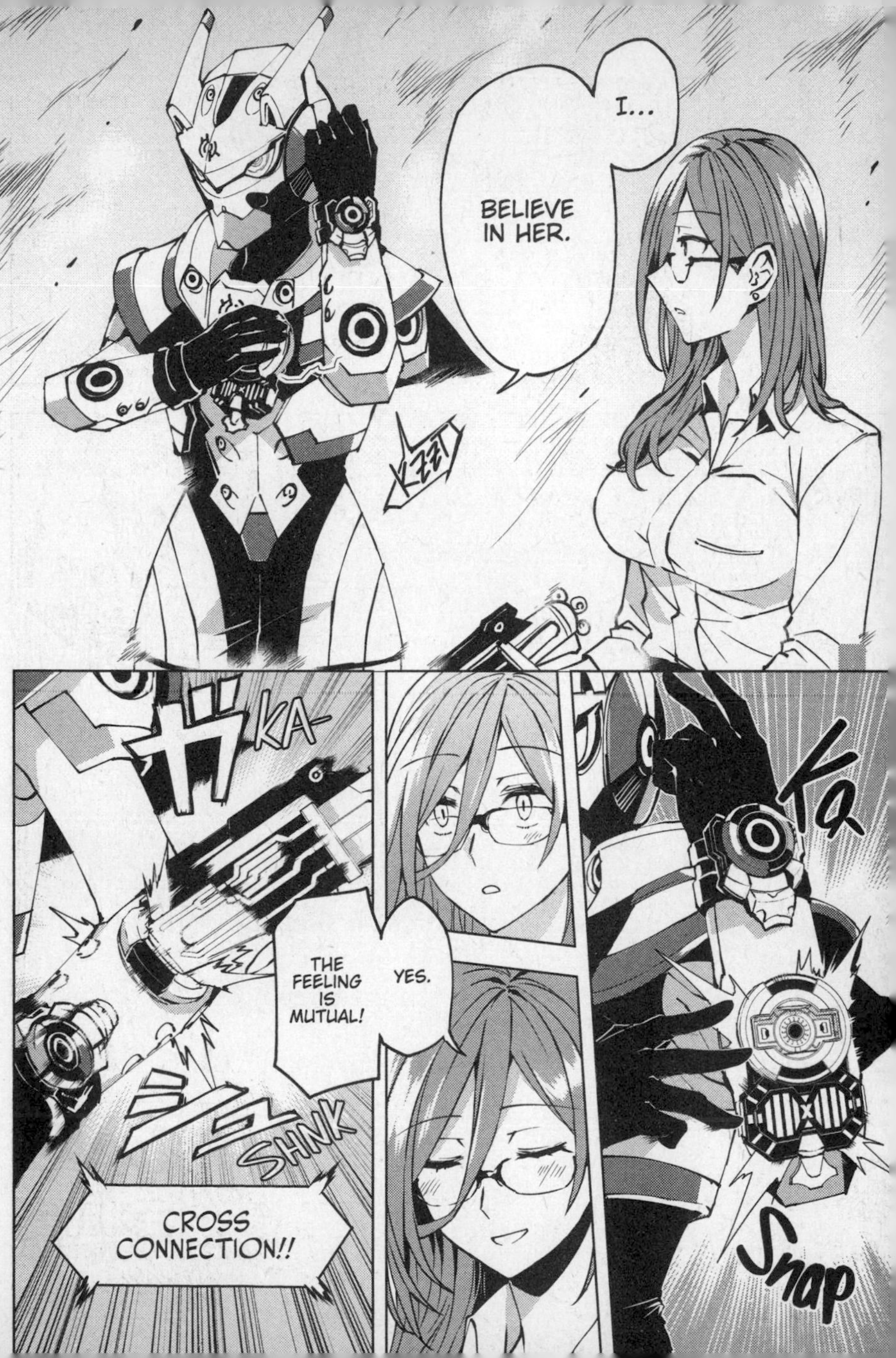
I...
BELIEVE IN HER.
KZZT
KA
Snap
YES.
THE FEELING IS MUTUAL!
KA-
SHNK
CROSS CONNECTION!!

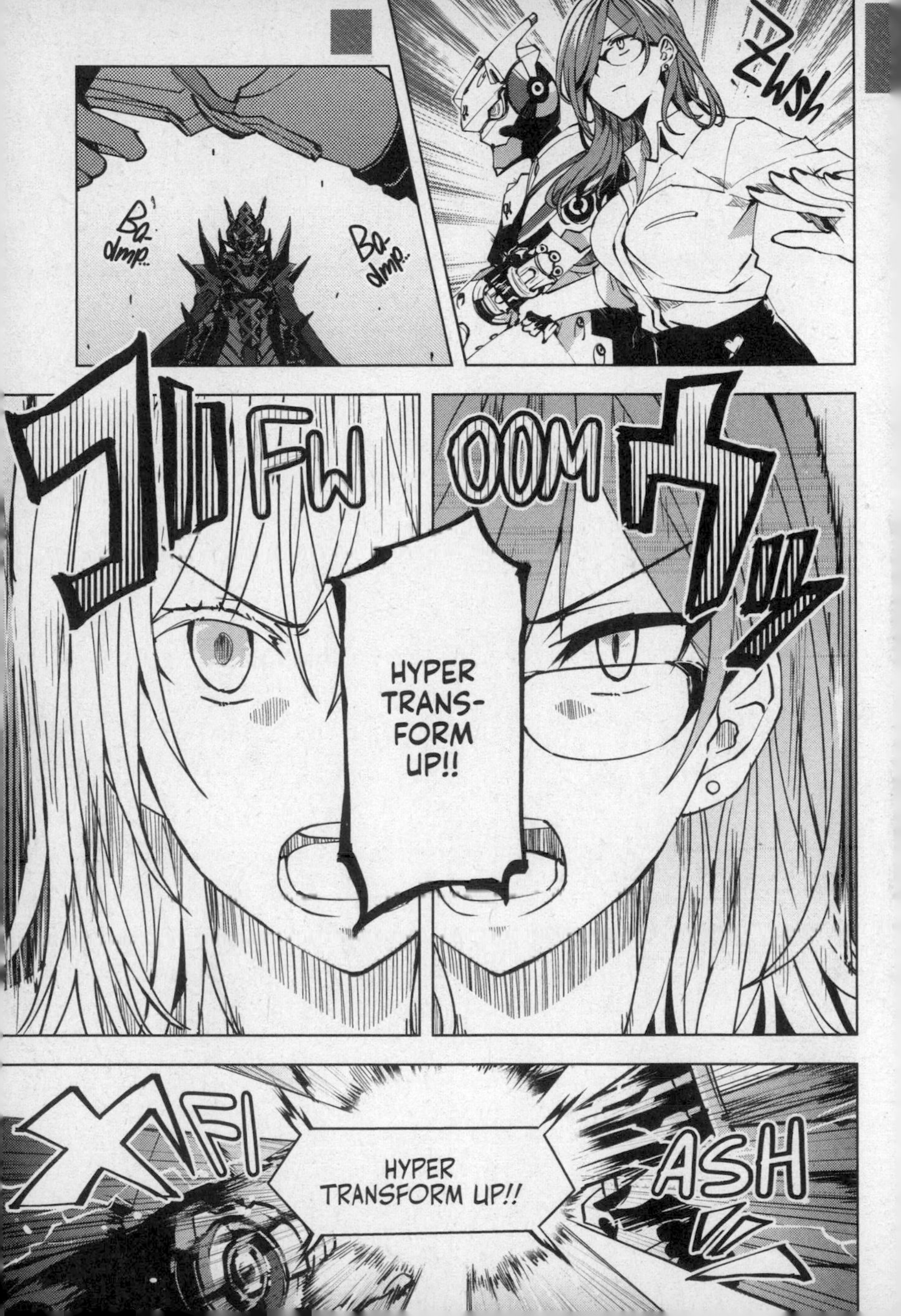
Zwsh
Ba-dmp...
Ba-dmp...
FwOOM
HYPER TRANS-FORM UP!!
FlASH
HYPER TRANSFORM UP!!

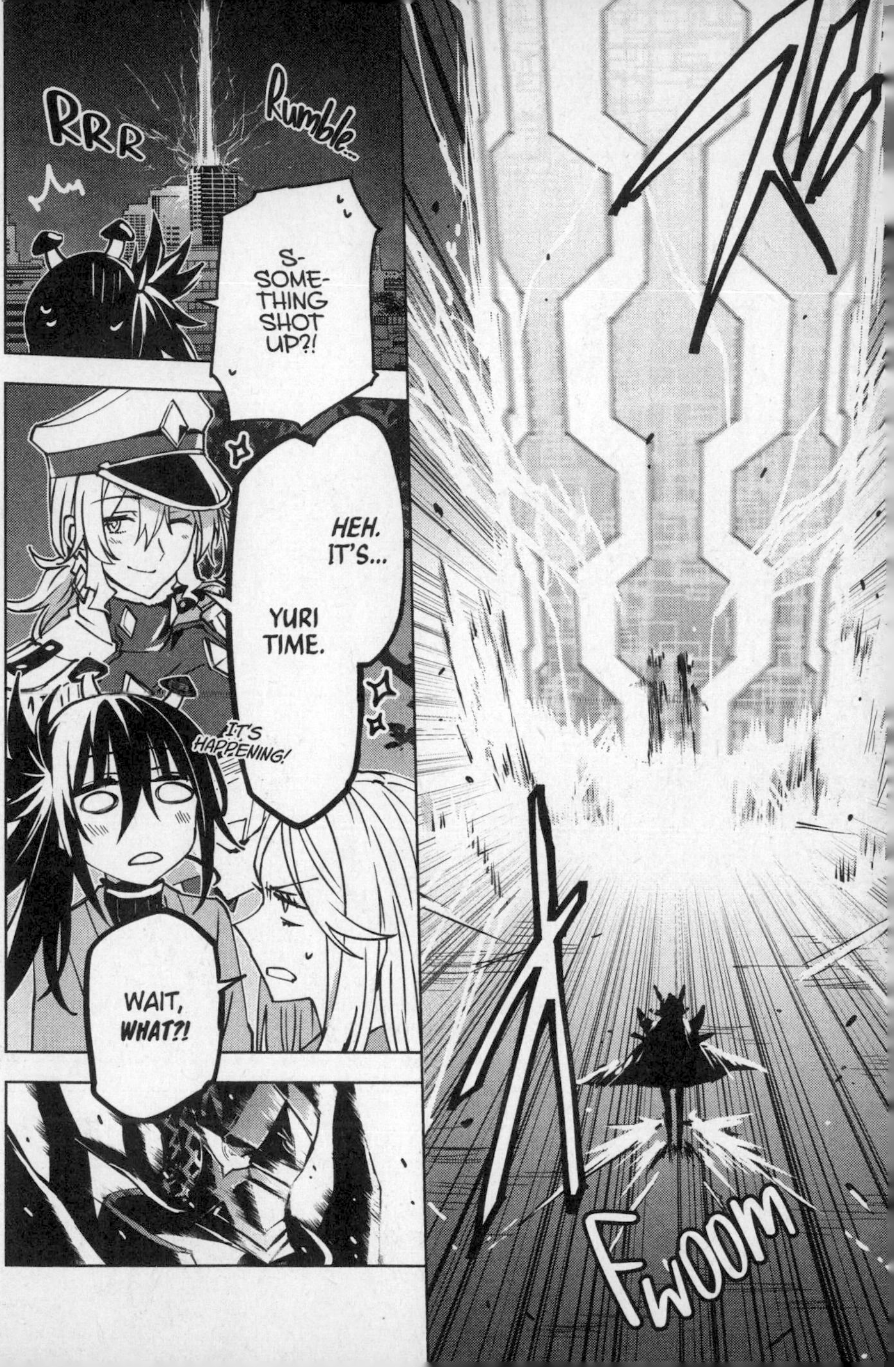
Fwoom
Rumble...
RRR
S-SOMETHING SHOT UP?!
HEH. IT'S...
YURI TIME.
IT'S HAPPENING!
WAIT, WHAT?!

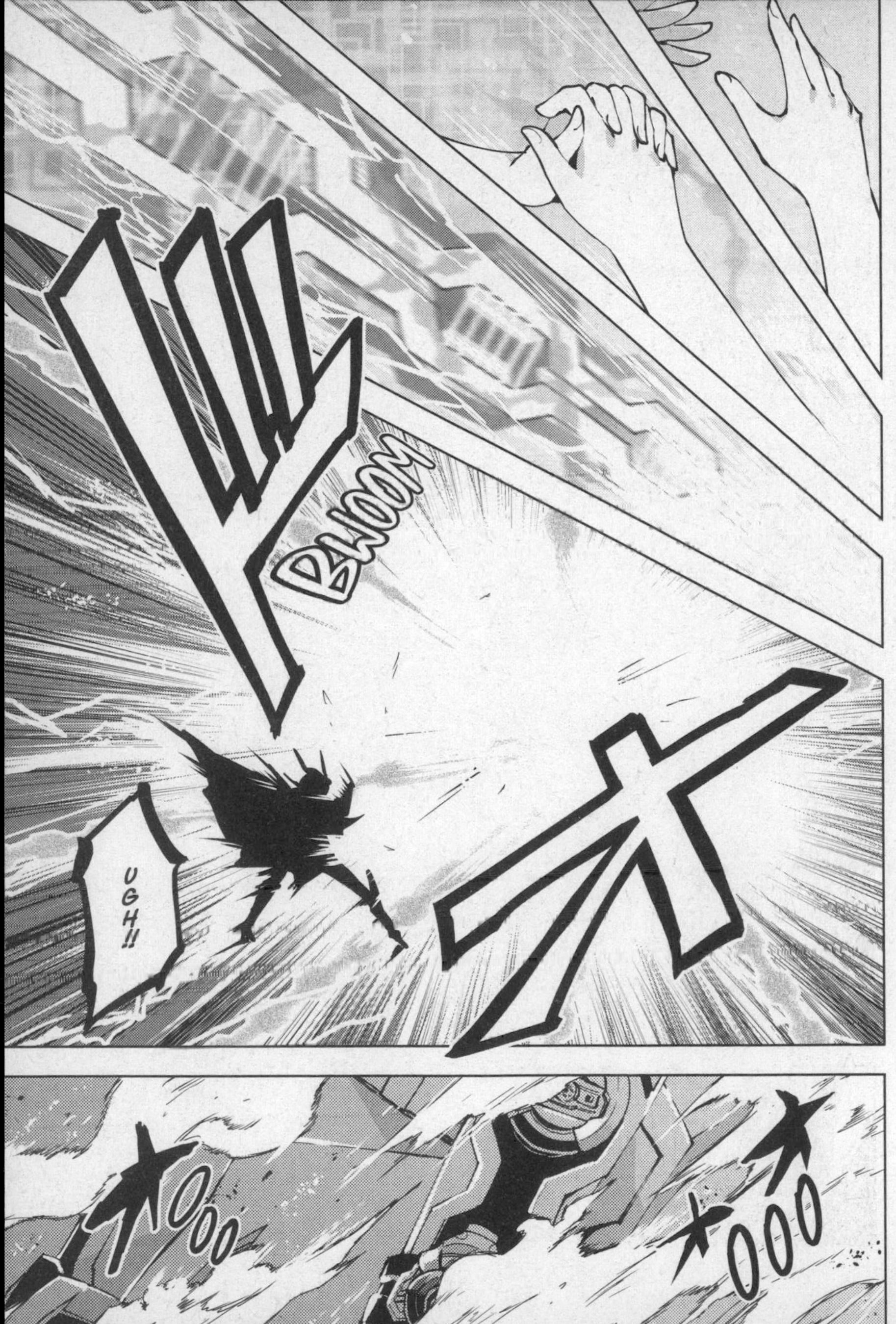
BWOOM
UGH!!

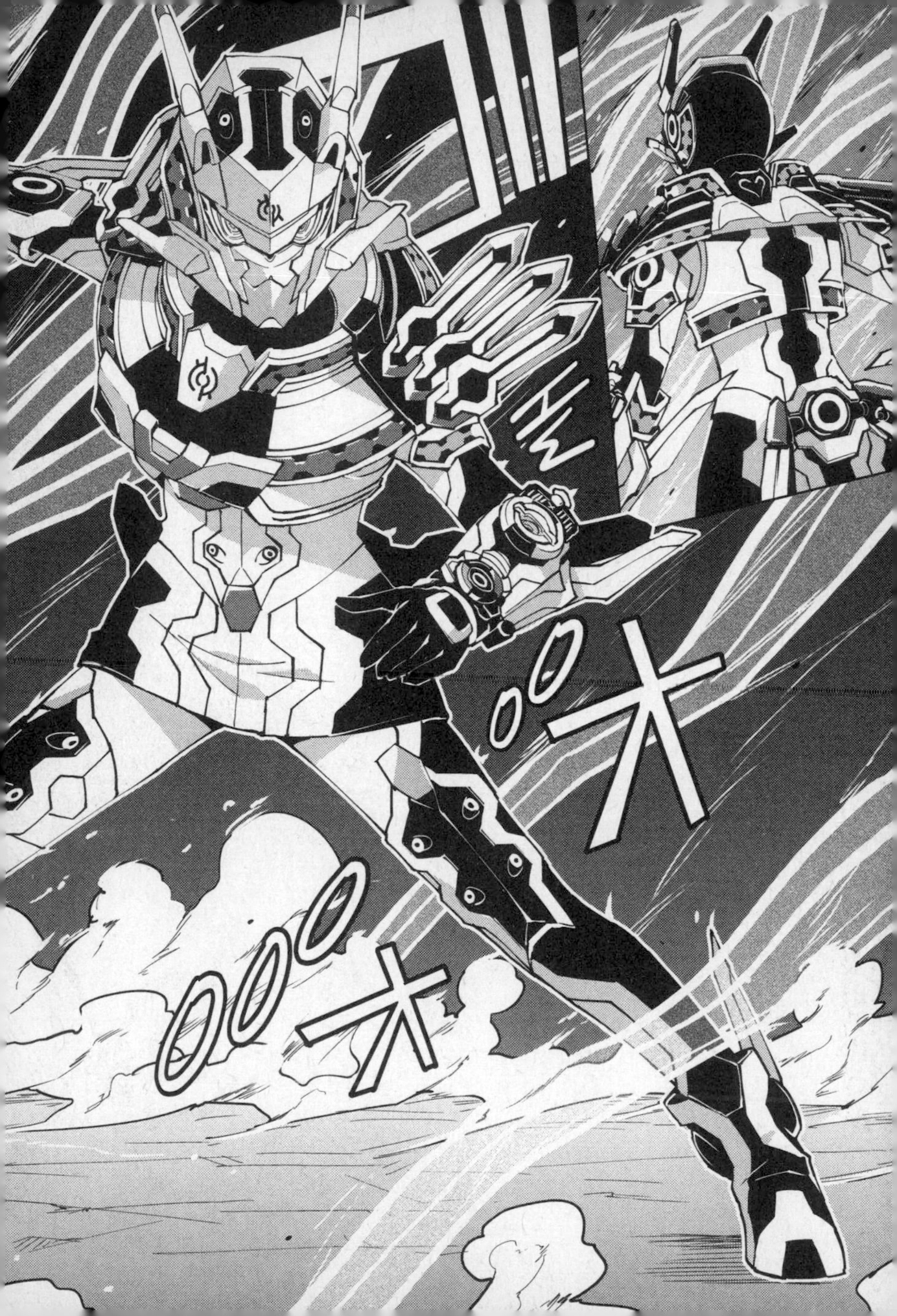

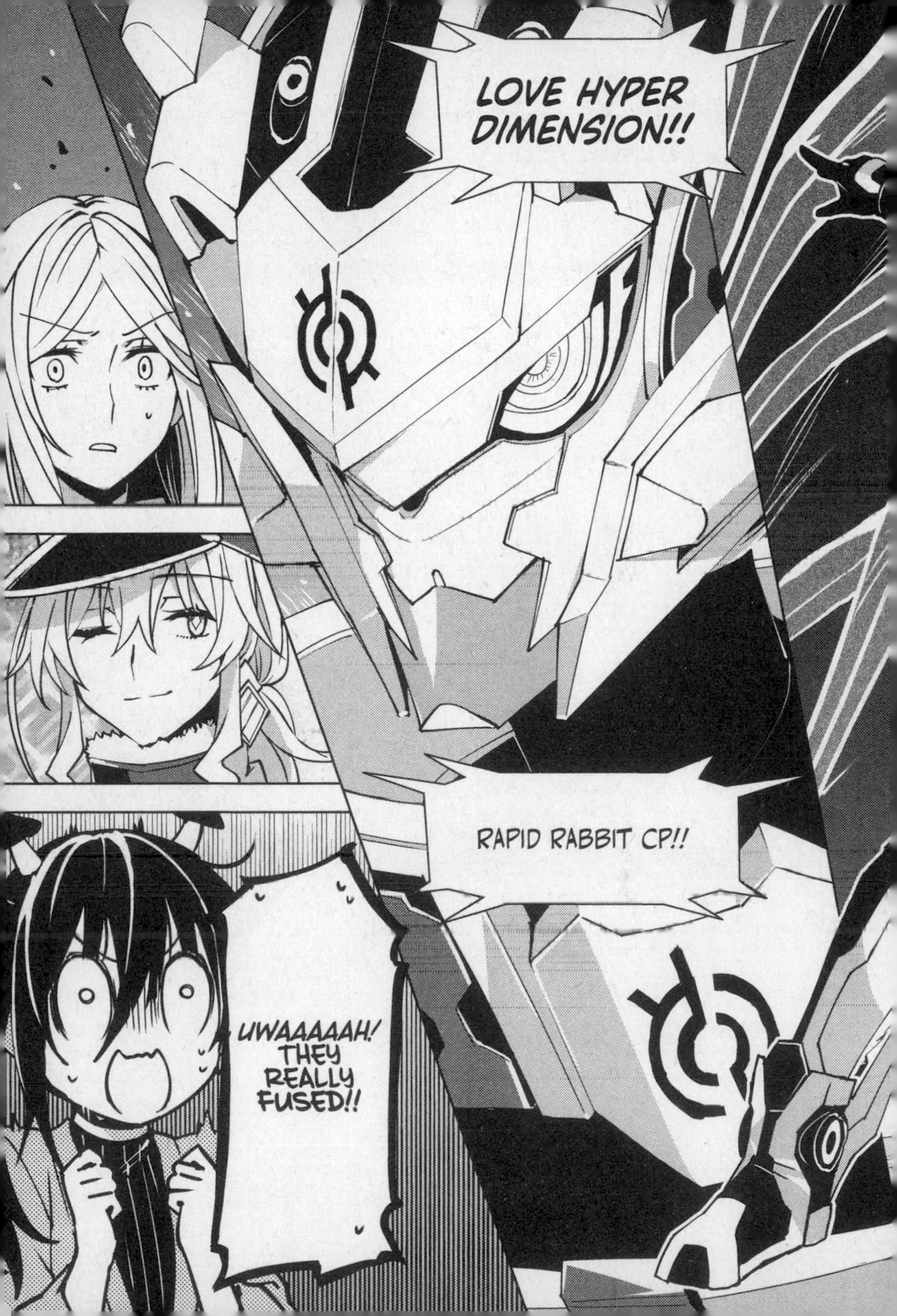
LOVE HYPER DIMENSION!!
RAPID RABBIT CP!!
UWAAAAAH! THEY REALLY FUSED!!

Be.
Beep

...!

IT CAN'T BE.

THAT SAME STRANGE ENERGY READING AGAIN...?

IS THIS... RESO-NANCE...?

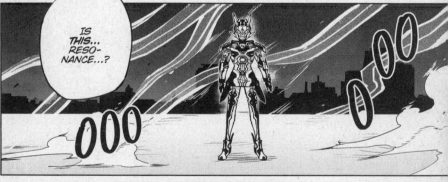

OOO

OOO

IMPOS-SIBLE...!

OOO

OOO

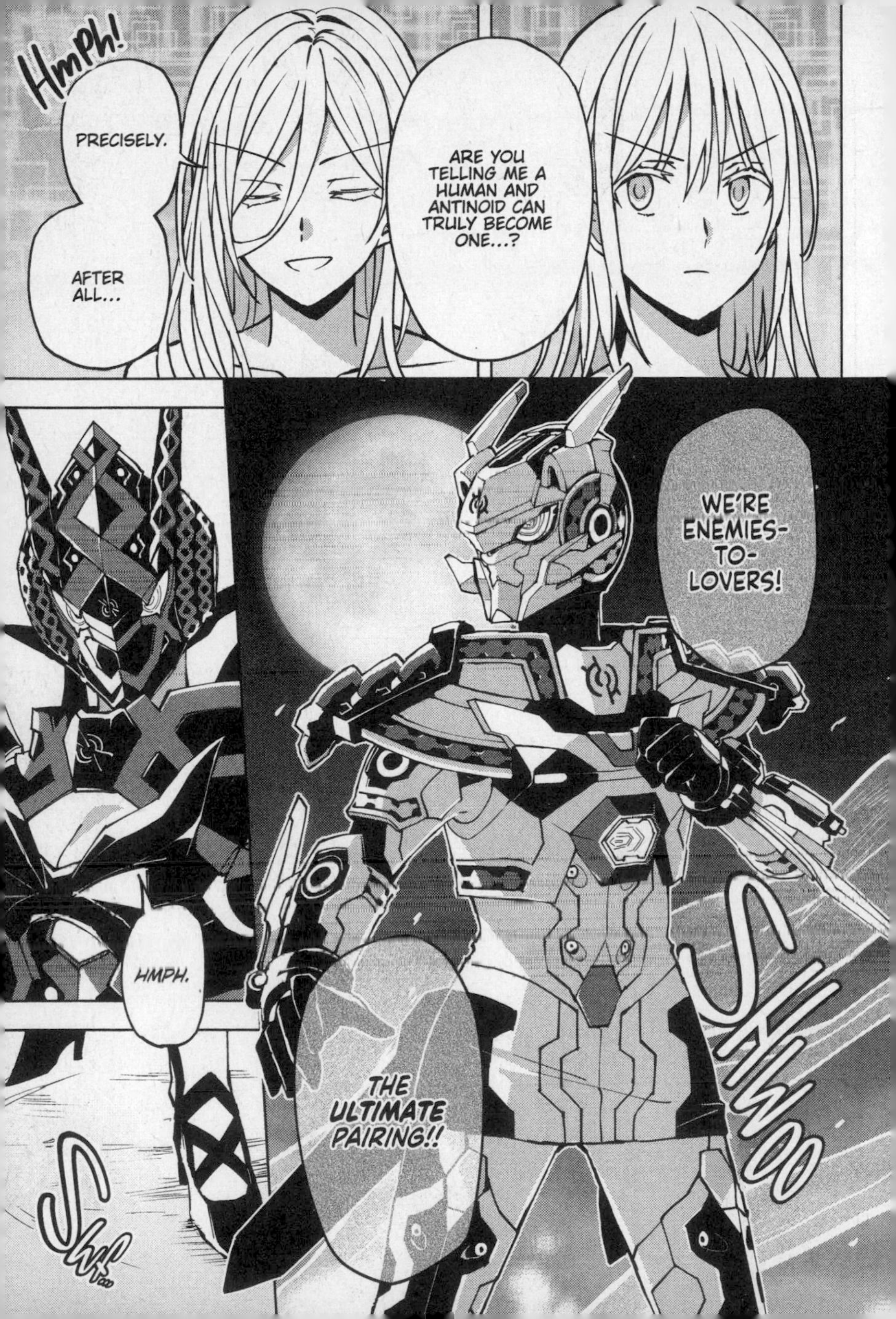
ARE YOU TELLING ME A HUMAN AND ANTINOID CAN TRULY BECOME ONE...?
Hmph!
PRECISELY.
AFTER ALL...
WE'RE ENEMIES-TO-LOVERS!
SHWOO
THE ULTIMATE PAIRING!!
HMPH.
Shf...

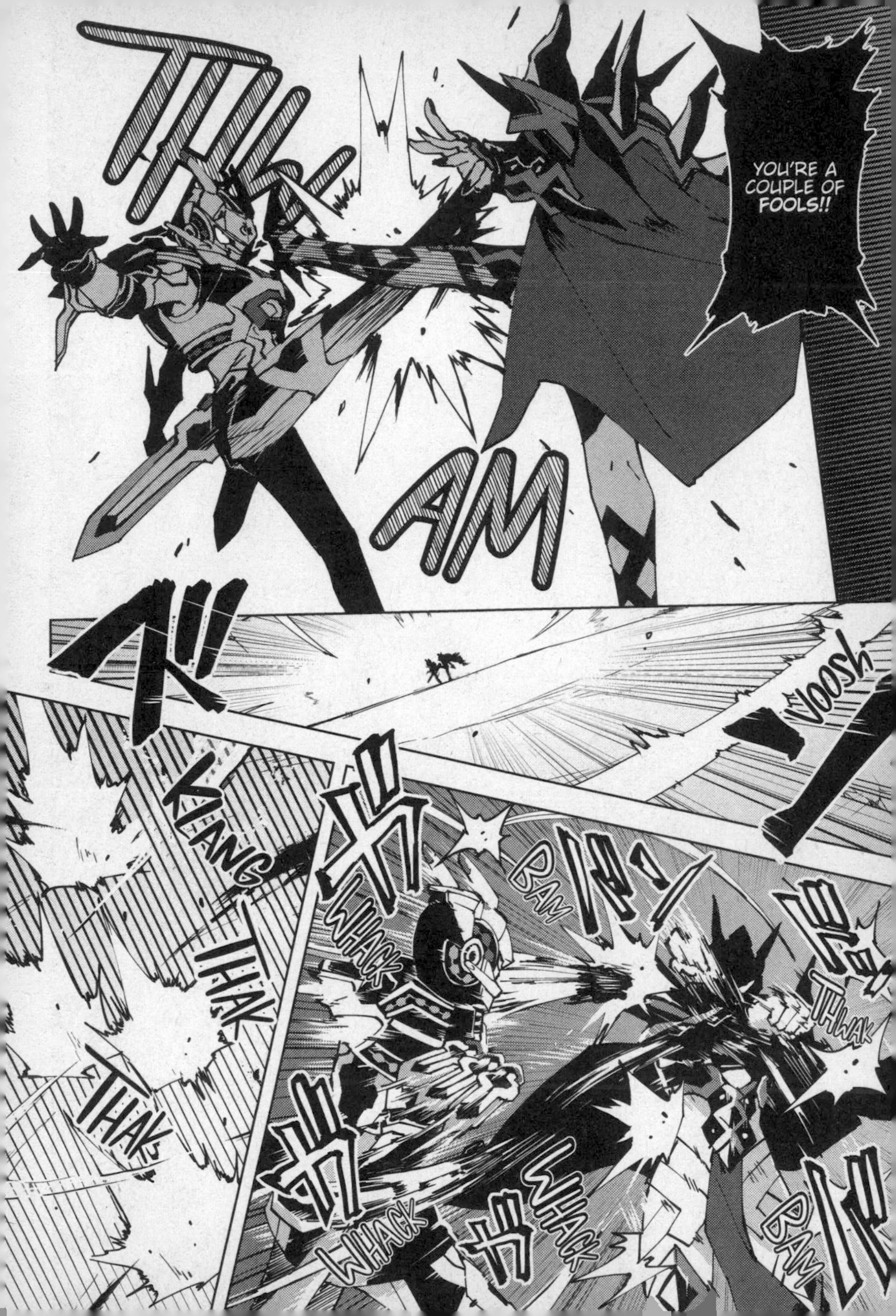
YOU'RE A COUPLE OF FOOLS!!
AM
VOOSH
BAM
THWAK
WHACK
BAM
WHACK
WHACK
KLANG
THAK
THAK

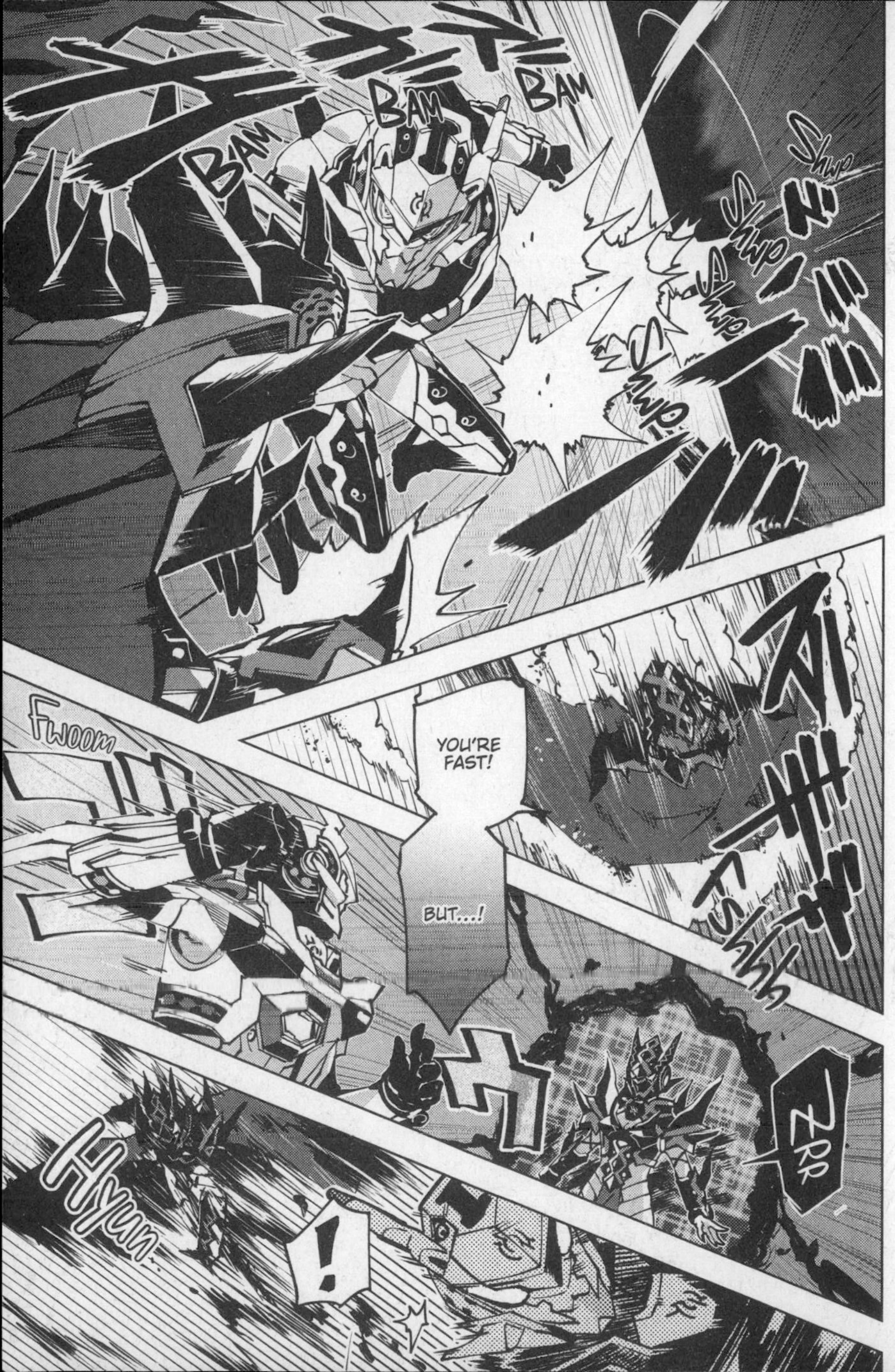
Shwp
Shwp
Shwp
Shwp
Shwp
BAM
BAM
BAM
Fshhh
YOU'RE FAST!
BUT...!
Fwoom
ZRR
Hyun
!

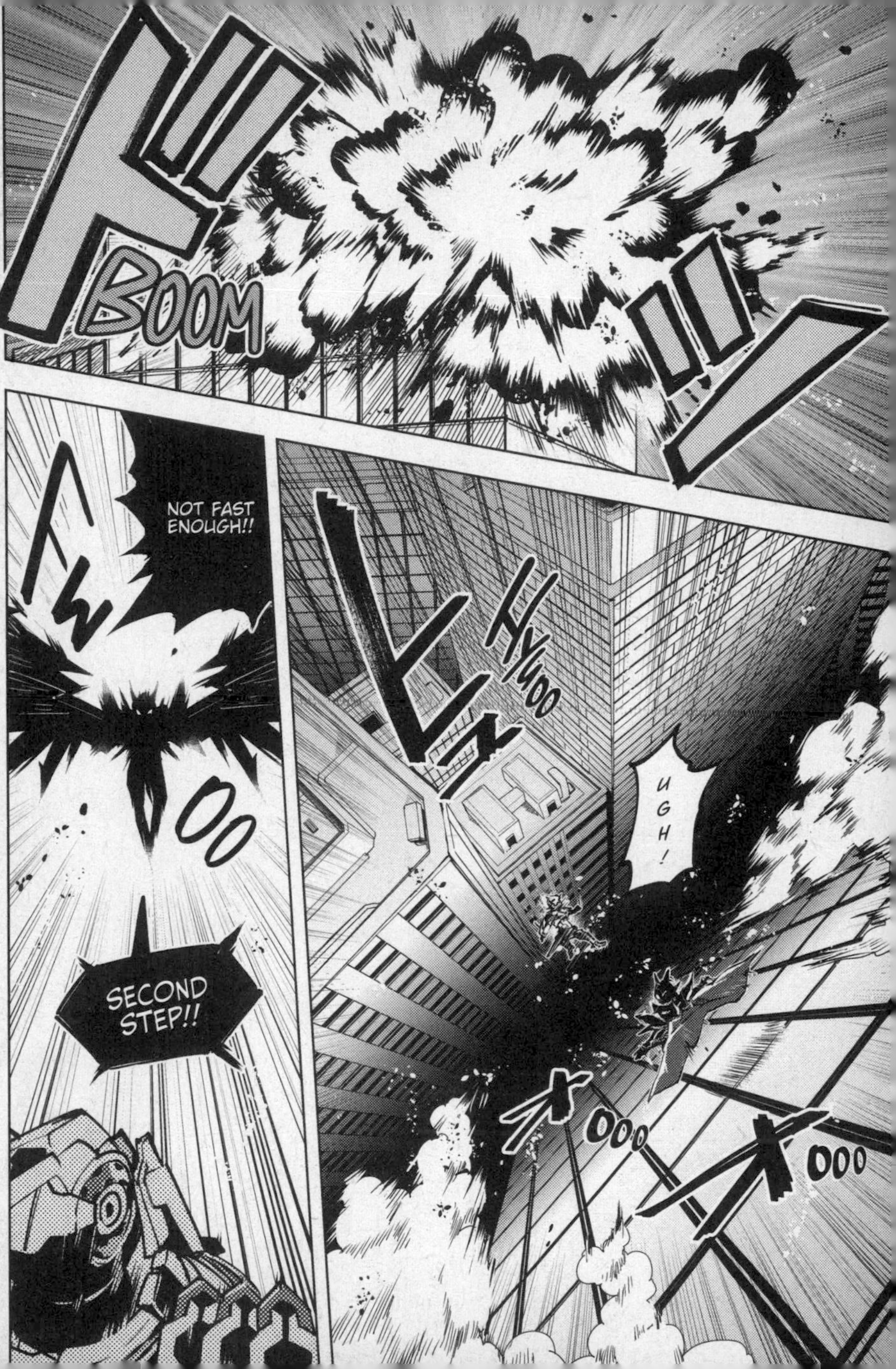
BOOM
HYUOO
UGH!
NOT FAST ENOUGH!!
SECOND STEP!!

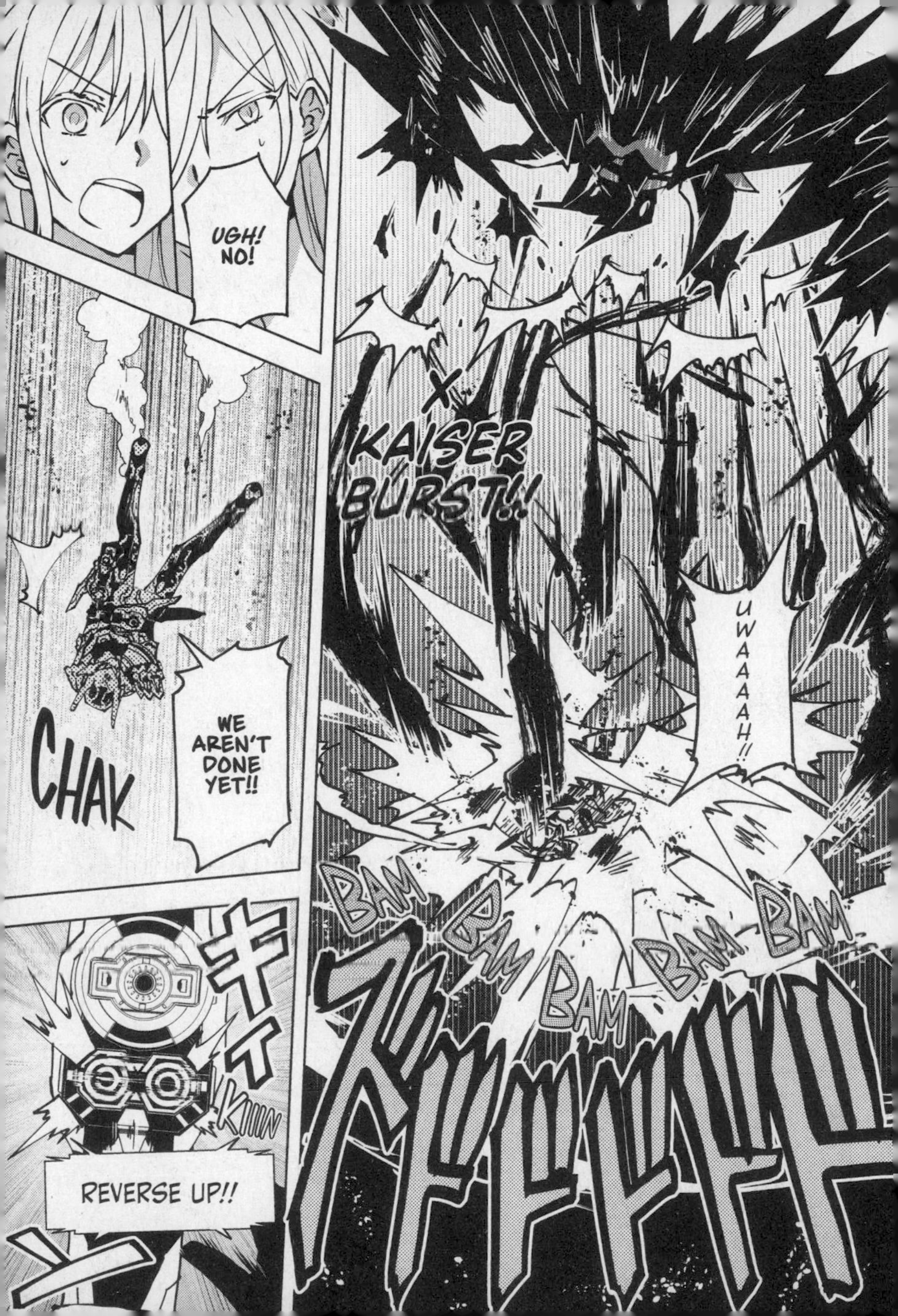
KAISER BURST!!
UWAAAAAH!!
BAM
BAM
BAM
BAM
BAM
BAM
UGH! NO!
WE AREN'T DONE YET!!
CHAK
KIIIN
REVERSE UP!!

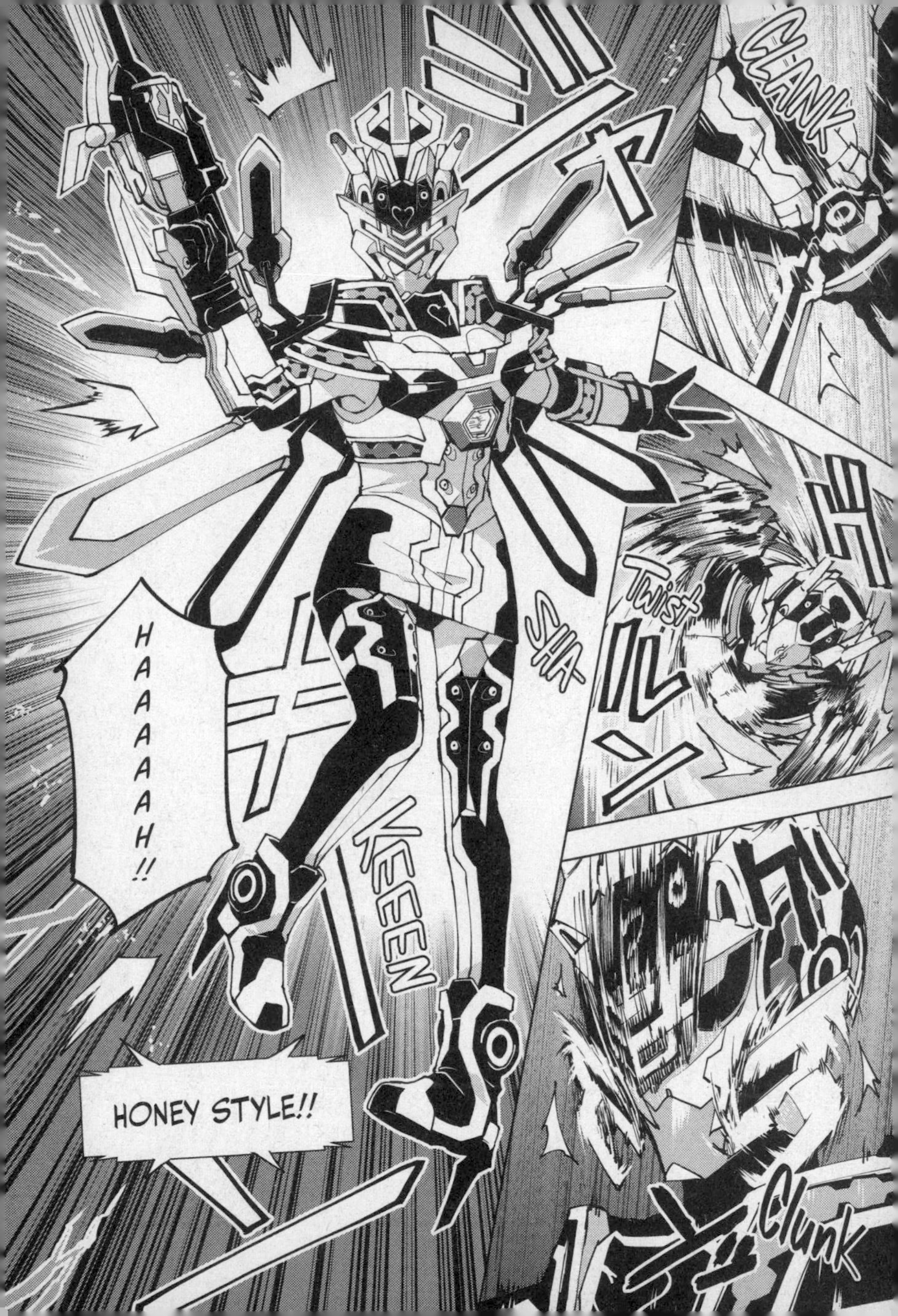
CLANK
Twist
Clunk
SHA
HAAAAAH!!
KEEEEN
HONEY STYLE!!

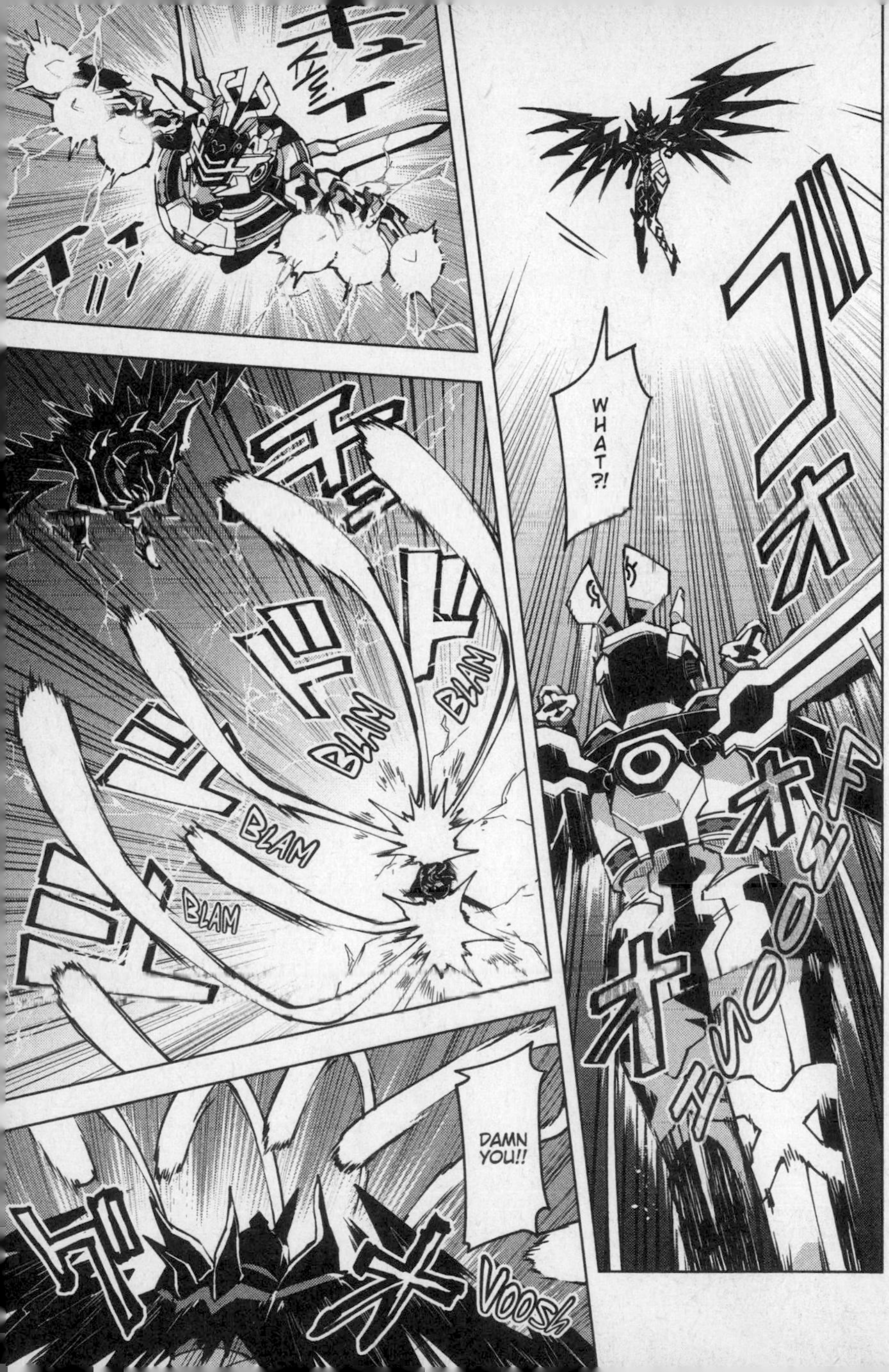
WHAT?!
FWOOSH
KYUI!
BLAM
BLAM
BLAM
BLAM
DAMN YOU!!
Voosh

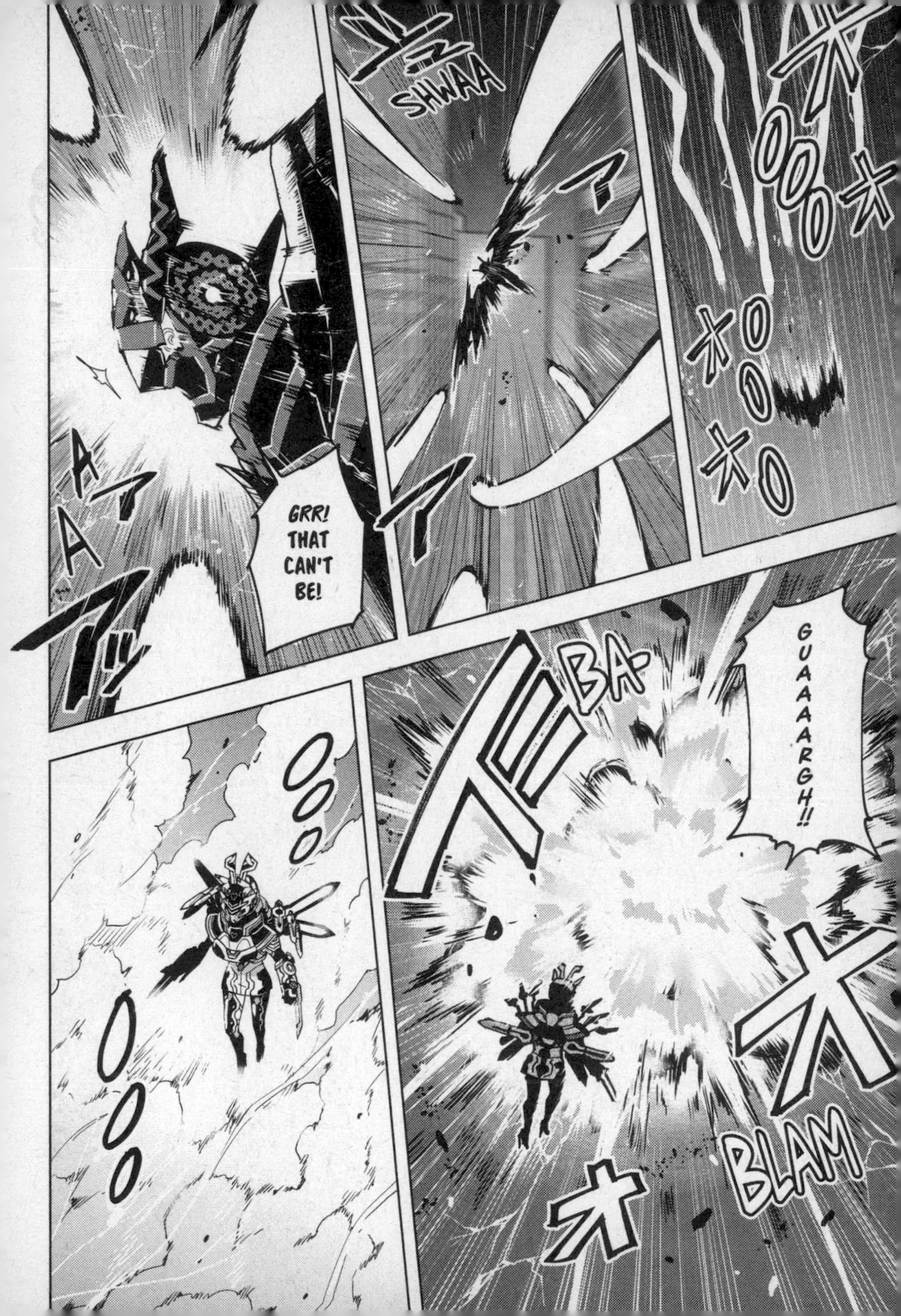
SHWAA
GRR! THAT CAN'T BE!
BA
GUAAAARGH!!
BLAM

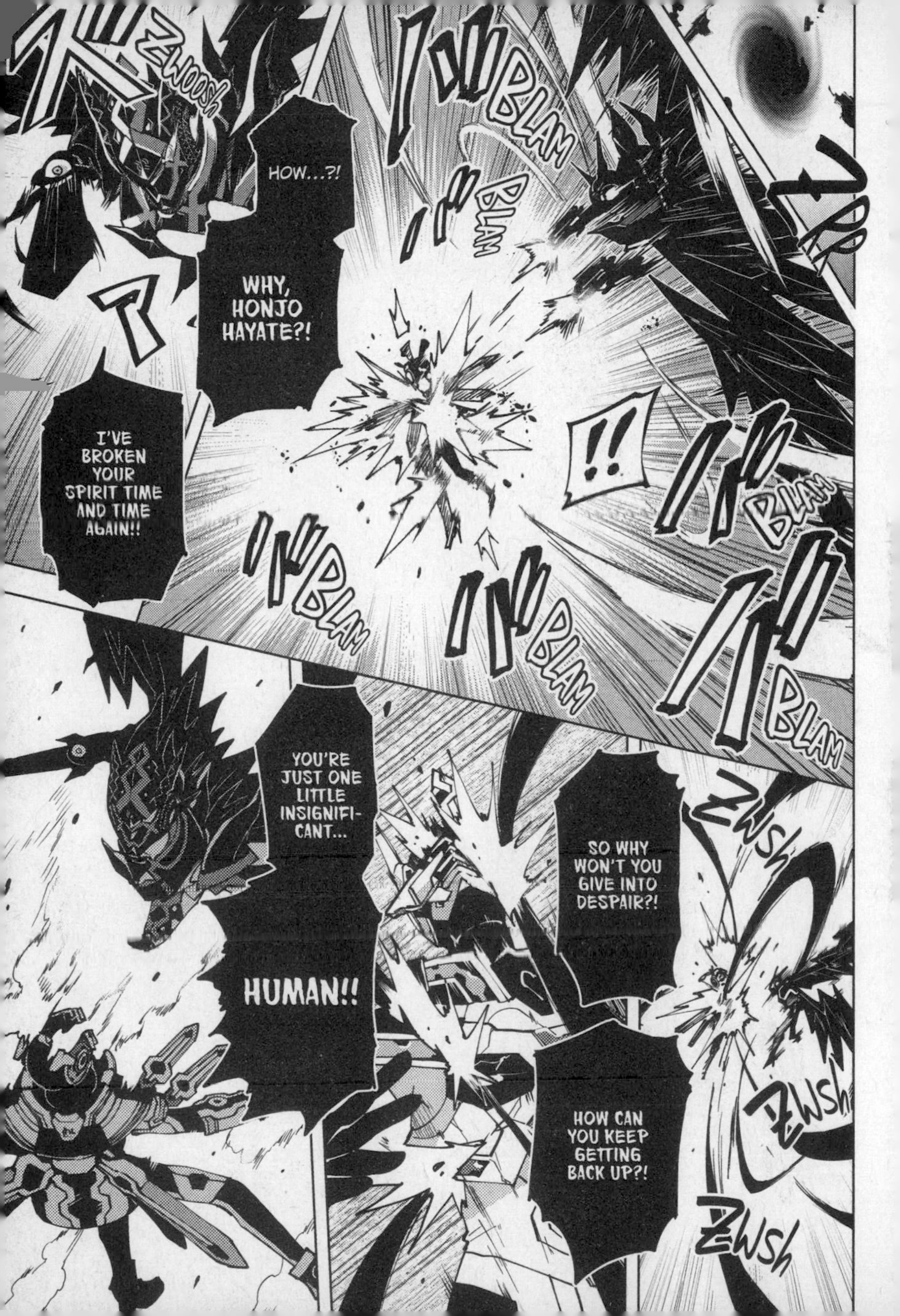
ZRR
BLAM
BLAM
!!
BLAM
BLAM
BLAM
BLAM
BLAM
WOOSH
HOW...?!
WHY, HONJO HAYATE?!
I'VE BROKEN YOUR SPIRIT TIME AND TIME AGAIN!!
ZWSH
SO WHY WON'T YOU GIVE INTO DESPAIR?!
ZWSH
HOW CAN YOU KEEP GETTING BACK UP?!
ZWSH
YOU'RE JUST ONE LITTLE INSIGNIFI-CANT...
HUMAN!!

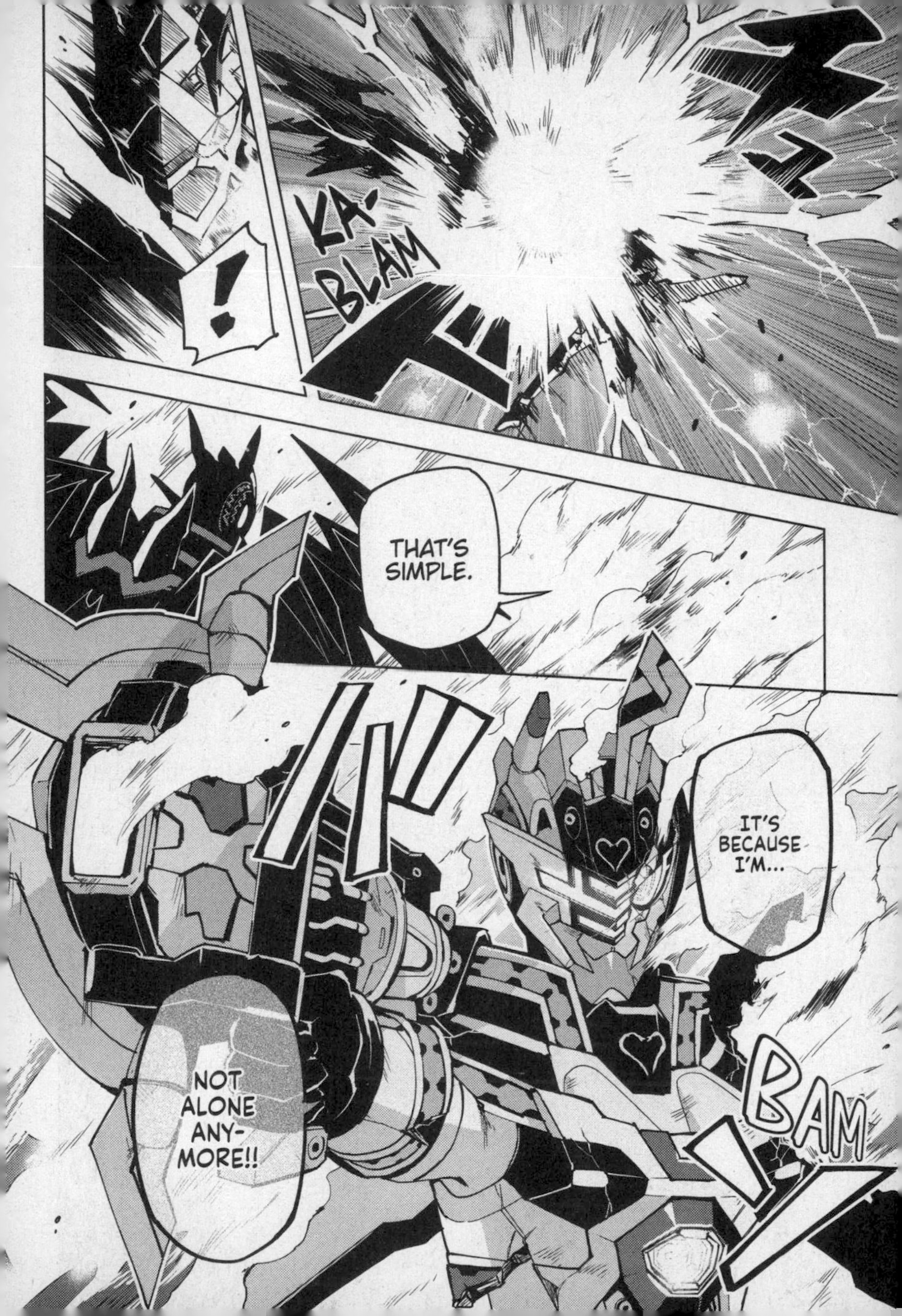
KA-BLAM
!
THAT'S SIMPLE.
IT'S BECAUSE I'M...
BAM
NOT ALONE ANY-MORE!!

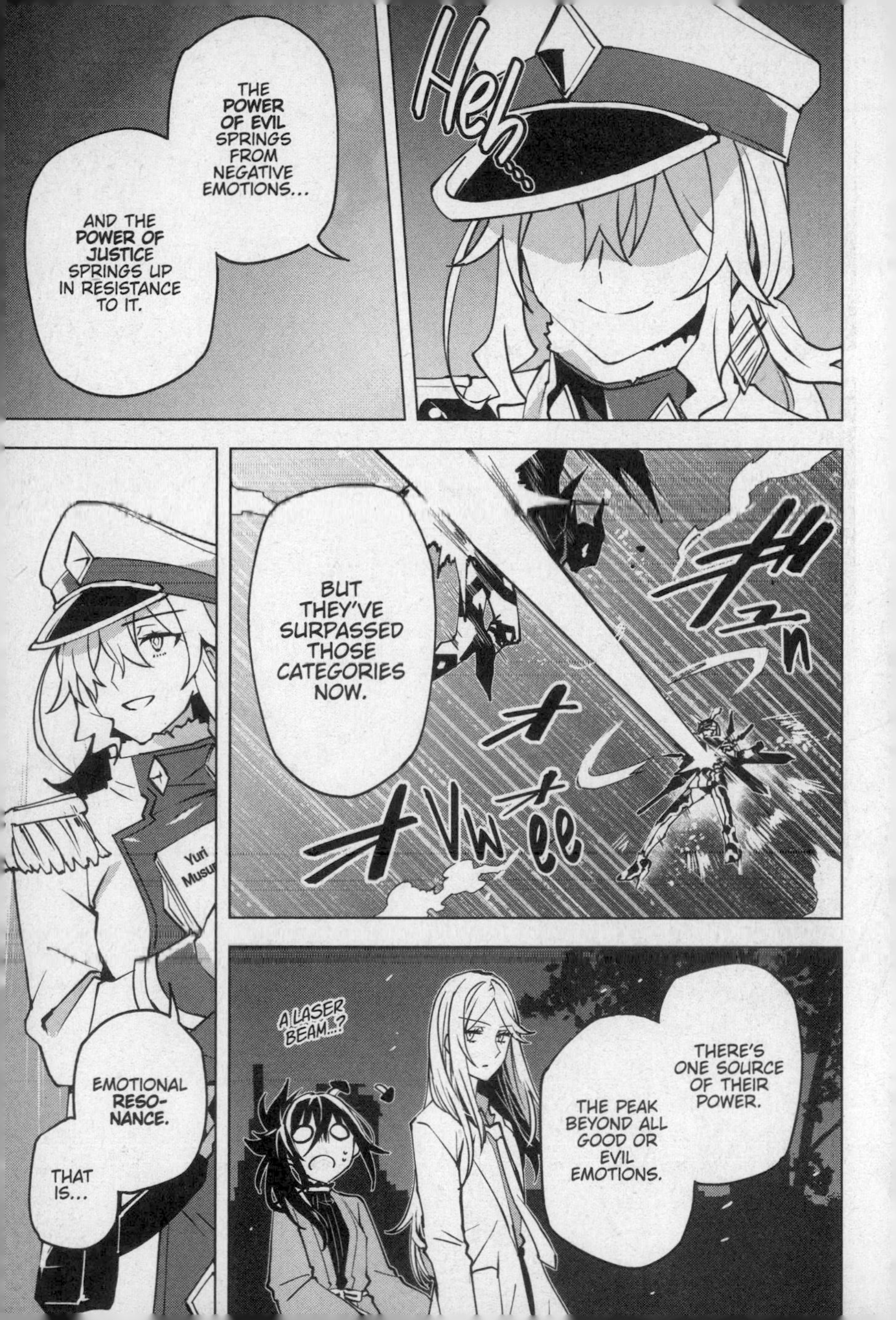
Heh...
THE POWER OF EVIL SPRINGS FROM NEGATIVE EMOTIONS...
AND THE POWER OF JUSTICE SPRINGS UP IN RESISTANCE TO IT.
BUT THEY'VE SURPASSED THOSE CATEGORIES NOW.
Vwee
n
THERE'S ONE SOURCE OF THEIR POWER.
THE PEAK BEYOND ALL GOOD OR EVIL EMOTIONS.
A LASER BEAM...?
Yuri
EMOTIONAL RESO-NANCE.
THAT IS...

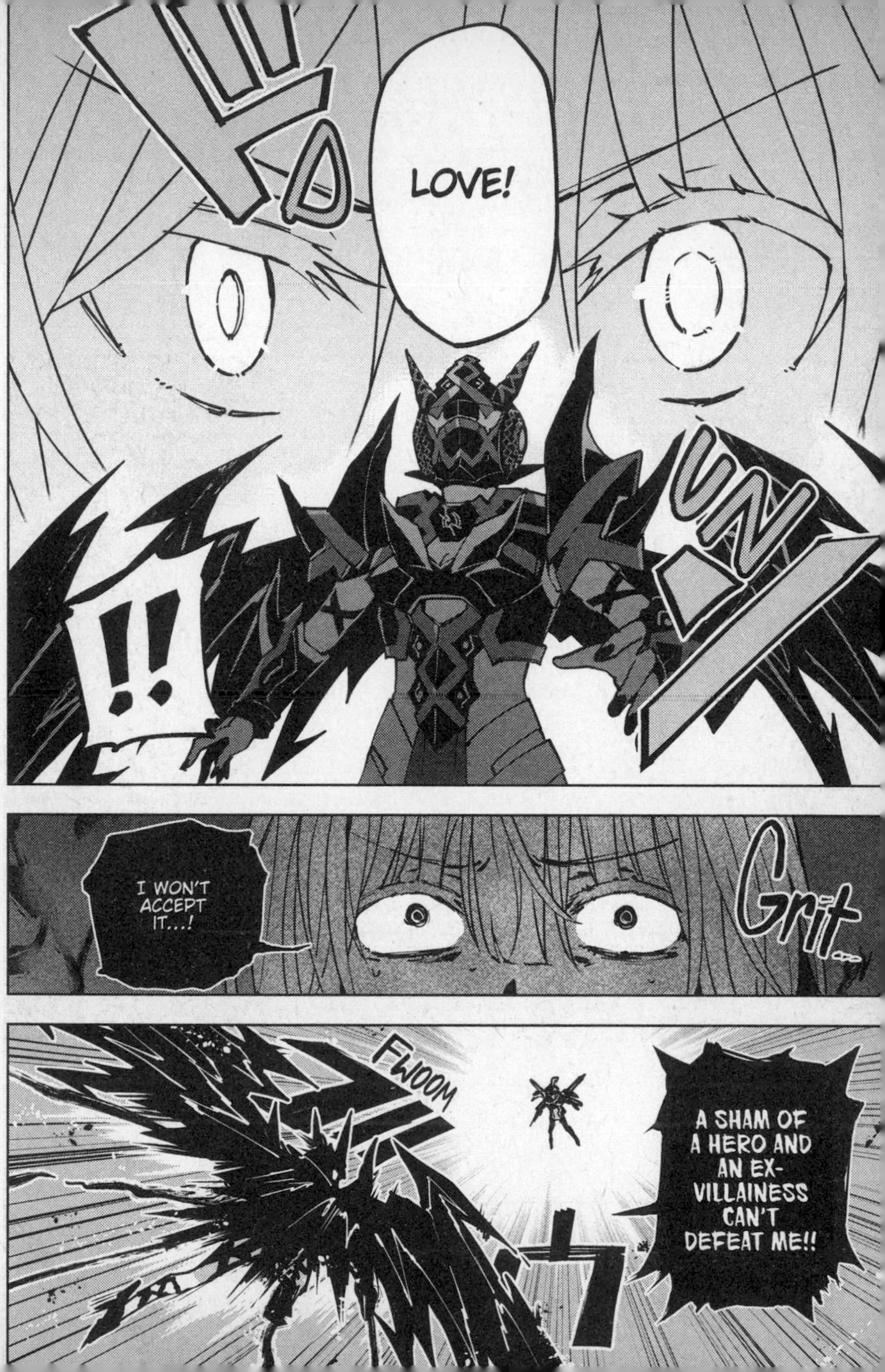
LOVE!
!!
Grit...
I WON'T ACCEPT IT...!
A SHAM OF A HERO AND AN EX-VILLAINESS CAN'T DEFEAT ME!!
FWOOM

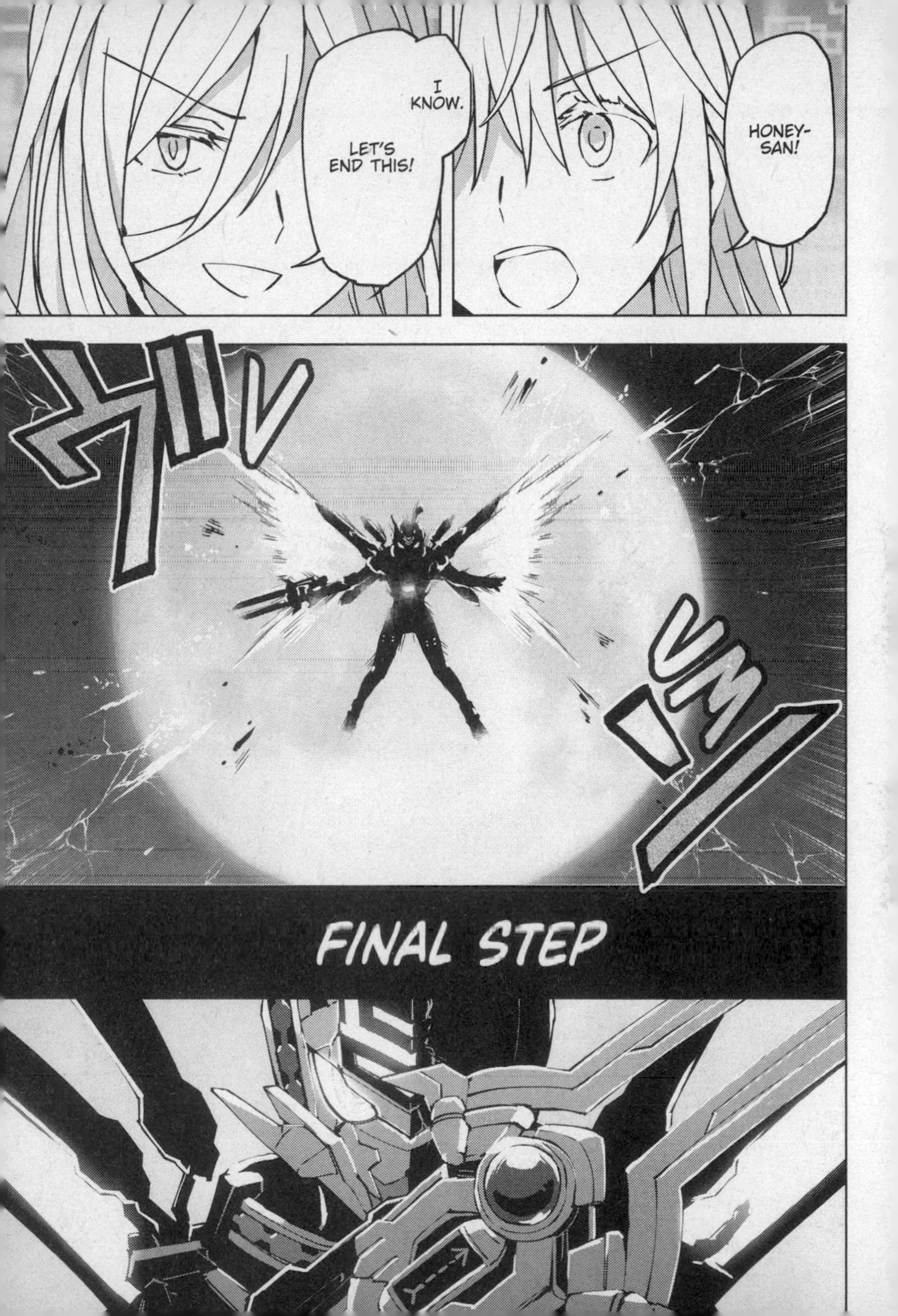
HONEY-SAN!
I KNOW.
LET'S END THIS!
FINAL STEP

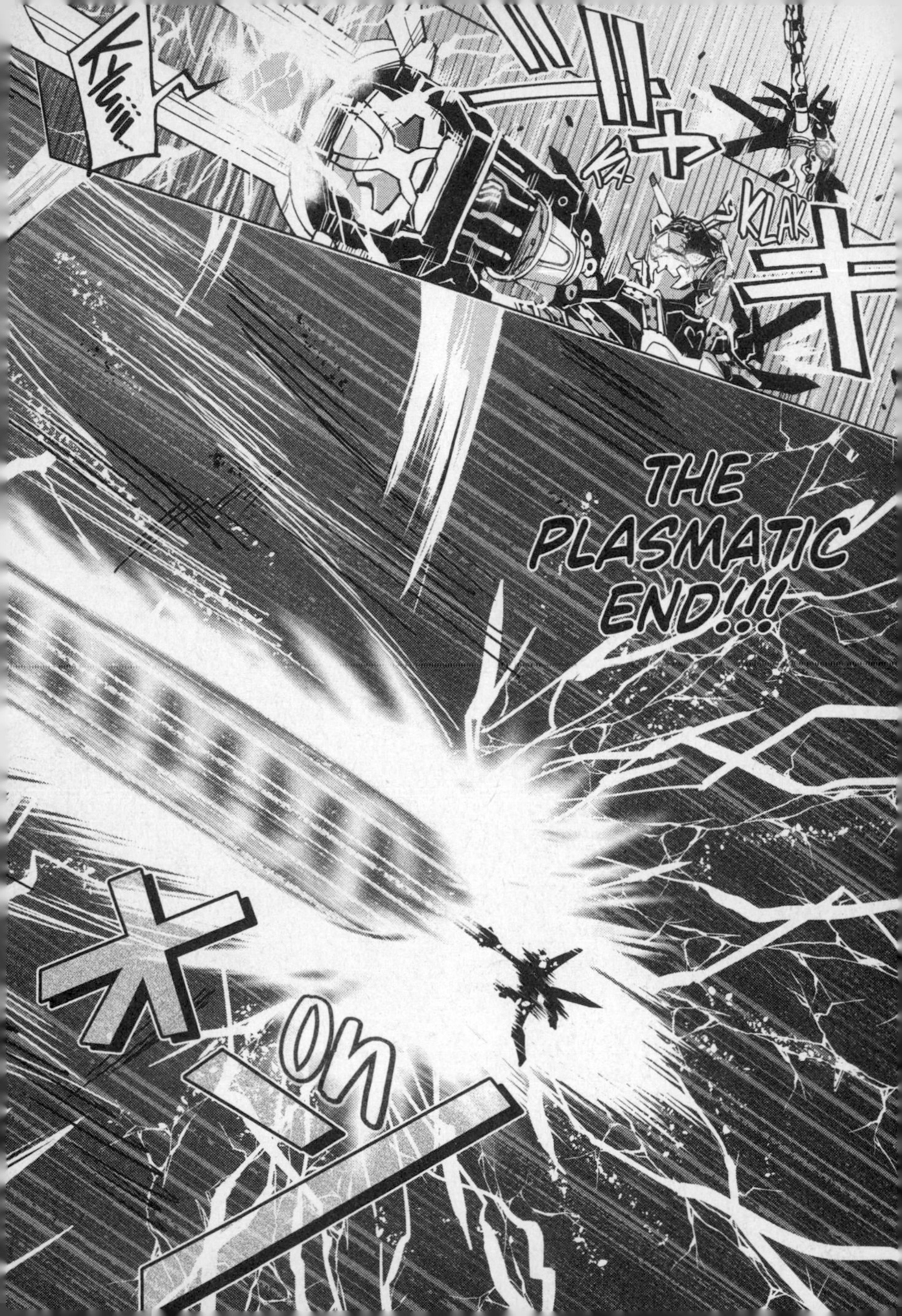
KLAK
KA-
KYUIII...
THE PLASMATIC END!!!

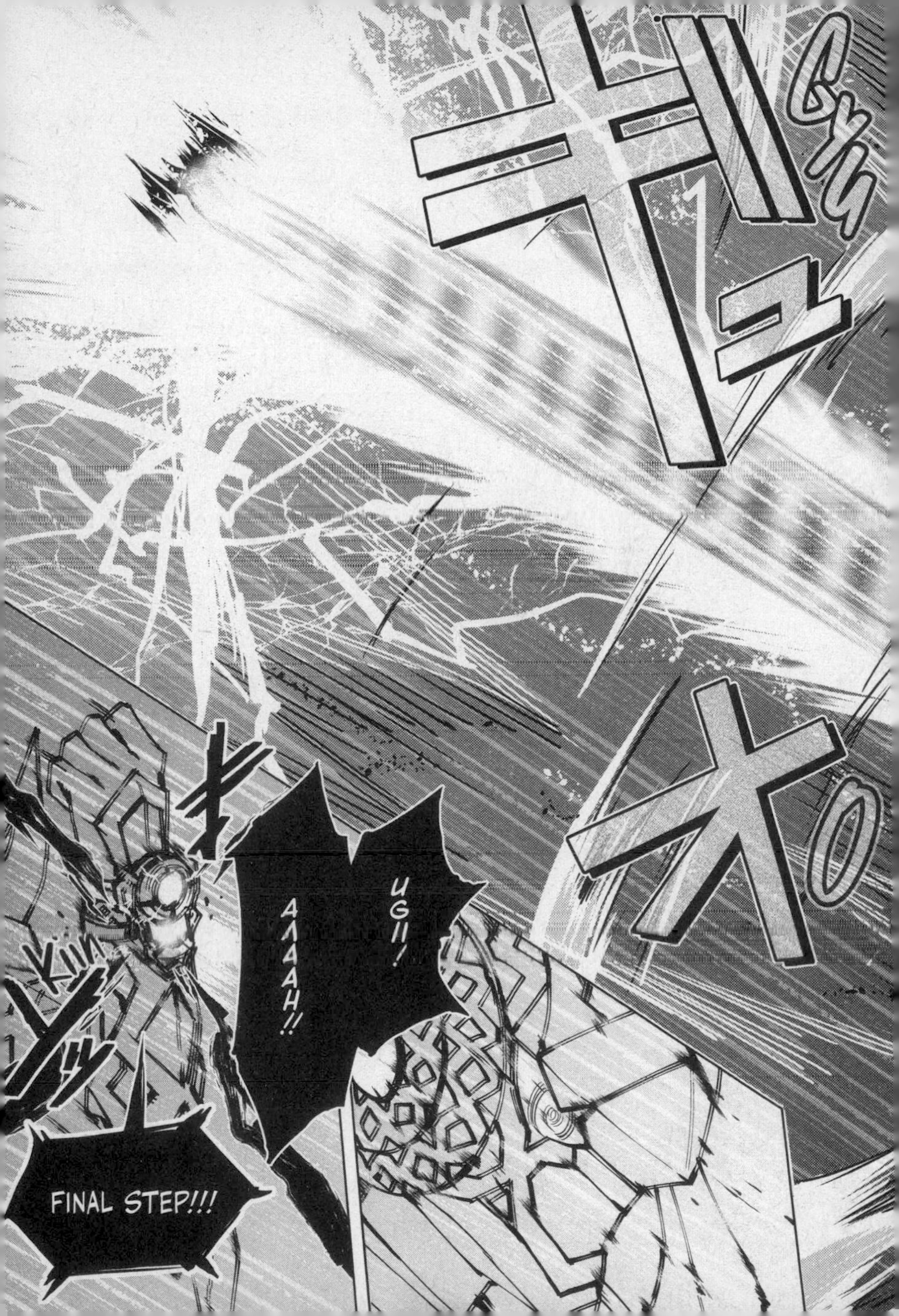
Gyu
o
UG!!
AAAAH!!
Kiin
FINAL STEP!!!

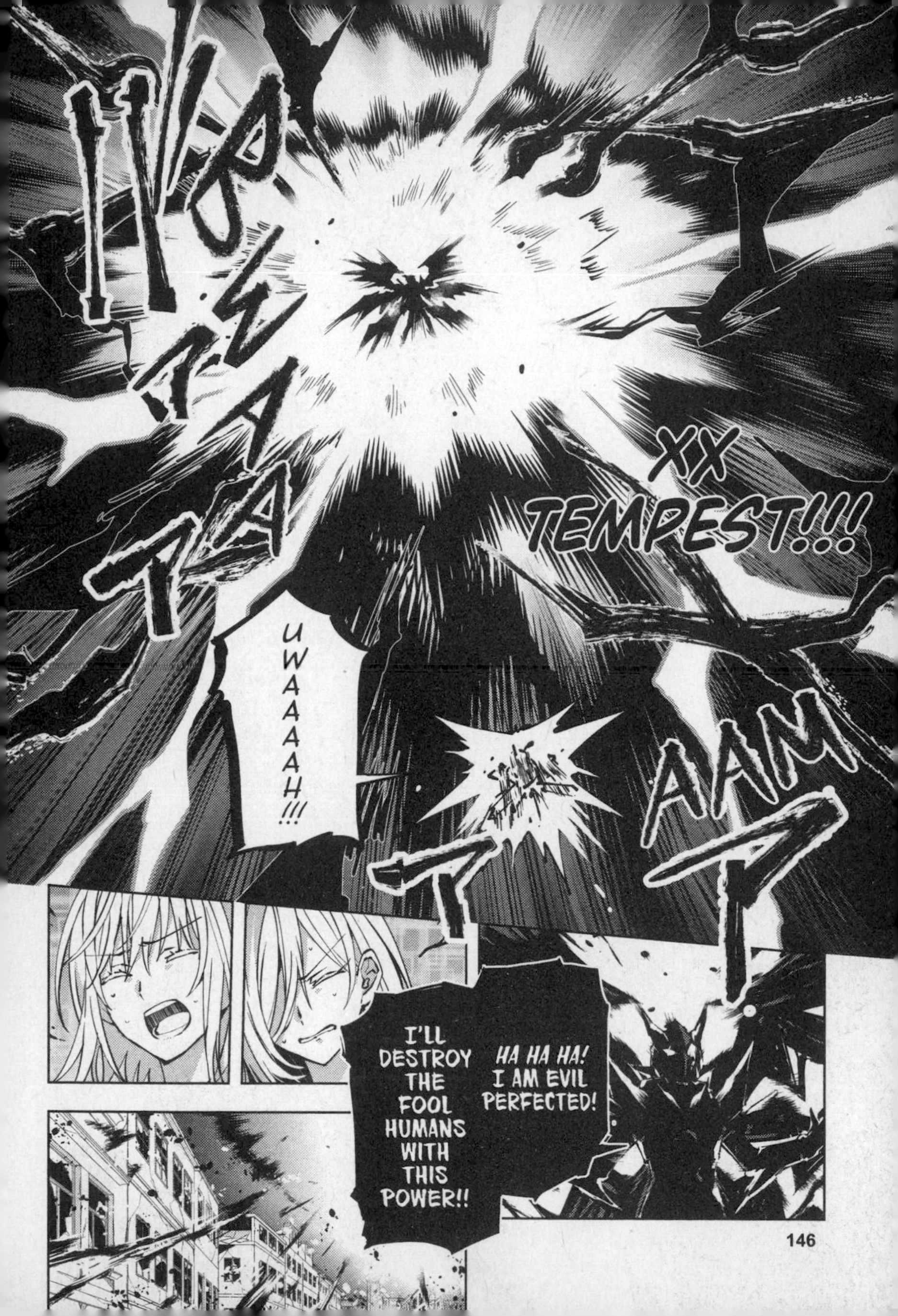
XX TEMPEST!!!
UWAAAAAAH!!!
AAM
HA HA HA! I AM EVIL PERFECTED!
I'LL DESTROY THE FOOL HUMANS WITH THIS POWER!!

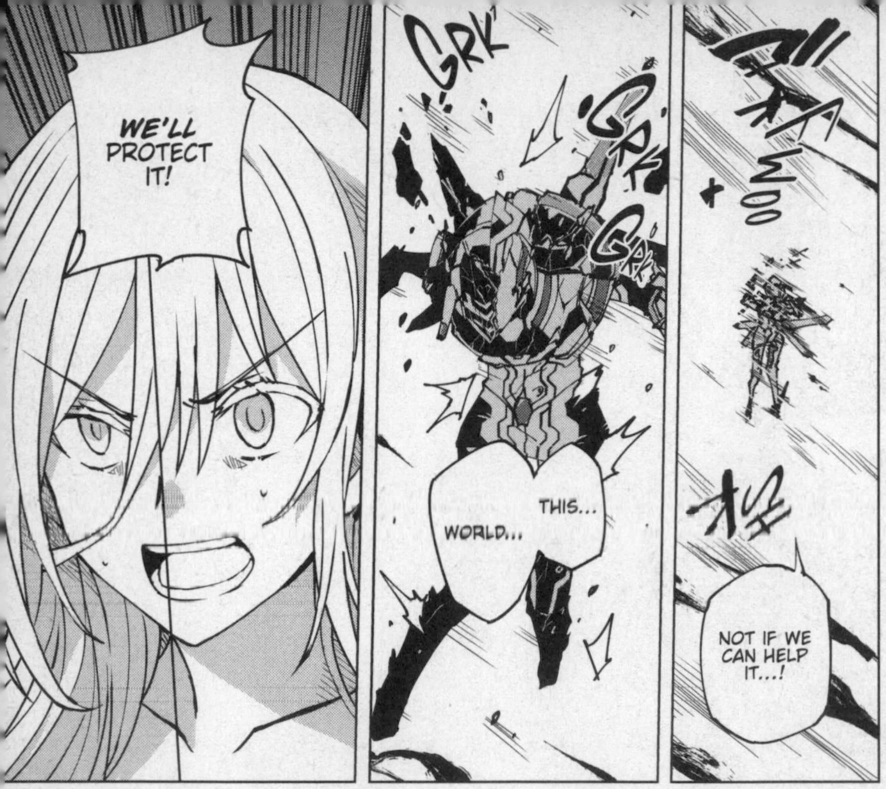
NOT IF WE CAN HELP IT...!
GRK
GRK
GRK
THIS... WORLD...
WE'LL PROTECT IT!

FINAL STEP

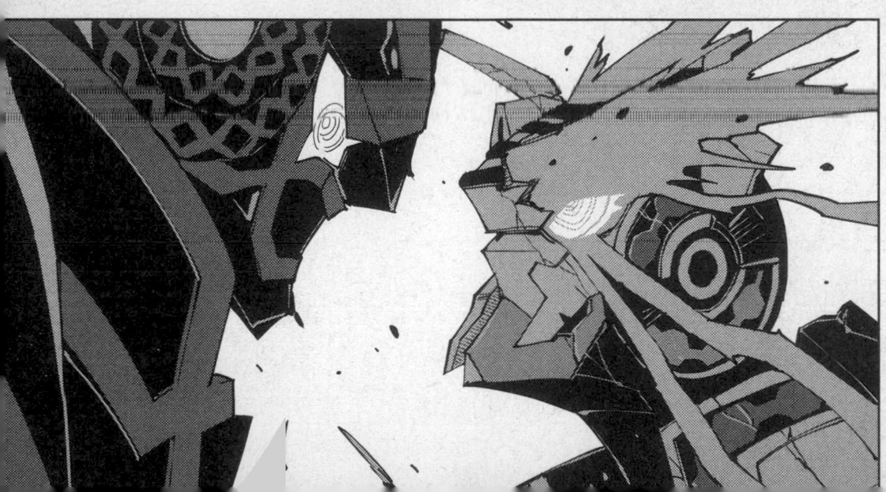

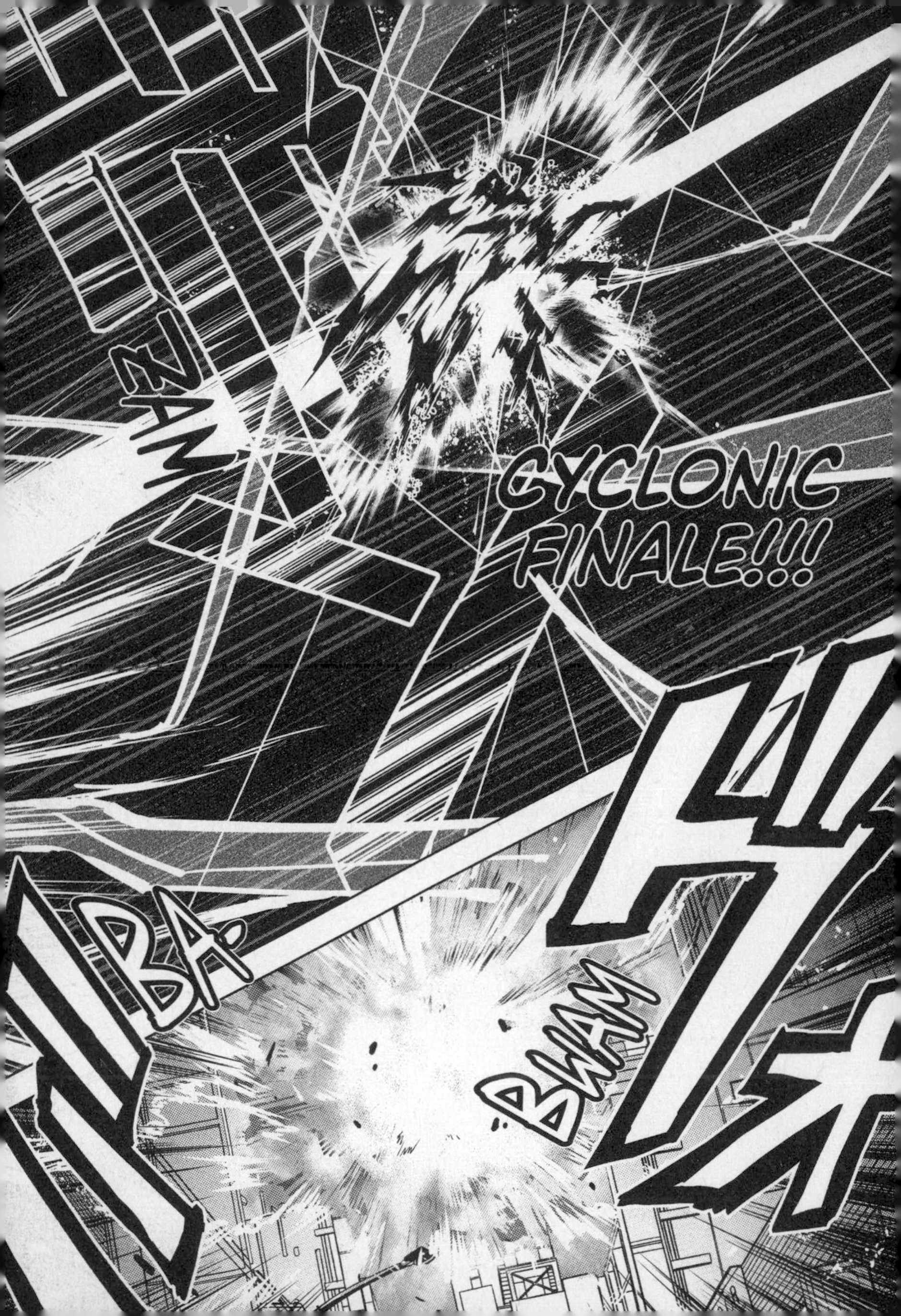
CYCLONIC FINALE!!!
ZAM
BWAM
BA

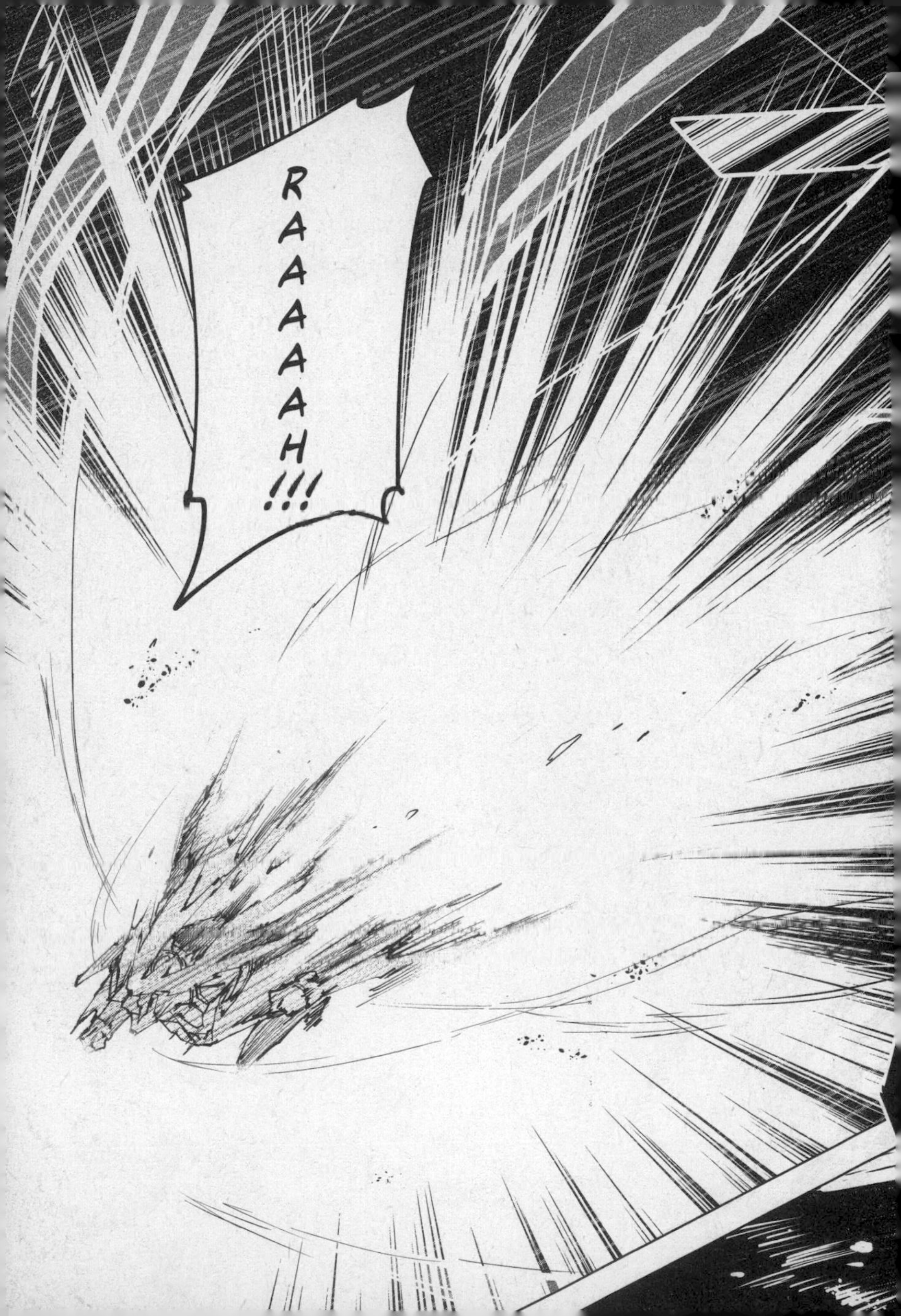
RAAAAAH!!!

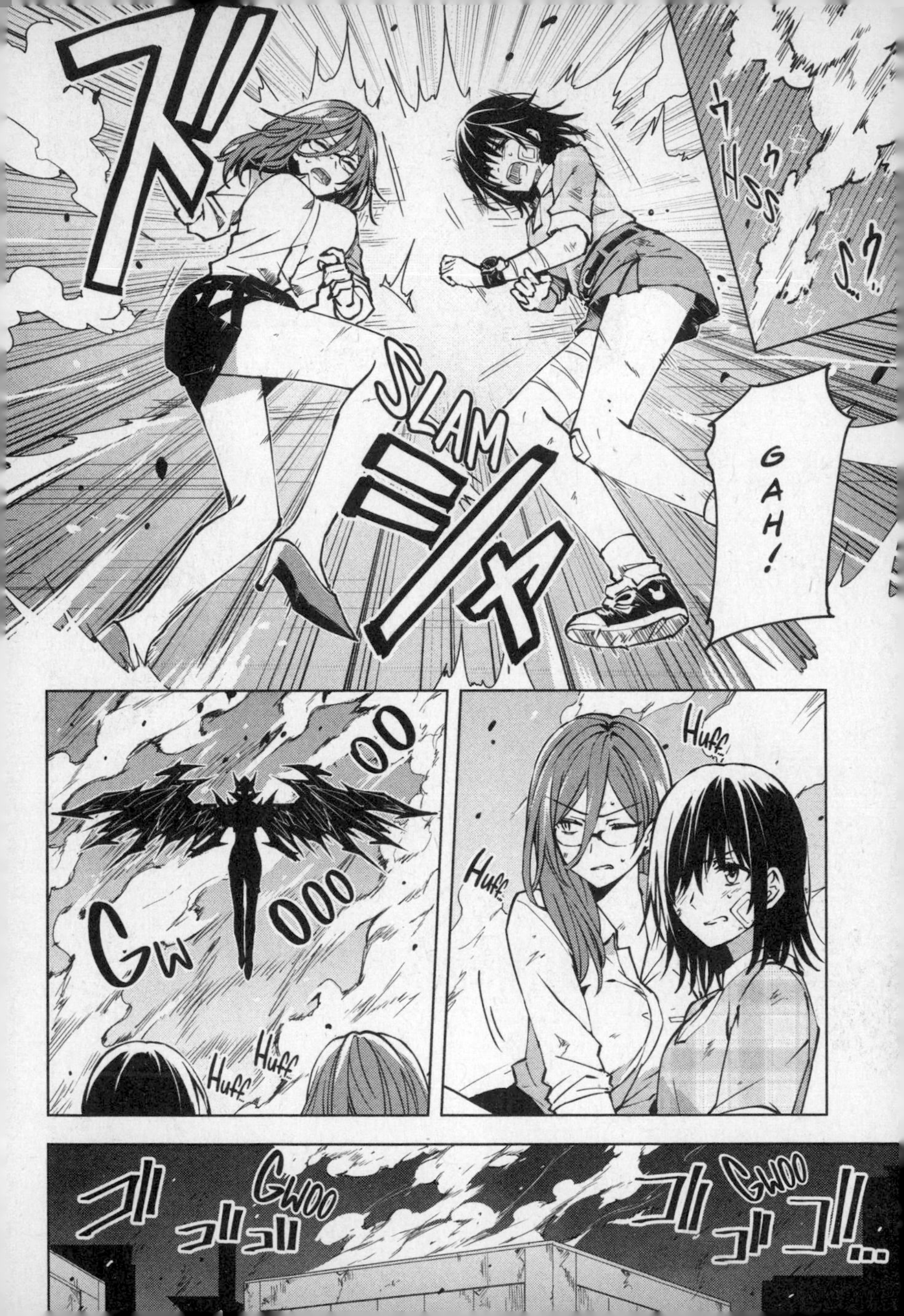
HSS...?
GAH!
SLAM
Huff...
Huff...
GWOOOOO
Huff
Huff
GWOO
GWOO

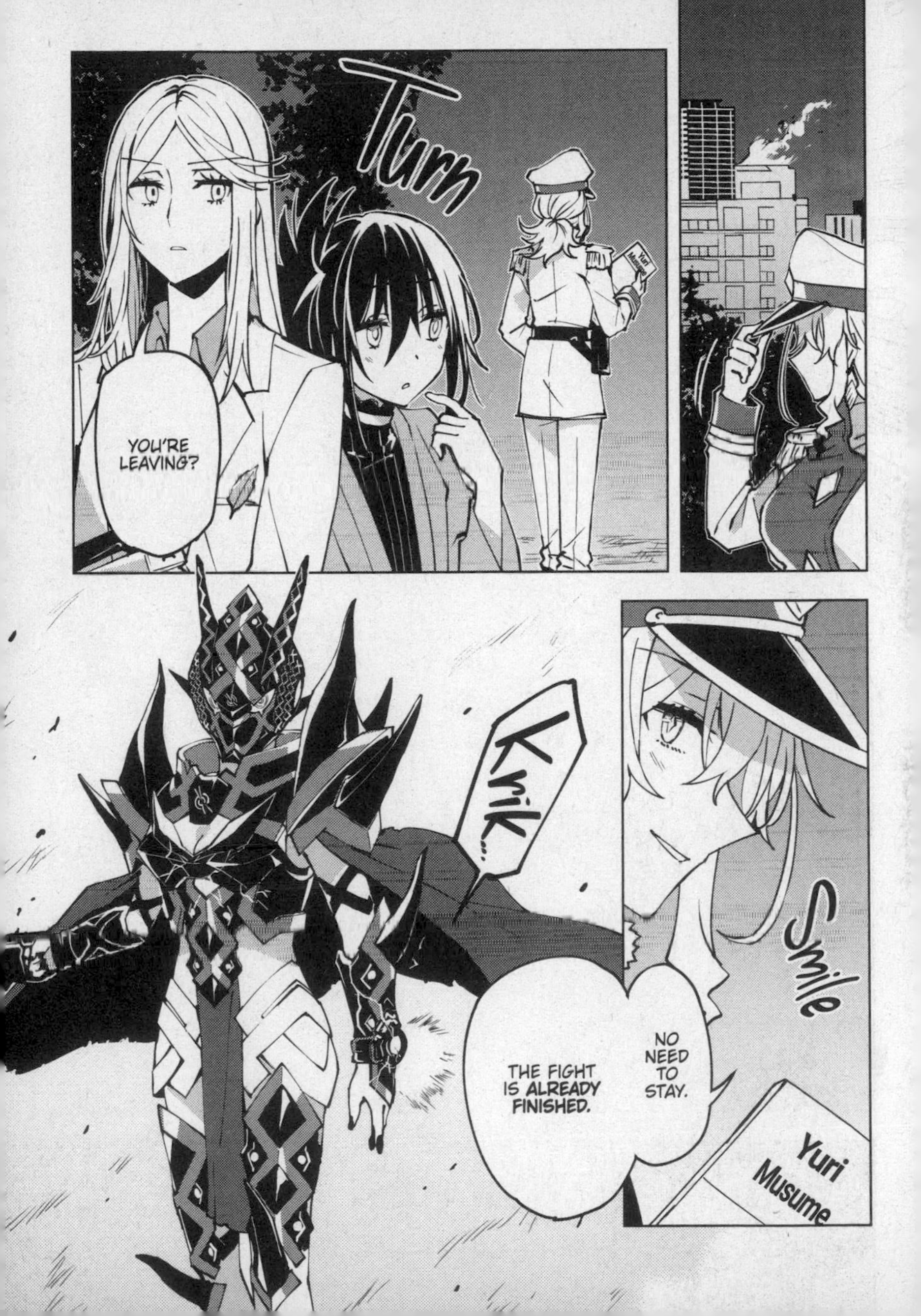
Turn
Yuri Musume
YOU'RE LEAVING?
Smile
NO NEED TO STAY.
THE FIGHT IS ALREADY FINISHED.
Yuri Musume
Krik...

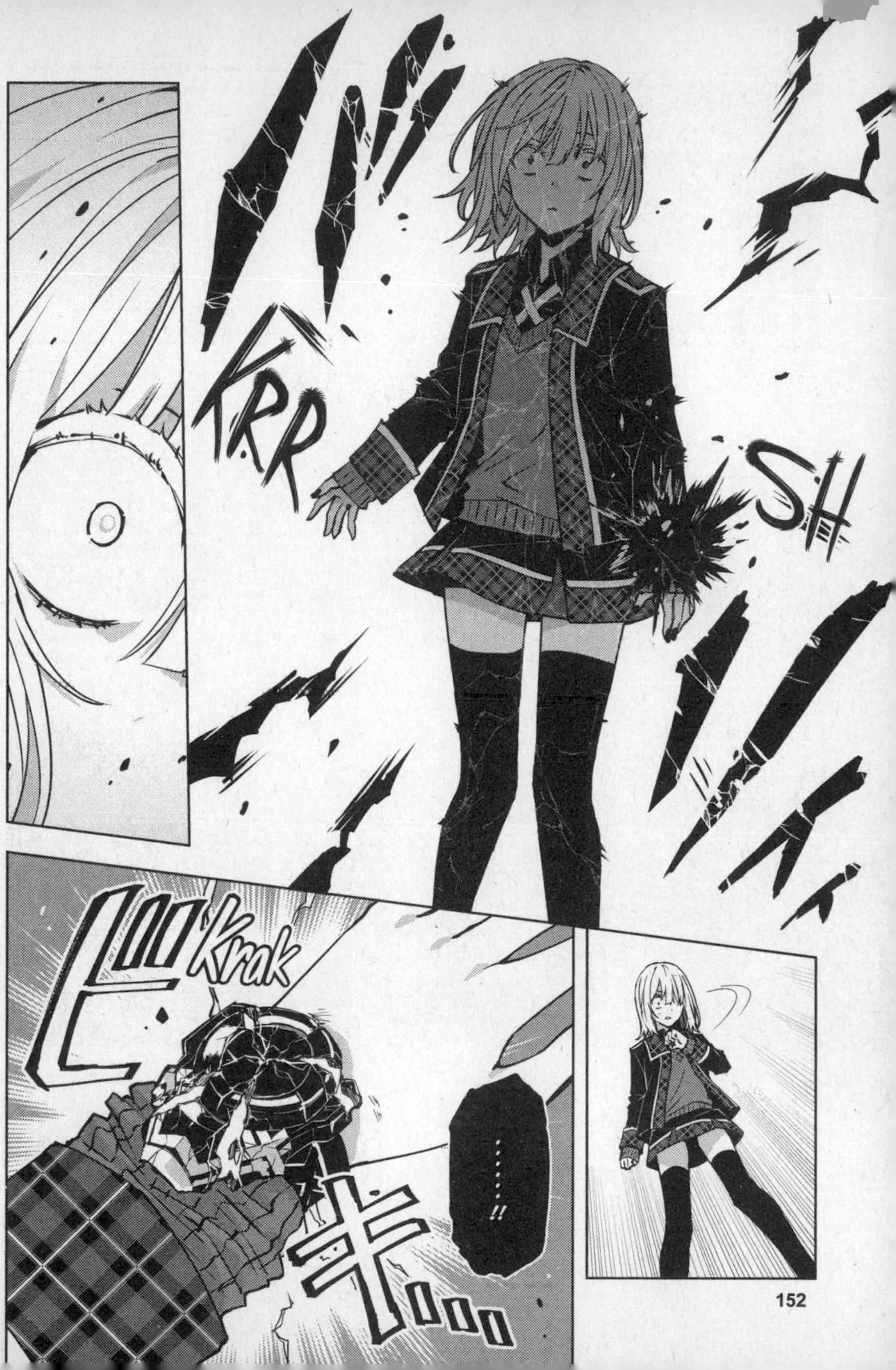

SH
KRR
Krak
......!!

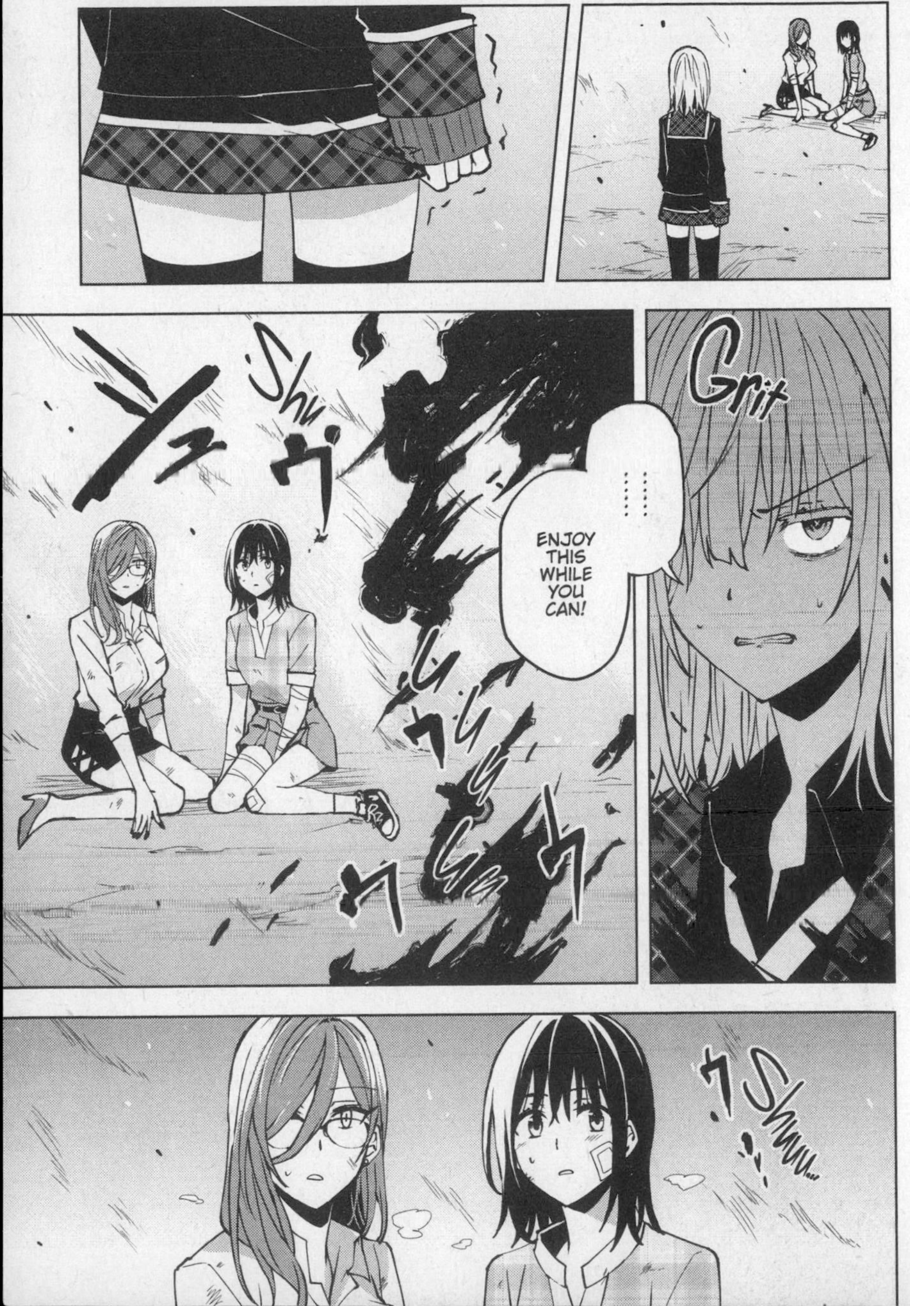
Grit
......
ENJOY THIS WHILE YOU CAN!
Shu
Shuuu...

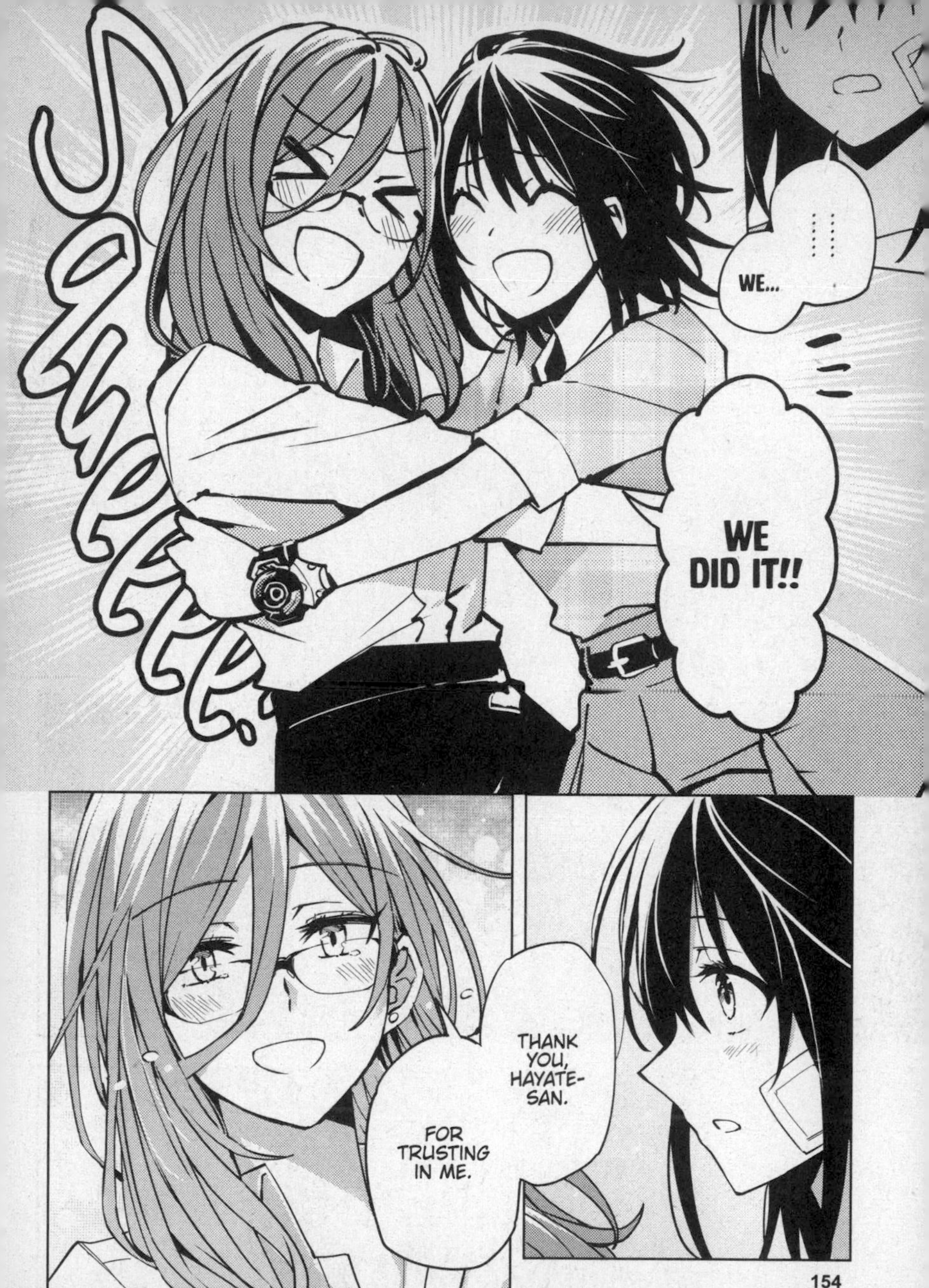
......
WE...
WE DID IT!!
THANK YOU, HAYATE-SAN.
FOR TRUSTING IN ME.

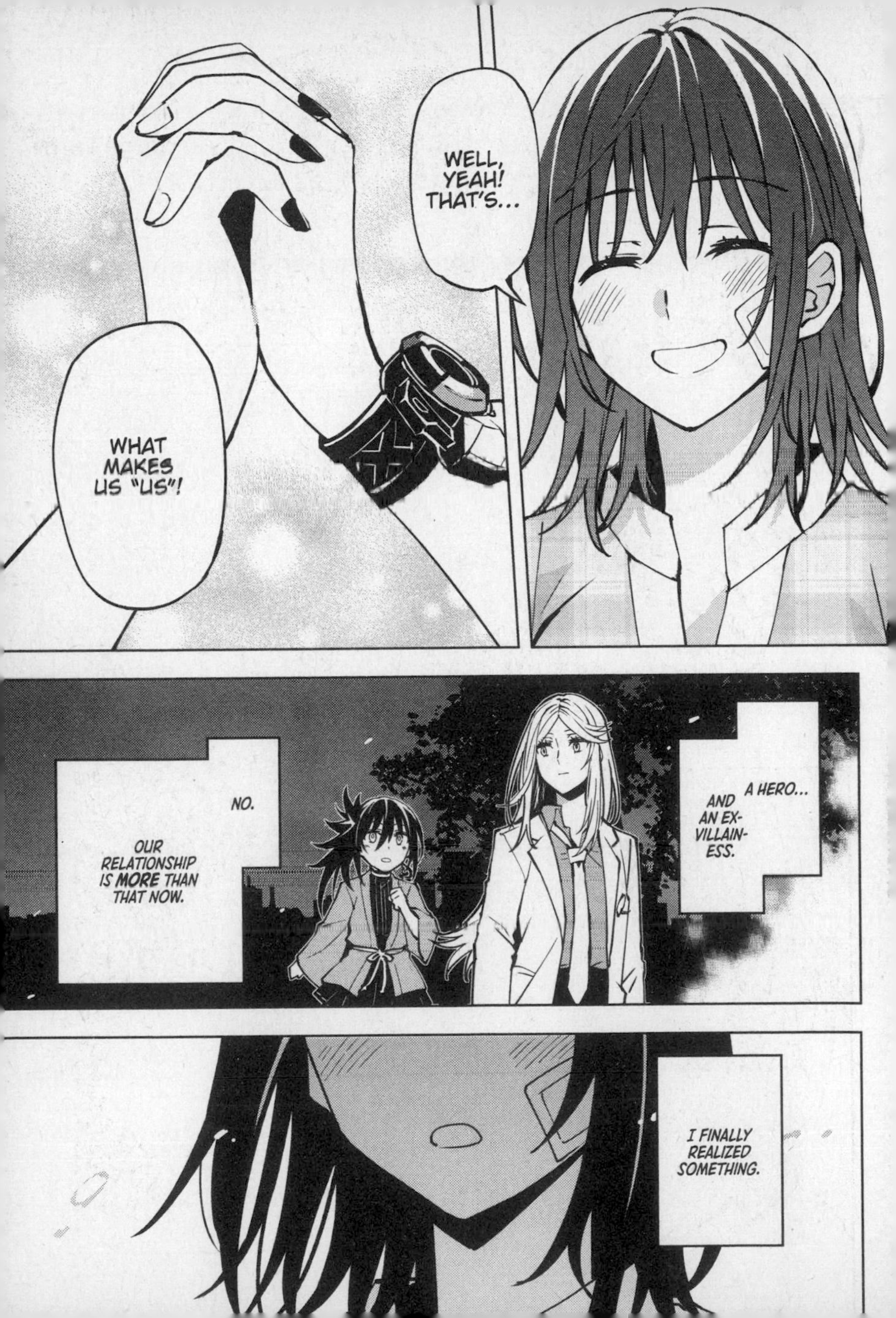
WELL, YEAH! THAT'S...
WHAT MAKES US "US"!
A HERO... AND AN EX-VILLAIN-ESS.
NO.
OUR RELATIONSHIP IS **MORE** THAN THAT NOW.
I FINALLY REALIZED SOMETHING.

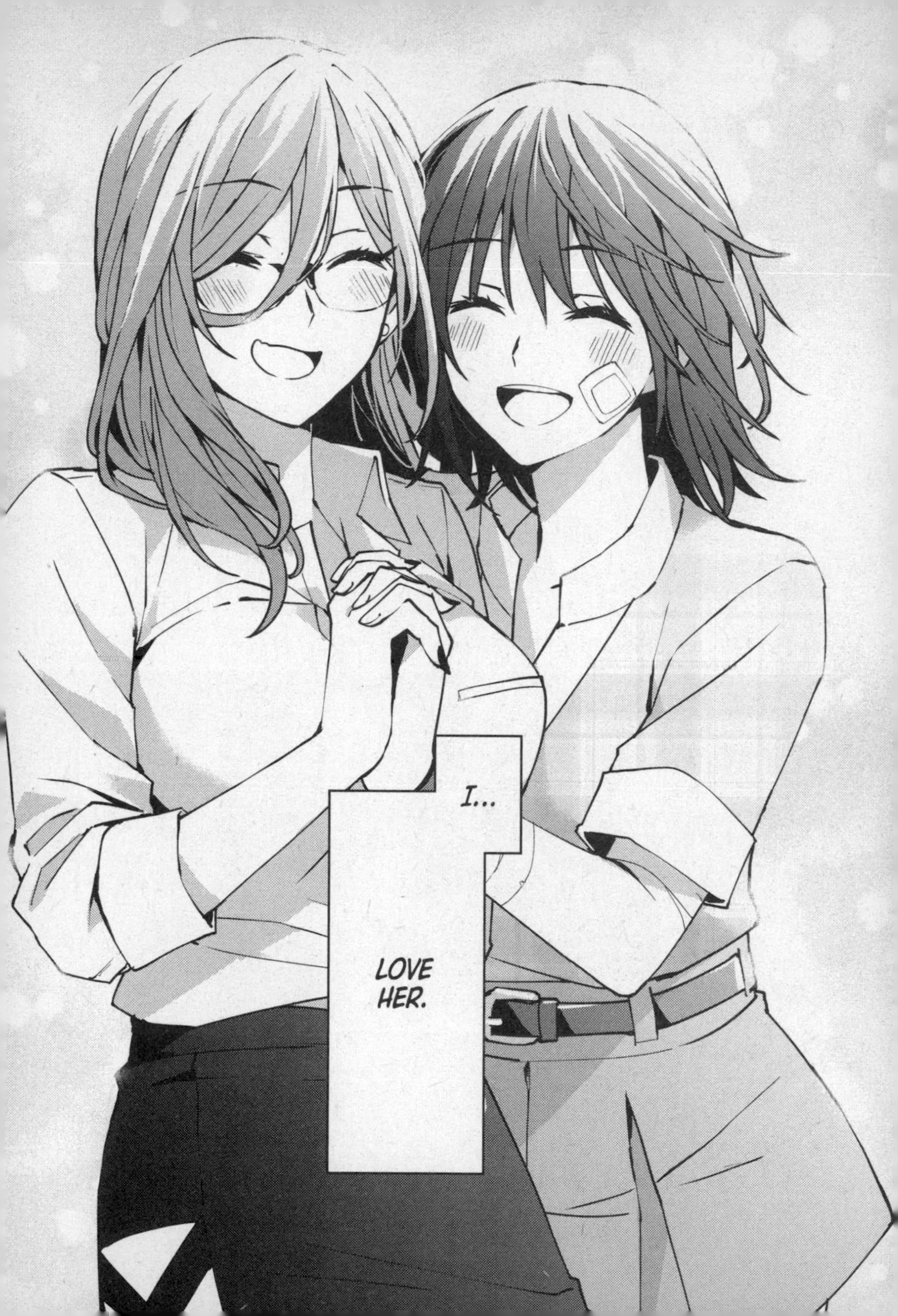
I...
LOVE HER.

SUPERWOMEN IN LOVE!

HONEY TRAP & RAPID RABBIT

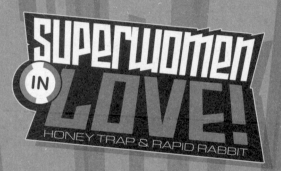

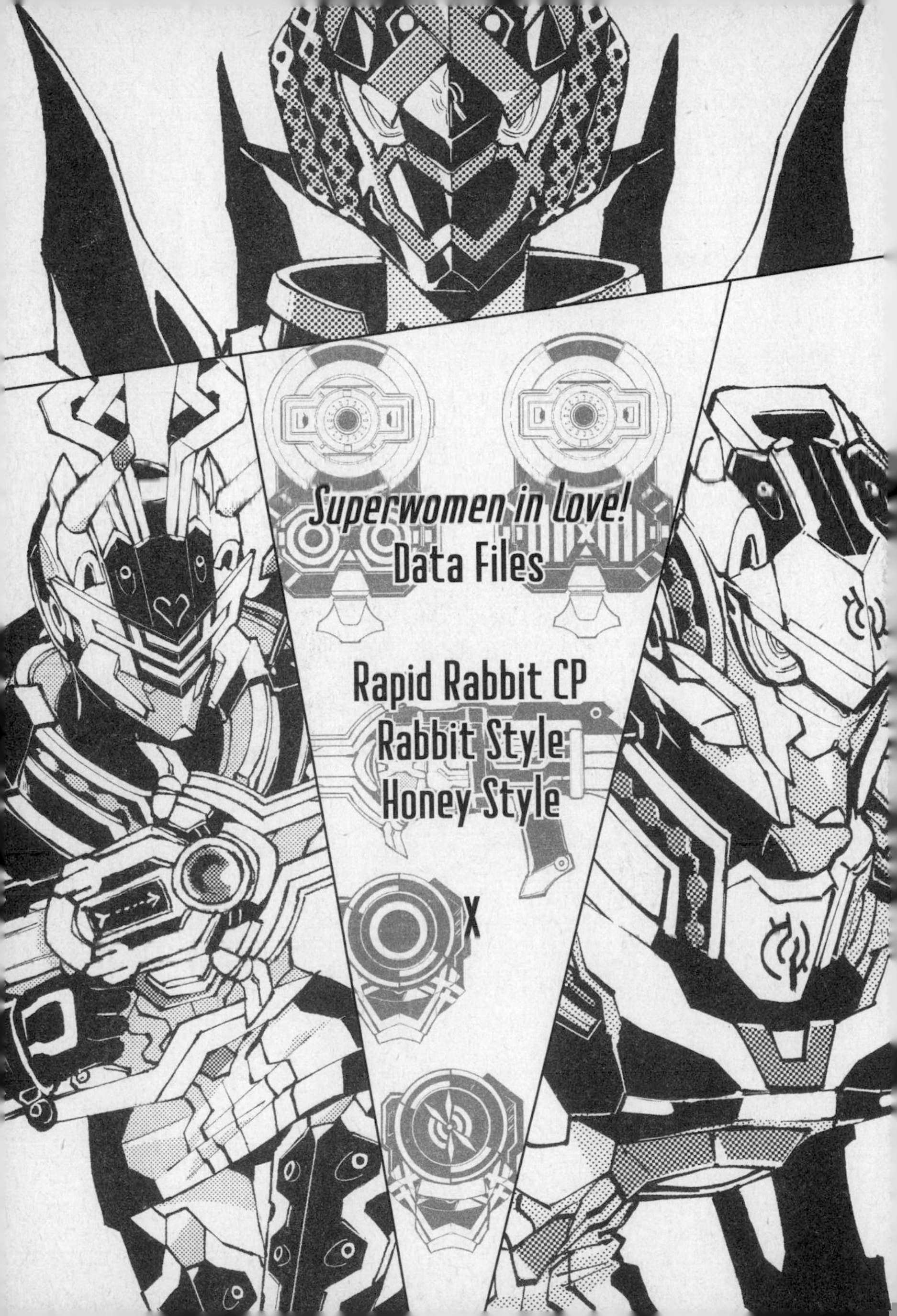
Superwomen in Love!
Data Files
Rapid Rabbit CP
Rabbit Style
Honey Style
X

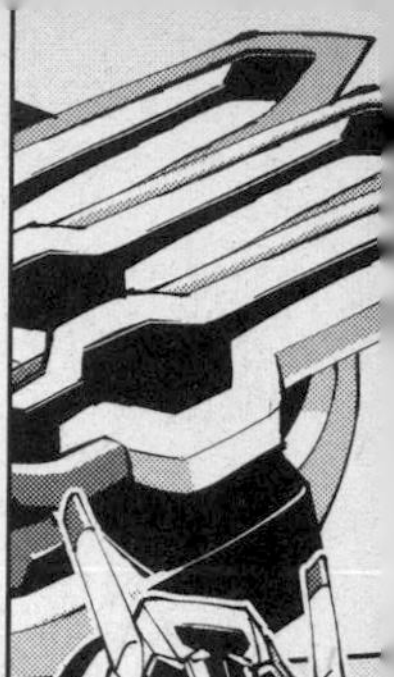

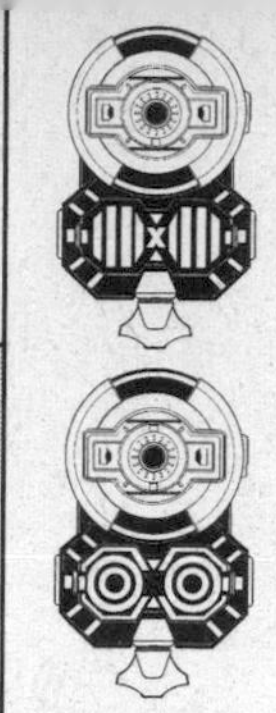

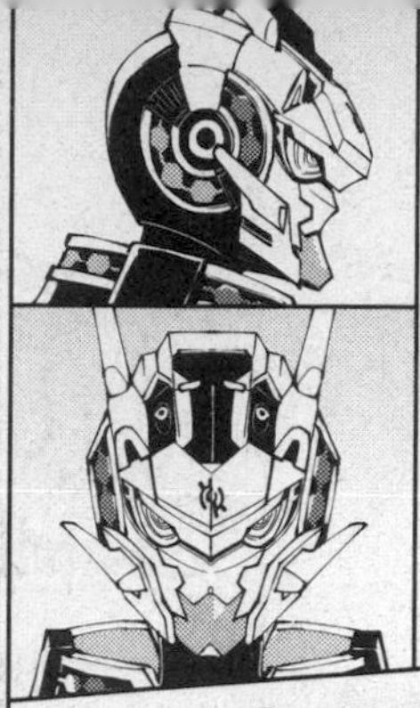

Transconnector

A dimension tool. Created by X, tuned and modified by Melt. Originally created by X to turn humans into Antinoids for her evil plan, but Hayate and Honey used its power to merge human and Antinoid against her, transforming into Rapid Rabbit CP.

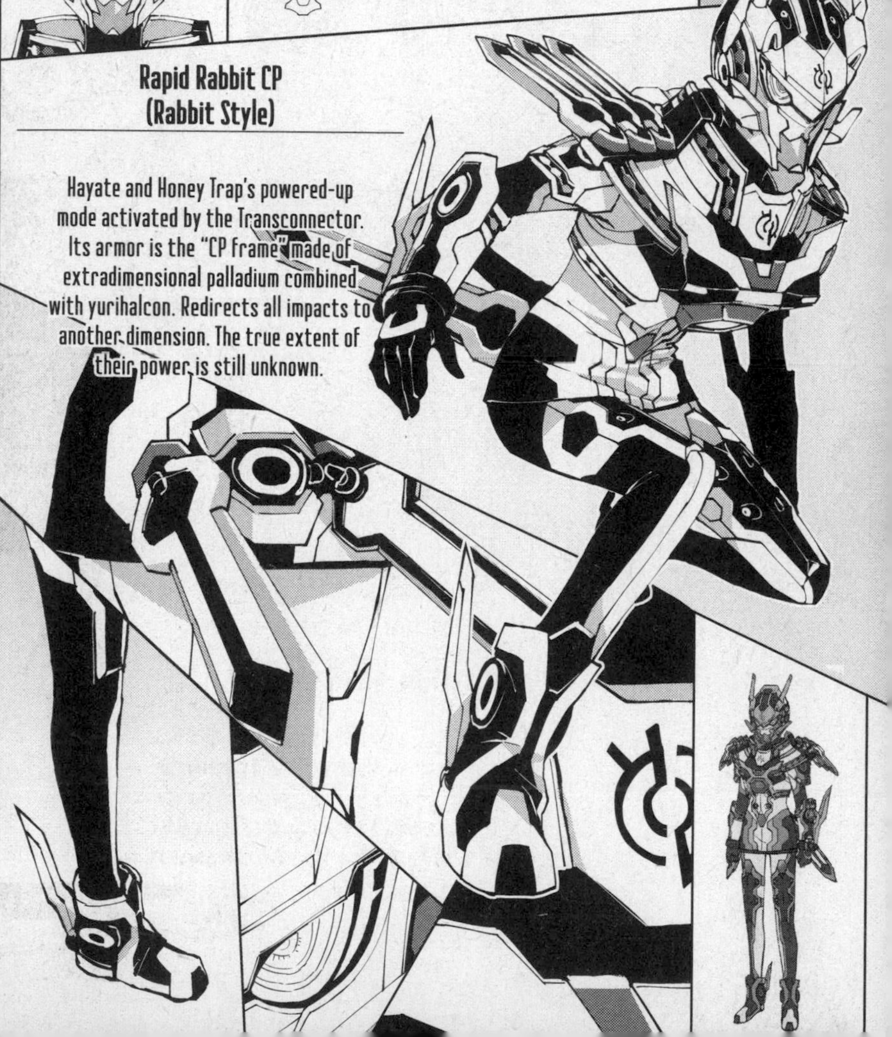

Rapid Rabbit CP (Rabbit Style)

Hayate and Honey Trap's powered-up mode activated by the Transconnector. Its armor is the "CP frame" made of extradimensional palladium combined with yurihalcon. Redirects all impacts to another dimension. The true extent of their power is still unknown.

Rapid Rabbit CP (Honey Style)

Rapid Rabbit CP's other form. Unlike Rabbit Style, which interacts with a higher dimension to draw out a speed surpassing the laws of physics, this form has flight and can shoot powerful beams from anywhere by compressing dimension energy.

Rapid Rabbit CP is neither hero nor kaijin. Depending on Hayate and Honey's resonance, it has the potential to evolve even further.

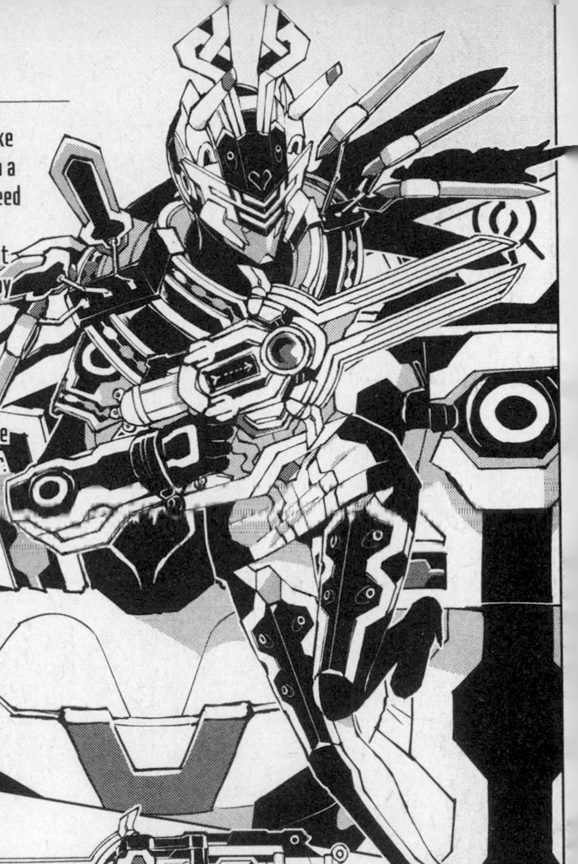

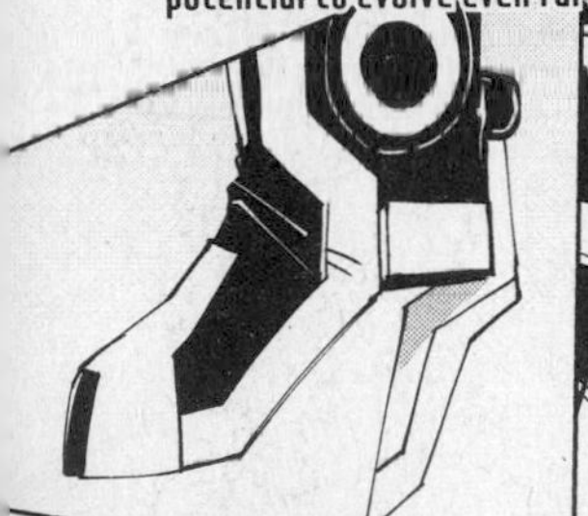

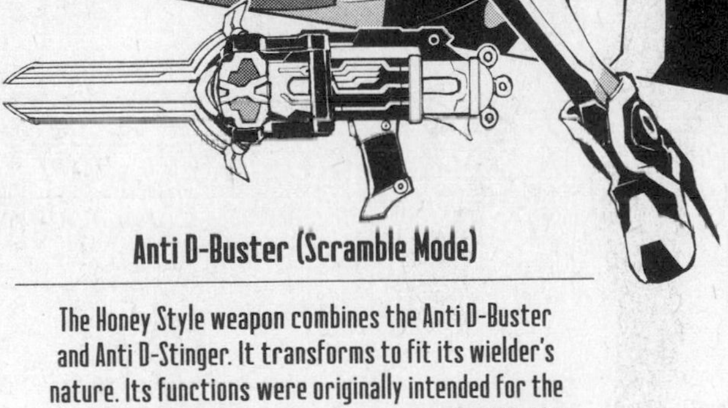

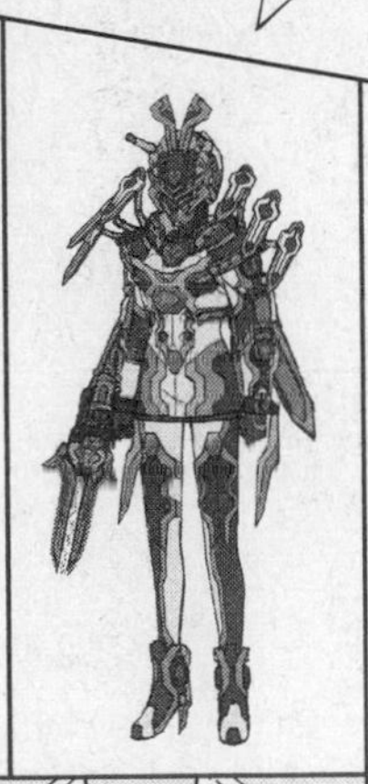

Anti D-Buster (Scramble Mode)

The Honey Style weapon combines the Anti D-Buster and Anti D-Stinger. It transforms to fit its wielder's nature. Its functions were originally intended for the kaijin-ified Orb Owl's future use, but when Rapid Rabbit CP obtained it, it changed into a powerful beam weapon.

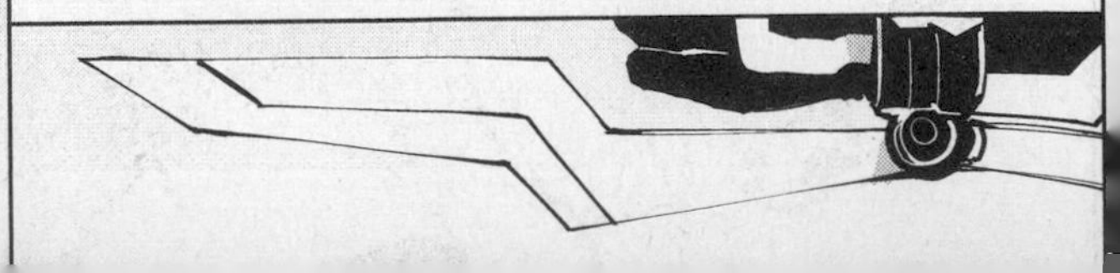

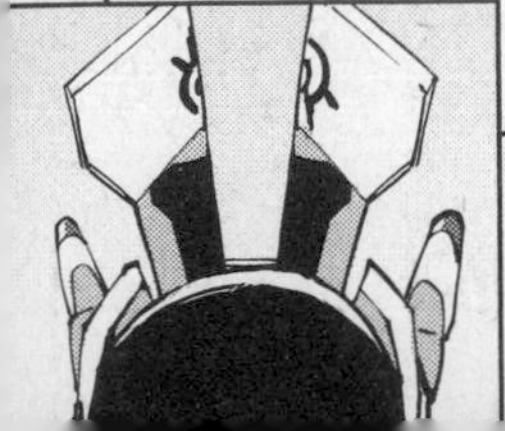

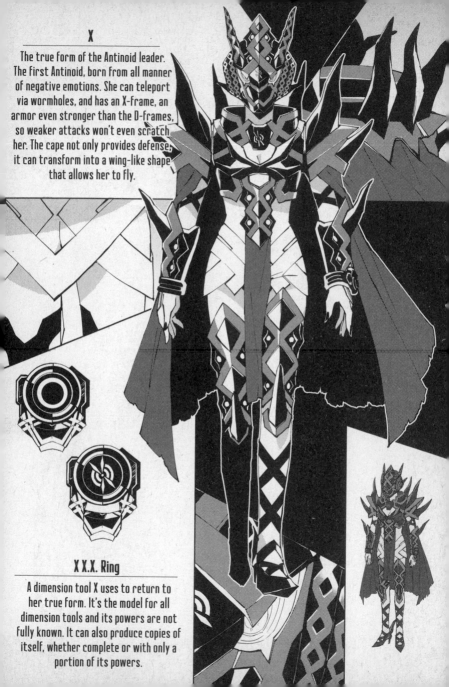

X

The true form of the Antinoid leader. The first Antinoid, born from all manner of negative emotions. She can teleport via wormholes, and has an X-frame, an armor even stronger than the D-frames, so weaker attacks won't even scratch her. The cape not only provides defense; it can transform into a wing-like shape that allows her to fly.

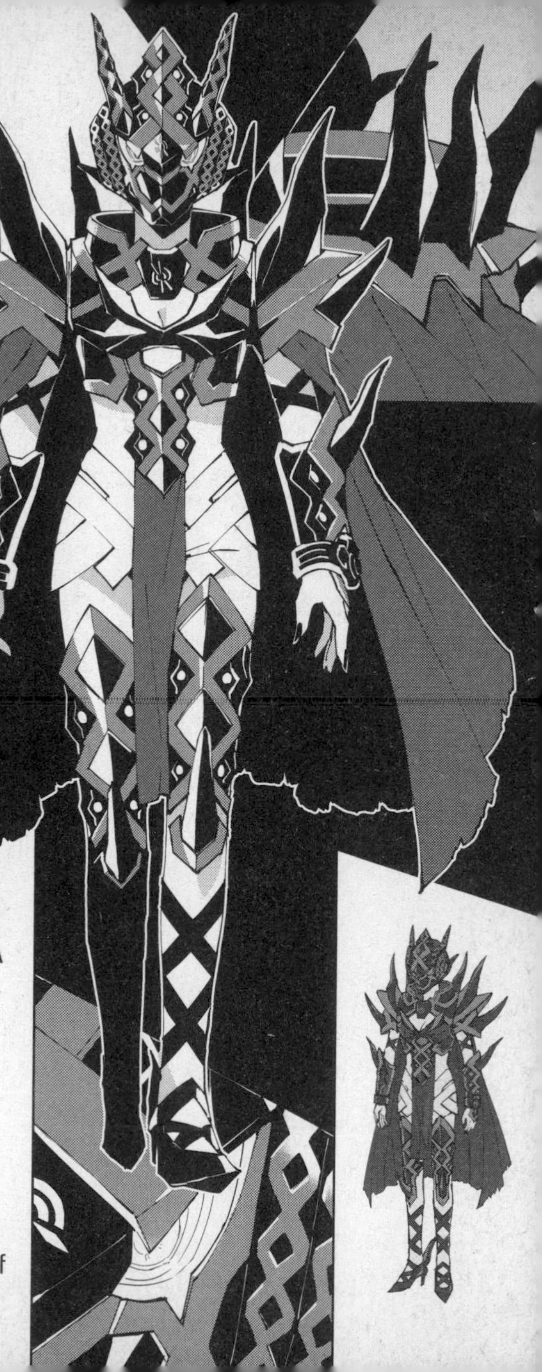

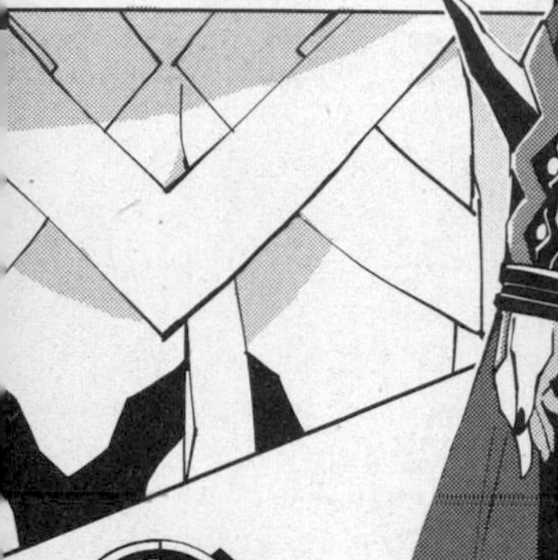

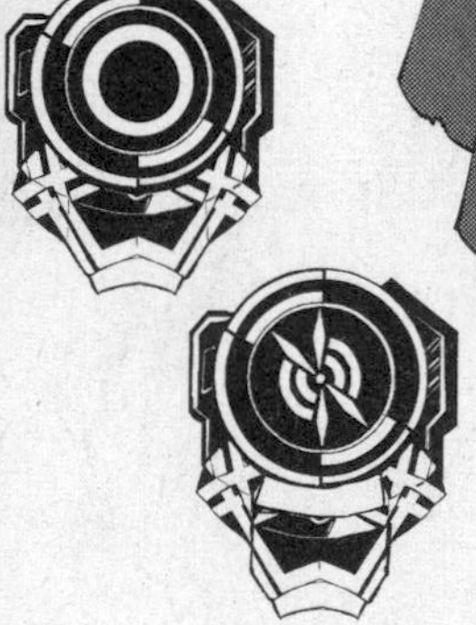

X X.X. Ring

A dimension tool X uses to return to her true form. It's the model for all dimension tools and its powers are not fully known. It can also produce copies of itself, whether complete or with only a portion of its powers.

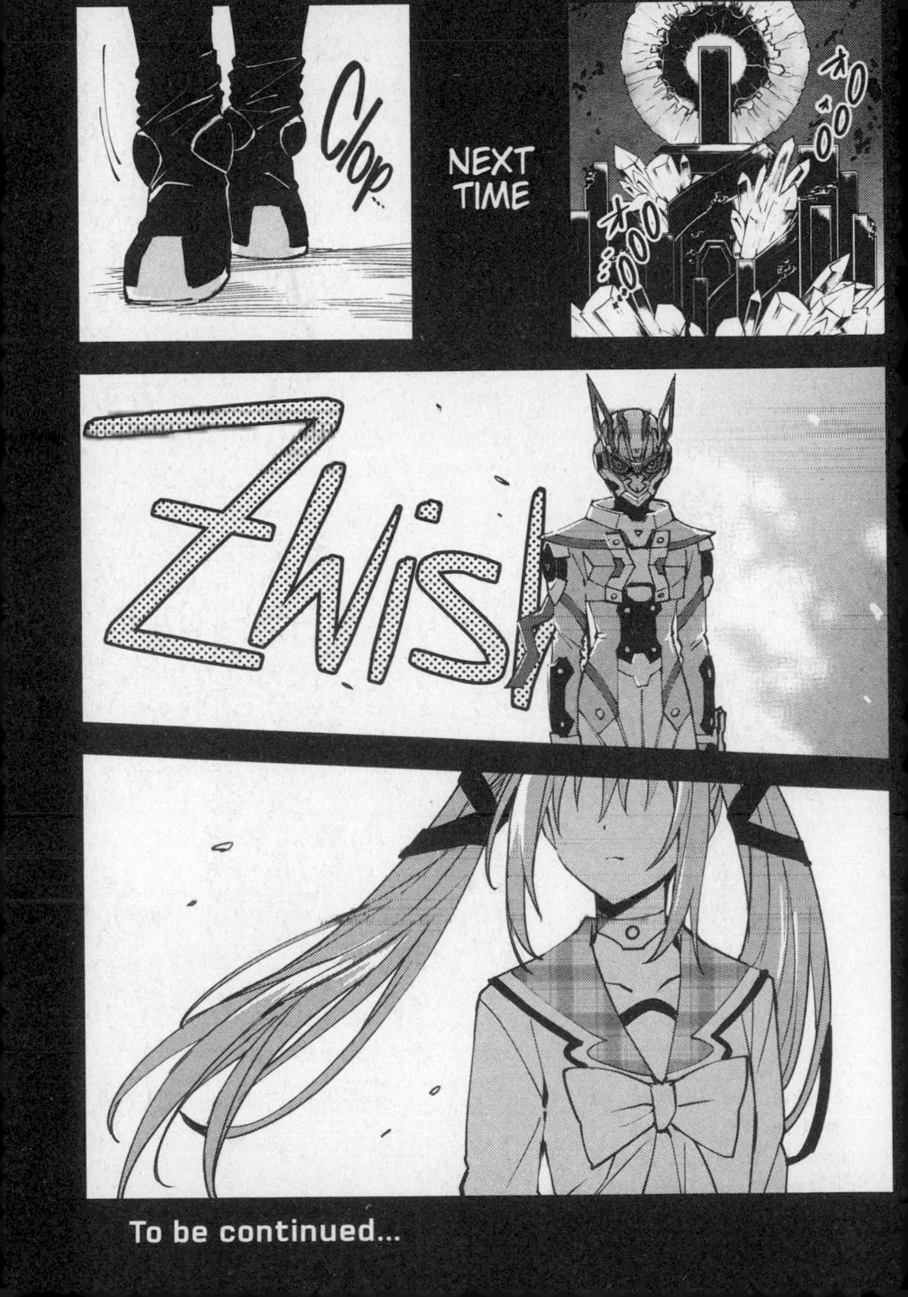
NEXT TIME
Clop...
Zwish

To be continued...

SEVEN SEAS ENTERTAINMENT PRESENTS

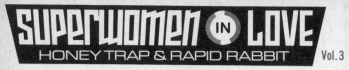

SUPERWOMEN IN LOVE
HONEY TRAP & RAPID RABBIT
Vol. 3

story and art by **SOMETIME**

TRANSLATION
Amanda Haley

LETTERING
Mercedes McGarry

COVER DESIGN
Nicky Lim

LOGO DESIGN
George Panella

PROOFREADER
B. Lana Guggenheim

COPY EDITOR
Dawn Davis

EDITOR
Shannon Fay

PREPRESS TECHNICIAN
iannon Rasmussen-Silverstein

PRODUCTION ASSOCIATE
Christa Miesner

PRODUCTION MANAGER
Lissa Pattillo

MANAGING EDITOR
Julie Davis

ASSOCIATE PUBLISHER
Adam Arnold

PUBLISHER
Jason DeAngelis

Hero-san to Moto Onnakanbu-san Vol. 3

First published in Japan in 2020 by Ichijinsha Inc., Tokyo.
Publication rights for this English edition arranged through Kodansha Ltd., Tokyo.

Seven Seas press and purchase enquiries can be sent to Marketing Manager Lianne Sentar at press@gomanga.com. Information regarding the distribution and purchase of digital editions is available from Digital Manager CK Russell at digital@gomanga.com.

ISBN: 978-1-64827-370-4
Printed in Canada
First Printing: December 2021
10 9 8 7 6 5 4 3 2 1

READING DIRECTIONS

This book reads from ***right to left***, Japanese style. If this is your first time reading manga, you start reading from the top right panel on each page and take it from there. If you get lost, just follow the numbered diagram here. It may seem backwards at first, but you'll get the hang of it! Have fun!!

1
2
3
4
5
6
7
8
9

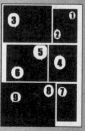

Follow us online: www.SevenSeasEntertainment.com